The Perennial Philosophy
Series

World Wisdom
The Library of Perennial Philosophy

The Library of Perennial Philosophy is dedicated to the exposition of the timeless Truth underlying the diverse religions. This Truth, often referred to as the *Sophia Perennis*—or Perennial Wisdom—finds its expression in the revealed Scriptures as well as in the writings of the great sages and the artistic creations of the traditional worlds.

The Timeless Relevance of Traditional Wisdom appears as one of our selections in the Perennial Philosophy series.

The Perennial Philosophy Series

In the beginning of the twentieth century, a school of thought arose which has focused on the enunciation and explanation of the Perennial Philosophy. Deeply rooted in the sense of the sacred, the writings of its leading exponents establish an indispensable foundation for understanding the timeless Truth and spiritual practices which live in the heart of all religions. Some of these titles are companion volumes to the Treasures of the World's Religions series, which allows a comparison of the writings of the great sages of the past with the perennialist authors of our time.

Cover: "Meeting of Sages", miniature from Mughal India, 17th century

THE TIMELESS RELEVANCE

OF

TRADITIONAL WISDOM

by

M. Ali Lakhani

Foreword by

Reza Shah-Kazemi

Introduction by

William Stoddart

The Timeless Relevance of Traditional Wisdom
© 2010 World Wisdom, Inc.

Library of Congress Cataloging-in-Publication Data

Lakhani, M. Ali., 1955-
    The timeless relevance of traditional wisdom / by M. Ali Lakhani ; foreword
by Reza Shah-Kazemi ; introduction by William Stoddart.
        p. cm. -- (The library of perennial philosophy) (The perennial philosophy
series)
    Includes bibliographical references and index.
    ISBN 978-1-935493-19-8 (pbk. : alk. paper) 1. Wisdom. 2. Conduct of life.
3. Religion. 4. Philosophy. I. Title.
    BJ1595.L25 2010
    202--dc22

                                                                          2010024505

Printed on acid-free paper in United States of America

For information address World Wisdom, Inc.
P.O. Box 2682, Bloomington, Indiana 47402-2682

www.worldwisdom.com

CONTENTS

Dedication and Acknowledgments

In the Name of the Most Compassionate and Most Merciful Reality:

There are many writings about traditional wisdom, but few that focus on its relevance to our times. While the essays in this anthology address traditional principles and values, they are also intended as a reminder of the "timeliness of the timeless"—for in truth nothing is more jarringly anachronistic than the profane.

I am indebted to the great sages and teachers within all the faith traditions, whose lives, works and teachings have inspired and guided my own. In addition to the teachers of more distant times such as Shankara, Honen, Lao Tzu, Plato, Plotinus, Ibn 'Arabi, Jalal ad-Din, Rumi, and Meister Eckhart, there are several guides in more recent times who have acted as beacons of light for me, particularly the revivifiers of traditional wisdom, and most notably Frithjof Schuon. These teachers, who all lived in different places and times, and who spoke of an essentially integrated Reality, are a reminder of the universal and perennial nature of wisdom. For those of us "who have eyes to see and ears to hear", their teachings summon us to find what is sacred within us so that we can discover its reflection around us. To the extent that their collective wisdom of the True, the Good, and the Beautiful, has resonated within my own heart, its influence will be evident in these pages.

Sacred Web would not have seen the light of day without the encouragement of, in particular, Seyyed Hossein Nasr, to whom I express my deep appreciation.

There are many individuals who have provided me with critical comments about my writing. I am grateful to them all. The responsibility for any errors in this book, however, remains my own. In particular, I would like to thank William Stoddart and Reza Shah-Kazemi for their helpful feedback and most especially for gracing this anthology with their introductory and prefatory remarks.

Finally, I thank my friends and collaborators at World Wisdom for their detailed attention to this manuscript, and for their assistance in making this publication a reality.

I dedicate this book of essays to my late parents, Ibrahim and Kulsam.

M. Ali Lakhani
Vancouver, British Columbia
June 2010

Foreword

By Reza Shah-Kazemi

The essays gathered here come from the pen of someone who can be referred to as a "perennialist": thus as one who is well aware of both the difficulties of living in the modern world, and of the mercies and graces which are present in every world and in every age. Rather than allowing himself to be dispirited by the difficulties, M. Ali Lakhani chooses instead to be uplifted by the mercies and to respond to the challenge of living in the modern world by imaginatively and intelligently applying traditional principles to contemporary problems. The journal he founded, *Sacred Web*, has now established itself as one of the foremost journals in the perennialist school of thought today. Its aim is not only to continue to make traditional principles available to seekers in the contemporary world, but also to apply those principles concretely to the complex and unprecedented issues generated by the modern, and now "postmodern", world.

In his book aptly entitled *The Eleventh Hour* (Cambridge: Quinta Essentia, 1987), Martin Lings drew attention not only to the negative aspects of the times in which we live, but also to their redeeming features, above all, the abundance of divine mercy which compensates for the extreme difficulty of pursuing a spiritual path—or even a religious path—in the contemporary world. This is precisely the principle evoked by the parable of the "eleventh hour" in the Bible: those who labored only during the eleventh hour were paid the same as those who labored during the whole day. The modern world, therefore, despite being dominated by anti-traditional principles, is by no means impermeable to the influence of the Sacred which is the very sap of Tradition. Rather, the compensatory mercy of the eleventh hour renders the Sacred accessible to those who sincerely wish to "swim against the tide", and to live according to the immutable principles of Tradition.

Lings also draws attention to the "wisdom" that comes with old age: the world in which we live is in a sense "old", inasmuch as it is so close to the end of this cosmic cycle, and the wisdom which is accessible in our time is the wisdom not just of the "ages" but of all places. Never has such an abundance of sacred literature been so widely available as it is in our times.

Moreover, in our times we have also been provided with keys to unlock the treasures of this traditional wisdom, and a compass to help us navigate the rich landscape revealed by this wealth of sacred literature. For part of this literature is constituted by the works of the school of thought known as *sophia perennis*, a school of thought perfectly proportioned to the universal scope of the sacred literature made available to us in our times, and in our times alone. This school of thought, inaugurated by René Guénon and Ananda Coomarswamy at the end of the 19th century, and perfected in the works of Frithjof Schuon, is often referred to as "traditionalist", a word which unfortunately evokes a sentimental attachment to the past and a refusal to rise to the challenges of the present. The term "perennialist", by contrast, more clearly implies the timeless aspect of the wisdom and holiness which define the essence of this school of thought. The perennialist is not simply one who harks back nostalgically to the traditions of a bygone age; rather, he is one who is resolved to assimilate and radiate, here and now, the perennial truths transmitted by Tradition. This is the challenge confronting the perennialist living in a world dominated by anti-traditional values; but it is also a world open, "from above", to the divine mercy, ever available to those sincerely seeking it.

The issues covered in this volume are considerable, ranging from a spiritual critique of fundamentalism to the metaphysics of poetic expression. In respect of poetry, we should like to draw attention to the fine essay, "'Standing Unshakably in the True": A Commentary on the Teachings of Frithjof Schuon (1907-1998)', which is an original exposition based entirely upon the German poems written by Schuon, and published as *World Wheel* (Bloomington: World Wisdom, 2006). This essay, and indeed most of the essays gathered here, can be read as an introduction to the writings of Schuon, coming as they do from one whose intellectual perspective is clearly fashioned by the metaphysics of this unparalleled authority.

If, to return to the work of Martin Lings cited above, it is true that "again and again, about this or about that, one has the impression that Schuon has said the last word", it is no less true that Schuon's works can serve as a perpetually fresh source of inspiration for those seeking not only to discern between the Real and the illusory on the highest levels of metaphysics, but to apply this spiritual discernment to the potentially bewildering complexities of a nebulous and ever-changing world. Lakhani's essays demonstrate, therefore, the value of what one might call "applied metaphysics". They will doubtless prove to be of great benefit in particular for those who are interested in seeing the manner in which "pure metaphysics" can be transcribed within the interface between the immutable domain of traditional principles and the indefinite vagaries of the modern world.

Introduction

By William Stoddart

During the last fourteen years, the bi-annual journal *Sacred Web* has become recognized as a voice to be heard in the field of comparative religion and spirituality. This is largely due to the skillful editorship of M. Ali Lakhani, who, for virtually every issue, has been able to garner an impressive array of learned and distinguished contributors.

The Prince of Wales publicly expressed his appreciation of the journal and even made a gracious contribution to its pages.

Every enterprise must have a "mission" or a "guiding principle" and, for Lakhani, this has been the "traditionalist" or "perennialist" point of view. In recent years, the term "perennialism" has gained a certain notoriety, but it is not to be assumed thereby that absolutely everyone is clear as to what it means.

The "traditionalist" or "perennialist" school was founded by the French orientalist René Guénon (1886-1951) and the German poet and artist Frithjof Schuon (1907-1998). Guénon was the pioneer, and Schuon the fulfillment or consummation. Schuon pointed out the analogy here with two other wisdom schools which had dual originators and expositors, namely, those associated with Plato and Socrates in 5th century B.C. Athens, and with Jalal ad-Din Rumi and Shams ad-Din at-Tabrizi in 13th century Turkey.

Basically, the message of Guénon and Schuon is that of *philosophia perennis* or the perennial philosophy. This term was first used in the Renaissance, at which time it signified the recognition that the philosophies of Pythagoras, Plato, Aristotle, and Plotinus incontrovertibly expounded the same truth as lay at the heart of Christianity. In more modern times, the term has been enlarged to include the metaphysics and mysticisms of all of the great world religions, notably, Hinduism, Buddhism, and Islam.

Forerunners of the perennial philosophy in the East could be said to be the Islamic philosopher/mystic Ibn 'Arabi (1165-1240), who explained with particular cogency how an "essence" of necessity had many "forms"; and also the Hindu saint Ramakrishna (1836-1886), who was intimately familiar, not only with Hinduism, but also with Christianity and Islam, and who knew that each one of these religions was a way to God..

The central idea of the perennial philosophy is that Divine Truth is one, timeless, and universal, and that the different religions are simply different—and providential—languages expressing that one Truth. The two symbolisms most often used to express this view are, firstly, the uncolored light and the many colors of the spectrum, which are made visible only when the uncolored light is refracted. Secondly, there is the saying that "all paths lead to the same summit". In this symbolism, the variety of religions is represented by the multiplicity of starting-points around the circumferential base of a mountain or a cone. The radial, upward, paths are so many ways to God. From this picture, one can see that the unity of the religious forms is a reality only at the dimensionless point that is the summit.

Following upon the two eminent originators of the traditionalist or perennialist school, there came two distinguished continuators, namely the Anglo-Indian Ananda Coomaraswamy (1877-1947) and the German-Swiss Titus Burckhardt (1908-1984).

Coomaraswamy was born in Ceylon (Sri Lanka) of a Tamil father and an English mother. He was educated in England. In his early days he worked in his homeland, but later he moved to the United States, where he became Keeper of the Oriental Collection at the Boston Museum of Fine Art, a post he held for many years. During the early and middle part of his career, Coomaraswamy gained an enviable reputation as a historian and connoisseur of Indian and Indonesian art. When, in the later part of his life, he encountered the traditionalist writings of Guénon and Schuon, it was a case of love at first sight. From the late thirties onwards, he became a powerful voice for "tradition" in the English-speaking world, writing several books and contributing many articles expounding the traditionalist or perennialist point of view to a variety of learned journals.

Titus Burckhardt was Schuon's oldest and closest friend. He was born in Florence, but he came from a distinguished family of Basel, the city in which Schuon was born. Burckhardt was one year younger than Schuon, and they were at junior school together in Basel. Burckhardt devoted his life to the study and exposition of the different aspects of Wisdom and Tradition. He and Schuon were destined to become intellectual and spiritual colleagues for many decades.

It seems appropriate to mention in passing that the perennialist school has been attacked on many sides. Sometimes, because of its universalism, it has been likened to the "New Age" movement, and sometimes, because its central principle is gnosis (the knowledge of God), it has been likened to the heretical "gnosticism" of the early centuries of Christianity. I will not take up space here to refute these ill-founded charges.

*

* *

René Guénon began writing his principal books in the 1920s, and Frithjof Schuon in the 1930s; each of them wrote over twenty books. From the start, however, their writings usually made their first appearance in the form of articles contributed to journals which could be called the predecessors of *Sacred Web*. These included, among others: the venerable *Études Traditionnelles* (Paris)—for a short time under the title of *Le Voile d'Isis*—which for many years was edited by Paul Chacornac; *Studii Iniziatici* (Naples), edited by Corrado Rocco; *Sophia Perennis* (Tehran); *Connaissance des Religions* (France); *Sophia* (Oakton, Virginia); *Caminos* (Mexico); *Religio Perennis* (Sao Paulo); and *Zeitschrift für Ganzheitsforschung* ("Journal for Holistic Research", Austria).

The first English-language journal dedicated to the perennialist writings was *Studies in Comparative Religion* (London)—for a short time under the title of *Tomorrow*—which was edited by Francis Clive-Ross. This journal was published from 1963 to 1984, and has recently been revived as an on-line journal by World Wisdom Books of Bloomington, Indiana.

Finally, in 1995, *Sacred Web* (Vancouver) made a welcome entry onto the scene. The focus of *Sacred Web* is encapsulated precisely by the title of this anthology, *The Timeless Relevance of Traditional Wisdom*. The journal quickly became a forum for articles by highly qualified contributors on a multitude of topics, ranging from metaphysics, spirituality, and sacred art, to every conceivable problem of the modern world.

Lakhani's perennialist background did not in any way constrain him in his capacity as editor. All manner of points of view found expression in his pages. There were differences, and sometimes conflicts, the latter occasionally spilling over onto the "Letters to the Editor" section. No number of *Sacred Web* was dull.

From the beginning, each number of *Sacred Web* was introduced by a long and meaningful editorial by Lakhani. With a lawyer's meticulousness, he patiently and conscientiously scrutinized the problems and ambiguities emerging from the multi-faceted modern scene, often concentrating on those that were being dealt with in the relevant number of *Sacred Web*.

Part One of this anthology consists of a selection of the editorials from *Sacred Web*. The editorials expound what is meant by "Tradition", and discuss metaphysical principles such as "verticality" and the underlying unity of religions, as well as metaphysical "problems" such as reconciling "evil" with the existence of God, and "the quest for moral certainty". Many of the editorials focus specifically on the application of metaphysical principles to the issues confronting modernity. These issues include such topics as fundamentalism, secularism, pluralism, scientism, the environmental crisis, and issues of sexuality.

In these essays, Lakhani approaches the chaotic world with both compassion and sensitivity, but what makes his writings so worthwhile is the fineness of his analyses. In any context, he always seeks the "principle" or the "essence" underlying the issue and, from this starting-point, proceeds, deductively, to define its effects. When appropriate, it is his custom to offer an opinion as to what the "cure" for some problem or other might be. His opinions are a combination of principles and commonsense, and always repay much pondering. The "Greek" method of objectivity and impartiality in defining and rectifying a problem is always visible. Bias stemming from sentimentalism is not the way of Mr. Lakhani.

*
* *

Part Two of this anthology includes several philosophical studies by Lakhani. The first one, entitled "The Metaphysics of Human Governance", is an excerpt from a paper which he gave at an international congress organized by the Institute for Humanities and Cultural Studies in Tehran in 2001. It was awarded the Institute's First Prize for the best essay submitted in the English language. In this article Lakhani makes a close examination of the classic problem of the relationship between spiritual authority and temporal power. In the old monarchies of Europe, this surfaced as the relationship between "Church and Crown", and many battles have been fought over it, the most notorious case in England being the fateful case of Henry VIII. Some centuries later, the even knottier problem of the relationship between authority as such and the new—and still elusive—concept of "freedom" began to be the subject of debate. On the question of freedom, Lakhani quotes the following insight from Frithjof Schuon: "Freedom consists much more in satisfaction with our particular situation than in the total absence of constraints, an absence scarcely realizable in the here-below, and which in any case is not always a guarantee of happiness."

The second essay in Part Two is a wide-ranging study of aesthetics entitled "The Metaphysics of Poetic Experience". In this section Lakhani's love and knowledge of literature become apparent. He takes as his subjects "a wide group of thinkers who are not always reckoned strictly of the Traditionalist school, Henry Corbin, Kathleen Raine, Philip Sherrard, Harold Bloom and Wendell Berry, and poets and writers ranging from those of Antiquity (such as Homer and Virgil), of the Medieval world (Dante), the Renaissance

(Shakespeare, Milton, and Metaphysical poets such as Donne, Herbert and Vaughan), the Romantics (Coleridge, Shelley, Blake), and the Moderns (Yeats, Hopkins, Whitman, Emerson), to many in the non-English writing traditions (Li Po, Rumi, Sa'adi, Attar, Hafiz, Shabistari, Kabir, Mirabai, Juan de la Cruz, Rilke, Neruda, Jiménez)", but Lakhani's own standpoint remains that of the *philosophia perennis*. "Poetry", he writes, "is the art of transcendence".

Further in his exposition, Lakhani recalls the following distinction: "It is noteworthy that while Plato emphasized the moral purpose of poetry, Aristotle focused on an aesthetic value associated with the unity of the artist's composition, and that while Plato denounced the purely emotive appeal of poetry, Aristotle allowed for its cathartic and cleansing values." Each of the philosophers emphasized, however, that poetry must necessarily be the vehicle of Truth. "Poetry... is understood as the radial reconnection of circumferential man to his Origin and Center".

Another essay in this section deals with the concept of "Universality" both in itself and within the context of Islam. I will refrain from describing it in detail as this is an article that the reader must savor and ponder for himself. Those who are unfamiliar with the Koran will be grateful for the many references to its resounding verses. The whole article is like a hymn to the opening words of the Koranic "Verse of Light": *Allahu nuru's-samawati wa'l-'ard*. "God is the Light of the Heavens and the earth."

The final article in Part Two is on education in the light of metaphysics and tradition. Before one starts to read it, one knows not to expect praise for anything resembling what is served up to students in the schools and universities of today! I have forgotten the exact words of Coomaraswamy's quip, but it went something like: "It can take a man only three years to get a Harvard education, but it will take him ten years to get rid of it!" Saint Symeon the New Theologian puts the point more elegantly, but equally pungently: "Anyone who thinks himself intelligent because of his scholarly or scientific learning will never be granted insight into the Divine mysteries unless he first humbles himself and becomes a fool." Following in the footsteps of the great, Mr. Lakhani takes no prisoners!

*

* *

Part Three of this anthology consists of Lakhani's reviews of three important books. The first one is *Science of the Cosmos, Science of the Soul* by William Chittick. This evocative title comes from the sub-title of Titus Burckhardt's highly-praised book on *Alchemy*. The present book is a discussion by an Islamic scholar of the two fundamentally different types of knowledge: the infallible spiritual or intellectual knowledge ("intellectual" in the sense of Eckhart's *Intellectus*) and the empirical "knowledge" gained from observing, hypothesizing, and experimenting. This empirical science—supported by an illegitimate extension of Aristotle's doctrine of science—stems from the humanistic outburst that was the 15th-century Renaissance and, even more directly—and more crassly—, from the avowedly anti-spiritual 18th-century Enlightenment.

Lakhani's second review is of *Conversations with Wendell Berry* edited by Morris Allen Grubbs. The review outlines, largely in Berry's own words, the themes that define his views as "an agrarian reformer and environmentalist, a cultural and economic critic, and a defender of communitarian and family values and lifestyles, whose ideas are rooted practically in a sense of fidelity of place and community and in a commitment to community-based living." With Lakhani's interest in the application of traditional values to modern life, it is easy to understand the importance he accords to Berry's ideas.

Tom Cheetham's trilogy on the French Islamologist Henry Corbin (1903-1978) is the occasion for an interesting discussion by Lakhani on Corbin, his philosophy, and his wide-ranging influence on many contemporary writers. Corbin was born a Protestant, but early on he immersed himself in Medieval scholastic philosophy and Platonism. The turning point in his life, however, came with his discovery of the writings of the Persian theosophic mystic Shihab ad-Din as-Suhrawardi (1155-1191), who founded the Suhrawardi *tariqa* (one of the earliest ever formed). Corbin declared: "Through my meeting with Suhrawardi, my spiritual destiny for the passage through this world was sealed. Platonism expressed in terms of the Zoroastrian angelology of ancient Persia illuminated the path that I was seeking."

Corbin was a prominent figure in the University of Tehran, the Sorbonne in Paris, and the Eranos Foundation at Ascona (source of the famous Eranos "Yearbooks"), and is much beloved today by the Temenos Academy in London. One of Corbin's many merits was to castigate Jung's failure to distinguish between soul (*psyche*) and Spirit (Eckhart's *Intellectus*), which in practice amounts to the "abolition" of Spirit. At one stroke Jung abolishes the very notion of, and thus the capacity for, objectivity and, by the same token, for spirituality. The chaos and damage resulting from this anti-Platonic act of blindness are incalculable. We are left stranded in a satanic waste-land where everything (truth, morality, art) is relative.

Corbin was a man of conscience. Late in his life, he was a favored candidate for election to the French Academy but, for the sole reason that he refused to withdraw his overt opposition to the statuary belief in evolution and progress, his candidacy was refused.

*

*   *

Enough has been said to indicate the wide-ranging scope of Lakhani's interests; but his editorials, philosophical essays, and book reviews on a dauntingly large variety of topics become so many reverberations of one underlying and all-governing vision. Though Lakhani's treatment of his many themes is free and unconfined, the same unitary message remains throughout. The message is the primacy of truth, and its inseparable concomitants: beauty and virtue. This brings to mind the following Buddhist story:

Introduction

It is told that once Ananda, the beloved disciple of the Buddha, saluted his Master and said: "Half of the holy life, O Master, is friendship with the beautiful, association with the beautiful, communion with the beautiful."

"Say not so, Ananda, say not so!" the Master replied. "It is not half the holy life, it is the whole of the holy life."

In like manner, the doctrine of Plato can be encapsulated in the phrase: "Beauty is the splendor of the Truth, and Truth is the essence of Beauty." Thoughts of this kind serve to evoke the world of Mr. Lakhani and his journal *Sacred Web*.

Part One:

The *Sacred Web* Essays

What is "Tradition"?[1]

"Tradition", in the special way that the term is used by "Traditionalists", refers to a particular worldview: a way of seeing the world that differs from the ordinary perception.

We ordinarily see the world as composed of mind and matter: of physical objects located in time and space, which we interpret with our minds and our senses (of which our technological instruments are but extensions).

By contrast, Traditionalists speak of a way of seeing the world in which mind and matter exist as part of a continuum of reality that involves a deeper dimension: a transcendent spiritual dimension of which the worlds of mind and matter are merely a projection—like waves upon the surface of an ocean.

The worldview of Tradition is of this deep ocean, of a Presence in which we all participate: of a Reality in which we live and move and have our being—or we can think of it as a Sacred Web, as it were, through which each strand of life is intimately connected to every other.

This worldview engages the realization that within each of us is a transcendent Center, a unique vantage point within our innermost selves, our Heart, from which the complete web of life can be seen, which is one with the transcendent Source from which all the different strands emerge and by which they are all held together.

It is the realization that what we do to the web of life, we do to ourselves, and that our outer disharmonies are but the projections of an inner malaise.

True peace or harmony can therefore only be found by an inner alignment with that deeper Reality that connects us all.

---

[1] This is a revised excerpt from a speech given by M. Ali Lakhani at the opening of the Sacred Web Conference on "Tradition and Modernity", held at the University of Alberta in Edmonton, Canada, on September 23rd and 24th, 2006.

3

One can therefore point to three fundamental differences between the ordinary understanding of the term "tradition" and the special sense in which the term "Tradition" (with a capital "T") is used by Traditionalists.

First: in its ordinary meaning, tradition refers to etiquette, custom, habit, or a conventional way of doing or seeing things; but in its special usage, Tradition is both a worldview and a way of being that reflects a sense of the sacred—the sense that the created world is a radiance of the Transcendent—one might call it the fragrance of the Divine.

Second: in its ordinary meaning, tradition looks to the past; but in its special meaning, Tradition is timeless (it proclaims the ineffable Truth which is true for all time). Therefore, Traditionalists sometimes speak of the Primordial Tradition or of the Perennial Tradition.

And third: in its ordinary meaning, tradition refers to that which denotes the conventional, the commonly accepted way; but in its special usage, Tradition refers to the Truth, which, though universally accessible, is far from common. The Path of Tradition—though there are many faith traditions, each with their particular pathways and practices—involves initiation into a hallowed spiritual Path, the commitment of receptive faith and the practice of invocatory prayer, and the full engagement of one's deepest being to the True, the Good and the Beautiful, to piety, virtue, and reverence for all that is sacred.

An Introduction to *Sacred Web*[1]

"Tradition" and "Modernity" are two separate outlooks by which to judge the state of the contemporary world. By "Tradition" we mean *sophia perennis* or primordial wisdom, those principles which are timeless and universal, not limited to any one faith or culture, and which reconnect us to our Origin and Center. Traditionalist writers have distinguished between the terms "contemporary" and "modern", the former designating that which is of the present age, be it traditional or modern, and the latter, particularly when used in contrast to Tradition, designating the ideology of "Modernism" or "that which is cut off from the Transcendent, from the immutable principles which in reality govern all things and which are made known to man through revelation in its most universal sense" (*Seyyed Hossein Nasr*).

To speak of modernity is to evoke a certain ambivalence. On the one hand, we are the creatures of our time and so we celebrate its outward achievements, its advances in the fields of science and technology, and in its social reforms. Judged in these terms, what we conventionally label as "modern" is an improvement upon the apparent anachronisms of the past. The outward accomplishments of the modern world, which for the most part are scientific and technological, are undoubtedly impressive, ranging from achievements in medical science, to computer technology, from nuclear power to space travel, and other marvels so wondrous that we, mere humans, might almost believe ourselves gods. As well, we note other forms of advancement associated with modernity, social reforms undertaken in the cause of basic human rights and freedoms, manifesting in movements promoting civil rights and gender equality, and causes ranging from multicultural pluralism to ecological consciousness and advocacy. And yet, on the other

---

[1] This essay is a revised version of the Inaugural Editorial for *Sacred Web*, Volume 1, published in July, 1998.

hand, despite these outward accomplishments, and despite great privileges of our era—which, arguably, confer upon us the equally great responsibility to make use of our gifts respectfully and for the betterment of the world and ourselves—we experience a profound malaise that has been termed "the malaise of modernity".

From this perspective, wherever mankind turns its gaze, it no longer witnesses "the countenance of the Divine". Instead, it is confronted by a world of increasing fragmentation and spiritual poverty: a world accultured by individualism and secularism, by hubristic scientism and materialistic greed, and by the allure of the superficial that is marked by the erosion of both interiority and verticality. This acculturation has led to a myriad of problems: the alienation of man from nature, of man from humanity, and of self from spirit. Veiled thus from his celestial Origin and Center, mankind in the grip of modernity is without anchor or rudder, buffeted by the storms of his passions. Decentered man, enslaved thus by his passions, lives in a qualitatively impoverished world, of augmented alienation and diminished humanity, a universe characterized by the cognitive and ethical relativism of postmodernism, the sclerotic dogmatism of secular and religious fundamentalism, and—what may be termed the defining feature of modernity—the loss of the sense of the sacred.

By contrast, to speak of Tradition is to admit of the Transcendent and thereby to evoke the sacred. In the words of Frithjof Schuon, "the sacred is the Presence of the Center in the periphery". A central premise of Traditional metaphysics is the ultimate integrity of Reality evident in this Presence, whose locus is none other than our innermost and transcendent Self—the "Heart". The goal of Traditional practices is therefore to realize Reality by discerning it and concentrating upon it—in other words, by becoming "Heart-centered". It is through the faculty of the kardial Intellect (which alone is receptive to the "first principles" of Tradition) that we can discern (or "divine") that which is Real; it is through the submission of the lesser (human) passions to the greater (spiritual) Will that we can hope to merit ultimate peace and freedom; and it is by rediscovering our spiritual foundation and the trust of sacredness which is our primordial heritage that we can begin to properly address the malaise of modernity.

Sacred Web has been conceived as a journal whose aims will be to identify Traditional "first principles" and their application to the contingent circumstances of modernity, and to expose the false premises of Modernism from the perspective of Tradition. The journal will encourage and invite legitimate debate in this area and will seek to examine the interaction between Tradition and modernity. It is hoped that the journal will be of interest to the Traditionalist and general reader alike, concerned about the issues of modernity.

The Importance of Spiritual Literacy[1]

So interpret, O possessors of eyes!

(Koran, 59.2)

The importance of "literacy" in the sense of the ability to read, write, and compute, is taken for granted nowadays, and there are many forms of literacy that exist, ranging from technological and computer literacy to media and consumer literacy. It is also generally accepted that these various forms of literacy enable individuals to better function in modern societies. From the perspective of Tradition, however, there is a more basic and indispensable form of literacy whose importance is mostly overlooked and largely unacknowledged by the modern world. This is spiritual literacy.

The importance of spiritual literacy is founded upon principles of Traditional metaphysics according to which Reality is perceived as an integrated whole, manifesting within a spiritual continuum in which we ourselves participate. As with other forms of literacy, spiritual literacy has its utilitarian justification: it teaches us that all things can be traced to their spiritual roots, thereby equipping us to seek more profound practical solutions to our everyday problems, from the perspective of their spiritual origin. But beyond this pragmatic value, there is a deeper significance to spiritual literacy: it is the font of purpose. For it is the spiritual perspective alone that illumines the full spectrum of meaning for man, endowing human relationships with an ethical dimension as well as conferring on each individual a sense of purpose or *telos*. The true justification for spiritual literacy resides in understanding that the realization of Reality is the true métier of man, a project which cannot be undertaken nor achieved without the possession and development of the spiritual faculty.

---

[1] This essay is a revised version of the Editorial for *Sacred Web*, Volume 2, published in December, 1998.

To speak of existence is at a certain level to speak of contingency and displacement, and to situate man in any given manifestation is to invoke a necessary correspondence between context and contingency. From one perspective, each creature exists at its own level, bounded by its own context and its own set of contingent circumstances. From another perspective, man is a "fragment of the Absolute", and all creation a theophany radiating through multiple levels of contingent reality from a Center or Origin which is Itself Absolute and to which all of creation (and man, uniquely) is connected. To define man within any given context is therefore to evoke two outlooks, one fragmentary and discontinuous, the other integrated and continuous, which, though seemingly mutually exclusive, coexist from the perspective of Traditional metaphysics. These form the weft and warp of reality. And it is in this coexistence, in the two worlds in which we must live at the same time, in the intersection between the vertical and horizontal dimensions of reality, that the genius of man and the true project of mankind reside.

It is from the name of the Greek messenger god, Hermes, the god of boundaries, to whom was given the power of movement between the different worlds, that we derive the term *hermeneutics*, designating generally that which is concerned with the interpretation of texts. It is in the full sense of man's contextuality that the term "text" is to be understood, in the Muslim sense of *ayat* or the Christian sense of *logos*, in which creation is a continuous utterance whose meaning we ourselves, as divine articulations, embody. In this sense, the notion of the text as "sign" is inadequate to convey the true scope of its meaning insofar as it merely denotes the "other" without embracing a participatory dimension that includes our innermost selves. Similarly, our understanding of "interpretation" in spiritual literacy has to extend beyond "cognitive understanding", which expression is inadequate to convey the experiential dimension of meaning that goes beyond the mere explanation of concepts. In Traditional terminology, therefore, "text" is understood as the "symbol" connecting the "cipher" by way of its archetype to its Center and Origin; while "interpretation" is understood as the experience of that which is "de-ciphered". Traditional hermeneutics is therefore a means of integrating the "two worlds", of "beyond" and "within"—uniting knowledge and being.

In a multi-dimensional world, it is one's level of engagement with reality that determines the quality of one's experience. It is in this respect that Tradition and Modernism part company. The approach of Modernism is anthropocentric: it proceeds outwards from man, who is at its center, and in search of a source and origin, and is premised on the belief that man can define the Infinite and know the Unknown—a viewpoint that would thereby deny the transcendent, and limit reality to that which is contingent. This is a doomed enterprise, as futile as attempting to arrive at the ever-receding horizon. By contrast, Tradition is theocentric: it proceeds outwards from God, who is the axiomatic Center and Origin of all creation, the transcendent and (because also immanent) integral Source and Font of Reality, and of knowledge, manifested by the continuous grace of ever-renewing revelation, of which the interior pole is the Intellect. From the Traditional perspective, therefore, knowledge and its objects are not the entitlement of man to be had for the taking but rather are gifts to be justified by the receiving. Accordingly, man is enjoined by Tradition to approach knowledge reverentially, mindful of its sacred nature and of its ability to retrace his path to the ultimate ground of Reality.

The faculties of man valued by Modernism (such as reason, logic and sense perception) are each viewed by Tradition as competent within their own limited realms, but as subordinate to the higher faculty of the Intellect, which alone has hermetic access to the celestial realms from which all things originate and to which all things return. The difference between the Traditional and Modernist outlooks lies in their different orientations, which account for their different interpretations of the world. The orientation of Modernism is towards the Peripheral, the Center being concealed from it by the opacity of the Veil. By contrast, the orientation of Tradition is towards the Center (located simultaneously both beyond and within), which reveals Itself through the translucence of the Veil. In each case, the Veil confronting the seeker is the same, but the way in which it is perceived is different. This difference in vision is a matter of receptivity, of faith, whose denial constitutes the denial of meaning itself. Faith in the Absolute Reality of which all the ancient traditions speak is therefore the central prerequisite for spiritual literacy, the Jacob's Ladder that connects us to Heaven. It is faith that holds open the door for the functioning of grace and deepens all the faculties of perception, including desire itself, transmuting knowledge into love. But in order for the seeker to ascend the Ladder, spiritual hermeneutics requires that such faith be marked by a quality of critical openness that keeps the eyes alert at every moment, with an awareness that guards against the lapse into forgetfulness. And therein resides the mystery of the Divine Invocation, the *dhikr* or *Om*, the "re-minding" of Prayer, or the Word that God utters, which ultimately is none other than our very Self.

Pluralism and the Metaphysics of Morality[1]

> We are spirits. That bodies should be lent us, while they can
> afford us pleasure, assist us in acquiring knowledge, or doing
> good to our fellow creatures, is a kind and benevolent act of God.
>
> (*Benjamin Franklin*)

How should a society organize itself? How can one properly resolve
the tensions between equal rights and individual freedoms? At the
root of both equality and freedom lies the question: What is morality? These are the fundamental questions underlying the pluralist
discourse in modern societies. The motto on the Great Seal of
the United States ("*E Pluribus Unum*") suggests a possible nexus
between pluralism and its metaphysical origins. The philosophy
of Dostoevsky's Ivan Karamazov ("If God is dead, then everything
is permitted") suggests a similar nexus between morality and its
spiritual foundations. Without this nexus, there can be only error.

There are two errors that must be guarded against in the pursuit of Truth or Reality. These are reductionism and relativism.
Both errors derive from a denial of the Traditional metaphysical
principle that Reality, being Absolute, can be neither reduced to
the conditions of existence (hence, reductionism) nor excluded
from it (hence, relativism). A corollary of this principle is that
Truth has a transcendent aspect (entailing Faith and mystery) as
well as an immanent aspect (manifesting as the intimacy of the
Spirit/Intellect). It is as dangerous, therefore, to isolate either of
these aspects as it is to ignore them. The isolation of Faith (or the
denial of the Intellect) is a reductionist tendency and can lead to a
sclerotic dogmatism—the tyranny of "fundamentalism", while the
isolation of the Intellect (or the denial of Faith) is a relativist tendency and can lead to an extreme subjectivism and anarchy—the
delusions of the hypertrophic self. The corrective of dogmatism is

---

[1] This essay is a revised version of the Editorial for *Sacred Web*, Volume 3, published in June, 1999.

deconstruction, and vice versa. Between these two, lies the field of engagement, the narrow pathway between reductionism and relativism, the Straight Path of Tradition.

Equality and freedom are two of the pillars of modernity. They are also two of its grandest illusions. For neither equality nor freedom can truly exist extrinsically in reality. Intrinsically (and from the Traditional perspective), they exist only as attributes of the spiritual dimension of reality: the Spirit is equally present notwithstanding its pluralism, and is freely present notwithstanding its formal limitations. To understand equality and freedom otherwise is to commit the errors of reductionism and relativism, respectively. Reductionism (the delusion of a false equality) is to seek equivalence between the Absolute and the contingent by reducing the Absolute to a contingent aspect of reality. Relativism (the delusion of a false freedom) is to seek liberation from contingency by denying the reality of the Absolute. Outside of its spiritual dimension, equality tends to become a homogenizing force that reduces itself to the harmony of the lowest common denominator, whatever that may be, however devoid of spiritual value; while, freedom tends to become a permissive liberalism that manifests in the privatization of morality, however devoid of virtue.

Much of the pluralist discourse centers on the term "value". Equality and freedom are touted as fundamental "values", and many a modern society is founded on "values" enshrined in a Bill of Rights or a Charter of Rights and Freedoms. But rights and freedoms must be rooted in ontological principles, that is, in the reality that corresponds to our innermost and transcendent Self. In other words, the sole criterion of worth is the Absolute, or its reflection within the core of our innermost Self—which we call the "Heart". It is this kardial intelligence that transmutes knowledge to love, and which is the essence of "virtue". Tradition therefore focuses on the ontological principle of "virtue" rather than on "values". To be virtuous automatically entails a limit on freedom, a limit that is sometimes expressed as conscience or responsibility. It incorporates the notion of a hierarchical society in which authority derives from virtue, in which diversity is embraced through the moral intelligence of love rather than atomized or homogenized by recourse to secular "values".

Tradition provides both the doctrine (*theoria*) and the method (*praxis*) for apprehending and conforming to Truth or Reality. From the perspective of Tradition, Truth is Presence, the meeting-point and intersecting Center of knowledge and love, of Intellect and will. This ontological reintegration of knowing and being expresses itself as "virtue". Morality from the traditional perspective is thus more than merely a form of good behavior: it is the love motivating the ideal of equality and the knowledge underlying the ideal of freedom. It is the Spirit that conforms ontologically to the principial Truth that it embodies.

"What Thirst Is For"[1]

It is good knowing that glasses are to drink from.
The bad thing is not knowing what thirst is for.

(Antonio Machado)

Whoever is desireless, sees the essence of life.
Whoever desires, sees its manifestations.
These two are the same.

(Tao Te Ching)

Man is compounded of both dust and spirit, and, like all creatures, he is covenanted concurrently to both time and eternity. This simultaneity, this admixture, inheres within the very fabric of creation and existence, of revelation itself. To exist is to be and, at the same time, not to be. Growth is a form of evanescence, dying a form of being born. Existence is now and, in a certain sense, forever. Form conceals essence, being resides within becoming, stasis abides in the heart of movement, reality is both present and fleeting, both beyond and within. And in this *complexio oppositorum* lies the paradox and ambiguity of spiritual expression: divine utterances, ourselves included, contain ineffable meanings. Words proclaim Silence.

It is this same ambiguity that clouds the nature of desire—a cloud of ambiguity which only the rays of the Intellect—the supernal Sun—can disperse. This is the ambiguity of *Maya*, the ambiguity of the Cosmic Veil. And at the heart of this ambiguity lies a choice given to all of mankind: to seek the fulfillment of one's desires in the beatific vision of the Sun's heavenly Light or to seek it in the tumult of the shadows.

From a metaphysical standpoint, privation and proximity, transcendence and immanence, the mystery of the Absolute and the radiance of the Infinite, are each embedded within the very

---

[1] This essay was the Editorial for *Sacred Web*, Volume 4, published in December, 1999.

structure of Reality. It is our "ontological distance from God" that constitutes our privation, and the possibility of our "ontological re-integration" within God that constitutes our proximity. "Things are in God and God is in things with a kind of discontinuous continuity" (*Schuon*), and Reality is therefore translucent with the radiance of God. Creation is understood in traditional thought to be a Veil through which—and in which—God is metaphysically transparent. Insofar as creation is separate from God, man is ontologically distant from the source of his existence and from the object of his salvation, which remains ever transcendent, mysterious, beyond reach. Yet, insofar as creation is a theophany, radiating the immanence of God, man—made in the image of God—has within him both the means and end of the fulfillment of his desires.

But what appears as translucent to the Inner Eye of the Heart is perceived as opaque by the Outer Eye of the mind or the senses. Therein lies the ambiguity of the Icon and the Veil, an ambiguity inherent in the process of the concretization of the Absolute, and its reversal. It is the Inner Eye that "dis-covers" the Beauty beneath the Veil. And it is "sacred desire" (or "spiritual thirst") that impels this discovery.

From the traditional perspective, since "all that exists tends towards perfection" and since "God is the Supreme Perfection", desires are satisfied only by the serenity of the Divine Presence. God is the sole and final refuge of lustful man. This is why Niffari exclaims: "I take refuge in the unity of Thy Quality against every quality". In the Islamic context, God is said to be both *Zahir* ("Manifest" or "Outward") and *Batin* ("Hidden" or "Inward"). He is revealed to the extent that man perceives Him through his Inner Eye, the Eye of the Heart—the Eye of the Intellect. For traditional man, there is no Truth without Presence, and there is no Presence until God is perceived in the "eternal now", both beyond and within: the world seen in a grain of sand, and a heaven in a wild flower.

One of the key attributes of Modernism is its profanation of desire. For, "He who knows God is disinterested in the gifts of God, and he who is negligent of God is insatiable for the gifts of God" (*Shaykh Ahmad al-'Alawi*). Modern man has an insatiable thirst for the gifts of God, but is blind to His Presence. Instead he perceives only the objects of his lusts, breeding through them a world of concupiscence, exploitation, commodification and wanton consumption—a world in which desire is reduced to the need for the instant gratification of individual wants and cravings, and the indulging of personal appetites. In such a world, the notion of the perfectability of desire as love, or the conformity of the soul to the Beauty of the Spirit, is all but forgotten—replaced by Modernist explanations of desire in terms of behavioral instincts, or the pleasure/pain principle, or libido, or the evolutionist's creed of the "survival of the fittest". These theories are reinforced and systematized through the tyranny of the modern media and its various seductions that fuel the monster of consumption, creating wants and desires that mankind never before even dreamed of. Lost in such a world is the respect for traditional values, for the nobility of the person, the sanctity of relationships, the wonder of life, and the appreciation that "everything that lives is holy". In a world of such wantonness, desires degenerate, pander to the unsalutary, and eventually erode the very foundations of society. In Cymbeline, Shakespeare observes:

> The cloyed will,—That satiate yet unsatisfied desire, that tub
> Both fill'd and running,—ravening first the lamb, Longs after for
> the garbage.

What, then, can fulfill this "satiate yet unsatisfied desire"? It is true that some traditional teachings have anathemized desire, but in so doing, they are in reality no more than condemning the desecration of desire—not desire itself. So, for example, when Bayazid exclaims "I desire not to desire", or the Buddha—who teaches that craven desire is the cause of all suffering—advocates "blowing out the flame of desire", the "desire for desirelessness" to which they aspire is itself a legitimate and necessary form of desire—a prolongation in the will of an apophatic discernment of the intelligence—and is another example of the *complexio oppositorum* referred to earlier. It is not until the final act of "letting go"—the initiatic "death" of the "psycho-physical *res*" which constitutes the crystallized being of man—that desire itself finally ceases, requited ultimately by Divine Presence (*visio beatifica*) or Mystical Union (*unio mystico*). But, till then, decentered man is enjoined, by force of his privative conditions, to desire. For thirst and privation are the conditions of existence. Man cannot overcome his privative conditions. To exist in a contingent and imperfect world is to partake of those very qualities. Man will thirst, hunger, bleed and eventually die. But something in man can transcend and survive the contingency and imperfections of his earthly existence. There is a connection between our worldly—sensual—desires (*eros*) and their intended end (*telos*). Worldly desires exist in order to be sublimated. The desire of man is prefigured in the desire of God. This is one of the many meanings of the famous *Hadith Qudsi* (a sacred or divinely-inspired utterance): "I was a hidden treasure; I desired to be known, so I created the world in order to be known." Creation then is a projection of God's desire into the world. In other words, God desires our existence precisely so that we may desire our return to Him, our Origin and Final Sanctuary.

Though man's lot cannot be overcome, it can yet be transcended by reconnecting our desires to their sacred Origin, a connection that is made through the golden thread of *Amanah*, the "Sacred Trust" of mankind. This is the true purpose of desire, whose fulfillment is both knowledge ("To know what is, and to know it in such a fashion as to be oneself, truly and effectively, what one knows"— *Guénon*) and vision ("Everything is perishing but His Face"— *Koran: 28.88*). Herein lies the meaning of the Koranic Covenant of Alast (*Koran: 7.172*) in which each departing soul, before being sent out into the world, affirms its sacred Origin—a witnessing that is subsequently reaffirmed by every practicing Muslim in the words of the Shahadah or "profession of faith": *La ilaha illallah* ("There is no god but God") and in the divine invocation or *dhikr*.

True knowledge (or Truth), because it permeates our very being, is none other than Love (that is to say, moral intelligence—or Virtue) and Vision (that is to say Presence—or Beauty): the True, the Good, and the Beautiful; *Sat, Chit,* and *Ananda.* It is through the cultivation of these qualities that desire, by grace and effort, is finally sublimated to its ultimate goal, the Pax Profunda, the "peace of God, which passeth all understanding".

Of Detachment and Spiritual Courtesy[1]

> The saint is effectively the void made for the passage of God.
>
> *(Frithjof Schuon)*

> He who clings to the Void
> And neglects Compassion
> Does not reach the highest stage.
> But he who practices only Compassion
> Does not gain release from the toils of existence.
> He, however, who is strong in practice of both,
> Remains neither in *Samsara* nor in *Nirvana.*
>
> *(Saraha)*

It is a curious fact of modern lives, particularly in urban societies, that people are increasingly hard-edged and jaded, burying their vulnerabilities deep within an exterior of toughness and resignation. Their detachment renders them capable of gazing vacantly at images of violence and depravity or of shrugging indifferently at news of war, famine or disaster. For them, in the words of Tennessee Williams, "happiness is insensitivity". This insensitivity—the detachment of modernity—is very different to the quality of detachment advocated by Tradition as a virtue. It is not a detachment of compassion and serenity, rather a paradoxical amalgam of unconcern and craving.

The detachment of Tradition, by contrast, is grounded in compassion, not in insensitivity. The basis for this detachment is a view of reality as both transcendent (hence the distance of detachment) and immanent (hence the intimacy of compassion). The acceptance of transcendence necessarily imparts the recognition of our own indigence and contingency in relation to the Absolute, producing a sense of wonder and humility that are all but lacking in the modernist outlook. At the same time, the acceptance of immanence

---

[1] This essay is a revised version of the Editorial for *Sacred Web*, Volume 5, published in July, 2000.

imparts an awareness of the integrity of reality, producing a sense of its sacred inter-relatedness and an abiding compassion for all things that is the very antithesis of insensitivity.

It is, from the Traditional point of view, fundamentally erroneous either to lose sight of our essential connectedness or to attempt to locate it outside transcendence and the integrity of reality. This is a principal error of modernism and a feature of modernity. By this, it is not suggested that to live in the contemporary world is necessarily to deny transcendence—merely that the denial of transcendence is a defining feature of modernism, the ethos of modernity—an ethos that has been characterized by contemporary commentators variously as narcissistic and apathetic. This denial, where it exists, lies at the root of modern humanity's conflation of compassion and passion, of joy and pleasure, of depth and intensity. And it is the cause of its tendency to reduce virtue to empty forms and gestures, and to favor subjective expressions of privatized morality or self-indulgent excesses of sentimentalism.

It is not difficult to understand how the denial of transcendence can lead to the postmodern excesses of relativism, subjectivism and, ultimately, nihilism. However, a more insidious threat to humanity lies in the modern inversion of transcendence—through abstraction, that is, the reduction of spirituality to its merely mental or psychic aspects, creating thereby a false detachment from the full spectrum of theophanic reality. Disconnected thus from its spiritual center, the soul's innate passion finds no opening into compassion, seeking in vain for its complement, becoming increasingly listless, and, though seeking outer pleasures, unable to find the inner wellsprings of joy. It is interesting to note that the *hesychasts* used the original Greek word *apatheia*, not to mean what we now call "apathy", but to mean "detachment" in the traditional sense of an absence of egoism and distorting passion—that is, dispassion and the purity of the heart. This is the "void made for the passage of God". It is only in such virgin soil that the flower of compassion—of love that is not self-contained but out-pouring and engaged—can grow. Contrast the disengaged "love" of abstraction. It was the statement of a clearly modernist sensibility that uttered

Ivan Karamazov's celebrated commentary on one of Jesus' central teachings:

> The idea of loving one's neighbor is possible only as an abstraction: it may be conceivable to love one's fellow man at a distance, but it is almost never possible to love him at close quarters.

How easy it is to love in the abstract! And how much more demanding it is to actualize the needs of love in the concrete context of our relationships and the exigencies of daily living! It is helpful to remember that in Christianity, the commandment to "love thy neighbor as thyself" is subordinate to "the first and great commandment" to "love the Lord thy God with all thy heart, and with all thy soul, and with all thy mind." According to traditional metaphysics, it is principle that informs process. It is the principial relationship of man and God on the vertical plane that gives meaning to all creaturely relationships on the horizontal plane. Humanity's love for the creatures of God is therefore grounded in the transcendental affirmation of humanity's love of God. This is not an abstract love, but a love that is animated, imbued with the presence of life. It is only by witnessing the spiritual basis of all life—the vision of creation as a theophany—that humanity can discover the criterion for the love of itself: not the narcissistic love that feeds on itself, but the selfless love that is fed by what it gives of itself. This is the criterion of loving the neighbor as oneself.

It is helpful to recall that, based on its etymology and in its traditional usage, the word "theoretical" (derived from the Greek *theoria*, suggesting "vision") does not signify an abstraction, as its modern usage implies, but rather imparts the sense of "presence" or an "envisioning" of reality. This is one of the reasons why traditional sages are often referred to as "seers". What distinguishes their perception from that of the common man is precisely their ability to "see" by looking beyond the "veil" of metaphysical transparency—to perceive the transcendent dimension and its pervasive manifestation in all things. It is only through the experience of spiritual intimacy that one can be initiated into the mysteries of existence.

This is why, in Vedantic terms, *ayam atma brahma* ("The Atman is the Brahman")—in other words, immanence is, paradoxically, an aspect of transcendence. It is interesting to note how the modern usage of the word "theoretical" suggests a distancing—through abstraction—of "reality", hence of God (or supra-formal, spiritual reality) and, *a fortiori*, of the "Self" (the divine or spiritual imprint within each human being), devaluing these terms and reducing them to their peripheral meanings.

Evidence of such a reduction is also apparent by contrasting the different outlooks of the traditional and modernist worlds regarding the term "humanism". Following Jacques Maritain, one can distinguish between two forms of humanism: the traditional (*l'humanisme intégrale*), which is premised on spiritual reality (or God) as the center of human existence, and the modernist definition, which views human beings as their own center and the center of all things. Traditional humanism, then, is a form of spiritual courtesy which is more than merely social or religious convention. In Islam, for example, the Arabic term for "humanism", *adab*, is usually translated as "courtesy". *Adab* signifies the manifestation of *ihsan*, that is to say, intrinsic beauty, projected in the sincere virtuous conduct (spiritual courtesy) of the individual, or in a culture and ethos of spiritual (or theocentric) humanism. It is an attitude of attention to the inner qualities which exist within all human beings as marks of their spiritual Origin. It is also an inner sensitivity to the divine image within each of us and a specific awareness of that spiritual Presence residing within each individual, no matter how faint or weak. By contrast, in the case of modernist (or anthropocentric) humanism, the impoverished view of reality, lacking any vision of a spiritual Presence, responds obliquely to the human soul's authentic need for order by producing merely the counterfeit of *adab* in the forms of societal norms of civility, privatized morality, and procedurally-regulated "values" or codes of behavior. These behavioral approximations of order and courtesy, being disconnected from their spiritual Center, are not the transforming "virtue" of Tradition "which wounds our nature as the plough wounds the soil" (*Schuon*), but represent merely a necessary—and sometimes conscienceless—pragmatism.

The distancing or abstraction that marks the detachment (a better term might be disconnectedness or apathy) of modernity is none other than our ontological distance from our spiritual Source—and therefore, in traditional metaphysics, also from our own humanity and our rightful place in the cosmos. It is this ontological distance that religion seeks to bridge, reconnecting us to our Center and Origin—as is evident from the etymology of the term "religion" (derived from the Latin root, *ligare*, signifying a binding).

True *adab*, on the part of human beings, is foremost a matter of the correct orientation. In traditional societies, human beings are oriented—both in intellect and will—towards the Source of Illumination, that is to say, theocentrically, towards the Supernal Sun. It is helpful to note that the Orient (from which the term "orientation" is derived) is the source of the physical light of the Sun—a felicitous metaphor for the discerning Intellect. Just as the sun illumines us, it enlivens us also. It is only by correctly orienting ourselves that we can begin to efface the darkness of our ignorance and to overcome our apathy and lassitude by reconnecting with the Light that radiates in all beings. In the words of Niffari: "You will not come out from your veil except through my Light".

The detachment of Tradition, then, is the voiding of all that is human in order to merit the grace of reconnecting with our spiritual Center—by entering into the Reality of the Light that transcends all metaphor. It is this Light of compassionate serenity that constitutes the core of our very being, radiating within us as true *adab*, the genuine spiritual courtesy that reconnects us to our Maker and thence to our fellow-creatures, and the foundation within humankind of its integral humanism.

Consecrated to the Sublime[1]

Now it came to pass, as they went, that he entered into a certain
village: and a certain woman named Martha received him into
her house. And she had a sister called Mary, which also sat at
Jesus' feet, and heard his word. But Martha was cumbered about
much serving, and came to him, and said, Lord, dost thou not
care that my sister hath left me to serve alone? bid her therefore
that she help me. And Jesus answered and said unto her, Martha,
Martha, thou art careful and troubled about many things: But
one thing is needful: and Mary hath chosen that good part, which
shall not be taken away from her.

(Luke 10:38-42)

A candle is not there to illuminate itself.

(Nawab Jan-Fishan Khan)

One sometimes encounters the view that human beings should
look to their own salvation and leave the world to its own fate. In
extreme cases, this view extends to an attitude that is completely
contra mundum, a retreat from all worldly relations, even a disregard for the body and the physical world it represents. In less
extreme instances, it manifests in an ascetic tendency taking the
form of voluntary privations and renunciations. To what extent is
this view justified from the standpoint of Tradition, and how is one
to integrate the necessary disciplines of Tradition with the demands
of living in the modern world?

Despite any apparent expressions to the contrary, the aim of life
for the Traditionalist is not to escape the world, merely to escape
the world as such. This is not a mere semantic distinction, rather it
represents a substantive difference in how one sees and experiences
the world. The "escape" is ontological, that is to say, it is a "passage from distinctive or mental consciousness to unitive or cardiac

---

[1] This essay is a revised version of the Editorial for *Sacred Web*, Volume 6, published in December, 2000.

consciousness" (*Schuon*), from a psychological level of self to an interiority that is spiritual, universal and therefore transcendent or participatory. It represents both a recognition of the metaphysical transparency of things and a reordering of our very beings to accord with that perspective of reality. One is not concerned here so much with our relative viewpoints that lead to our respective individual and psychological experiences of living, rather there is in the eyes of Tradition a transcendent dimension accessible to each of us, which integrates and effaces our subjective experiences of reality within an objective and participatory view of the world that alone merits the appellation "Real." In all ages and cultures there have existed a few privileged human beings who have attested to experiencing this "other" transcendent world, in comparison with which the solid world of our senses appears insubstantial and illusory. It is as though the common experience of living is but a rude dream from which we must awaken. In Hinduism, this is one of the meanings of *maya*, the *samsaric* world of illusion and forgetting—the cosmic dream. Similarly, in Islam, one can cite the famous *Hadith*: "All who live in this world are asleep, and when they die they awaken."

But through the subordination of the terrestrial to the celestial, there is a devaluation of immanent reality, and in this devaluation lies the potentially erroneous disregard of the mundane for the sake of personal salvation. Erroneous because, though Traditional metaphysics invites us to discern the reality of transcendence— the source of the illumination that pervades and constitutes this world—it teaches us also to appreciate how all that it immanently pervades and illumines is sacred and holy by the very grace of its illumination. Once enlightened, the self experiences its deepest core as universal and participatory and therefore is incapable, by virtue of the compassion that constitutes the essence of its universality, of renouncing the world—with which it is, in this sense, co-extensive. This is why all traditions identify sanctity with salvific compassion. Herein lies the nobility of the *boddhisattvic* ideal: to recognize the salvific nature inherent in all creation and to conform oneself to that nature by becoming an instrument of grace for the salvation of all beings.

In Eckhart's controversial reading of the famous passage in *Luke* about Mary and Martha, he anticipates the Reformation's critique of monasticism by refusing to read the words of Jesus as a repudiation of *praxis*/action (as represented by Martha) in favor of *theoria*/contemplation (as represented by Mary). Instead he sees Martha as the more spiritually mature because of her ability to combine the "one thing needful" (apprehending and conforming to her "real" nature) with her cares of the world—that is, attending to the mundane, but not at the expense of necessary interiorization. Martha pleads with Jesus about her sister, not because she selfishly wants Mary's help, but because she wants her to awaken from the paralysis of a partial view of reality—one that wallows in transcendence and forgets that God is also in the details of His creation. She wants Mary to be with God in the world, to be like her, "among cares", yet not "within cares." And Jesus' response, in Eckhart's reading, means: "Be reassured, Martha, she has chosen the better part, which will lose itself in her. The highest thing that can happen to a creature will happen to her. She will be as happy as you." For Eckhart, then, happiness lies in the maturity of combining work and spirituality, of living in both worlds at the same time, not merely in "basking in religious feelings."

The more conventional reading of the Mary/Martha passage is to fault Martha with being too "cumbered" to attend to the "one thing needful." But does this imply an abandonment of the cares of the world in the cause of personal salvation? From the traditional perspective, Eckhart's reading is not incompatible in an essential sense with the conventional interpretation of the text. It is not the world we have to exclude, but our cumbersome, "intermediary" selves. Not renunciation that we must achieve, but detachment. The goal is not to flee the world but to be detached from it, to be "unencumbered" in the sense of becoming an empty vessel, a channel, a passage for Light. As Eckhart states: "For all who are active in the light are soaring toward God, free and unencumbered of all that is intermediary. Their light is their works and their works are their light." The focus on the "one thing needful" (the attunement of our selves to what is essential, to becoming a passage for light) is precisely what is required of us in order to see the world afresh, with new eyes that give it its proper worth. It is this *metanoia* or transformation of our very being that gives us a new way of seeing the world, one that enables us to embrace it, not passionately but compassionately, so that what once seemed ordinary and mundane, with the grace of vision, becomes extraordinary and radiant. This is the process of the development of theophanic vision, which Li Liweng expresses poetically as follows:

> First we look at the hills in the painting,
> Then we look at the painting in the hills.

Both "hills" and "painting" must be seen. God must be seen as a real presence in the world—or, more accurately, the world must be seen as a projection of the divine. It is in this manner that the world can be viewed as sacred, so that each task, indeed our very lives, become acts of worship consecrated to the sublime.

How is this to be achieved in the modern world? The world we live in offers us great freedom, perhaps more so than in any other period of history. Technological advances have improved our material comforts, information, health and quality of life, all of which has served to increase our freedom. Yet our freedom has paradoxically diminished as it has grown. Our traditional foundations have gradually eroded as our material pursuits have expanded. There is an addictive quality to these pursuits. We are seduced by the illusory world and, as we satiate ourselves, our malaise grows. As our pleasures increase, our joys diminish. Our freedom is curtailed by the pressures of living, the demands of time, and the compulsions of the material world. As these pressures, demands and compulsions grow, so too does our sense of apathy and spiritual discontent. Modern lifestyles, with few exceptions, allow little room for traditional pursuits. Such pursuits are often regarded as anachronistic and are increasingly privatized.

Given the destabilization—perhaps, more accurately, eradication—of the Traditional world, one may ask whether it is any longer realistic for human beings, except by retreating from the world, to live consecrated lives. The answer depends on how one apprehends the nature of reality itself. In the famous words of Abu Sa'id al-Kharraz: "God cannot be known except as a synthesis of opposites." This *coincidentia oppositorum*, which is central to the Traditional understanding of reality, contains the key to the art of living. Just as one is required to apprehend the divine as both Absolute and Infinite, transcendent and immanent, hidden and manifest, stern and compassionate, Father and Mother, so one is required, like Martha (in Eckhart's interpretation), to live in "both worlds" at the same time. We can—in fact must—be *in* the world, yet not *of* it. Granted that our relationship with the world is predicated by both our perception of it as well as our spiritual temperament, and that these may at times lead us away from the world; also, that there are spiritual disciplines that appear to deprecate the mundane where that relationship may otherwise be overemphasized; yet, in all this it is important to remember that any intermediate stage of spiritual growth which corresponds to a movement away from the world is eventually surpassed by a return to the world precisely because "There lives the dearest freshness deep down things" (*Hopkins*).

What, then, are the methods by which we should relate to the world? There are two necessary methods, both interrelated, and neither involves a renunciation of the world, but rather requires a special engagement with it. The first method is aimed at refining our quality of perception, and requires us to discern what is Real—which in turn requires the exercise of our innate intelligence, through the remembrance of our Origin, the visualization of its Presence symbolically and anagogically, and an acknowledgment of our End and the purposes it shapes. This entails, not a retreat from the world, but an ability to integrate it with the transcendent Source of its illumination—to see ourselves and the world in the light of the Spirit. Once we can perceive the Alpha and Omega, the *Awwal* and *Akhir*, co-existing in the here and now, in the very core of our being and in the minutiae of living, then our "doors of perception" can be said to be cleansed. Once we can perceive the One who "fathers-forth whose beauty is past change," then can we truly yearn to "praise Him". We are merely journeying through the world, and we must do so, ever mindful of our Destination, yet rejoicing in the reminder of its Presence amid our surroundings.

The second method is aimed at disciplining our will, and requires us to conform ourselves to what is Real—which in turn requires us to be true to Reality by becoming—or, more accurately, *being*—what we know and thereby conforming our wills to our intellects and also integrating the two domains which these faculties represent, namely, praxis and *theoria*. Again, this requires a quality of engagement with life that is the very antithesis of its renunciation. We must honor God within His creation by conforming to our Adamic self and by avoiding the hubristic choice of Iblis. As human beings, we are composed of both dust and spirit, an amalgam that is both worldly and transcendent, both carnal and divine. As such, we are capable of incarnating within us either that which is infernal or angelic. Our choice is clear. We must, within the crucible of our very beings, discover the basis of harmonizing the essential principles of Truth within us to the innate Beauty or Virtue that is our spiritual heritage. Though shaped by a transcendent Power, we are not without free will. In a very real sense, we have the ability to fashion our own ends. Just as there is no quietistic retreat from the affairs of the world in the traditional notion of spiritual maturity, so there is no corresponding idea of fatalism. According to the well-known Sufi saying, one must "trust in God, but tie one's camel first." But the "tying of one's camel" should not be an act of transgression from the praxis dictated by *theoria*. "Know Thyself," said the oracle. For only by knowing what is sacred within ourselves can we know what is sacred in all things. It is this gift of knowledge that makes humanity the stewards of creation and accountable for its care. We are free precisely in order that we may attend to the "one thing needful" and thus conform intrinsically to our archetypal natures, no matter what the extrinsic conditions and contingent circumstances of modernity may be.

What does all this mean in practical terms? First, we must learn the art of spiritual literacy. As with any other form of learning, this requires guidance and an attitude that facilitates learning. We must develop within ourselves a receptivity that attunes us to our intellectual intuitions so that we can begin to perceive the world as a theophany, radiating the divine. Second, we must incarnate within ourselves those qualities of virtue that harmonize our independent and free wills with our spiritual intuitions and sensibilities. This too requires guidance, as well as grace, forbearance, perseverance, and the rigors of spiritual discipline. For the human will is recalcitrant and refractory. It is easily tempted and can seduce the other faculties to serve its own ends.

By refining our faculties of perception and disciplining our wayward passions, we can hope to attain self-mastery in our lives, like the divine charioteer of the *Bhagavad Gita*. By these methods we may hope to achieve our real purpose in this our terrestrial abode: to allow ourselves to be illumined by the transcendent light of the Spirit so that, like candles in readiness, we may be lit by its flame, and our Presence light up all the dark and empty corners of this world. Let us conclude with words of Nasir Khusraw:

> The sun has the power of turning stone into ruby
> Which no force of elements can turn again
>   into its original state—
> I am like that ruby now, and the sun is he
> By whose light this dark world becomes lit.

"Fundamentalism": A Metaphysical Perspective[1]

> ...In religion, What damned error, but some sober brow
> Will bless it and approve it with a text,
> Hiding the grossness with fair ornament?
> (William Shakespeare, *The Merchant of Venice*, III.ii.77)

History is replete with examples of those who have desacrated and degraded religion, sadly and ironically in the name of religion itself. Wars, massacres, persecutions, and the destruction of sacred works of art, have all been sanctioned by religious authorities throughout recorded history, fueling skepticism about the legitimacy, and claims to moral authority, of traditional religion. The infamy in history of the Crusades or the Inquisition, or more contemporary examples such as the demolition of Babri Masjid or the Bamiyan Buddha, and countless political wars rooted in religious differences—including the more recent turmoils in the Middle East, the Balkans, Northern Ireland and Sri Lanka—all add to the evidence of the skeptics. But these actions, many of which are forced to wear the badge of religion, are in fact defamatory of authentic religion. We must be careful not to reject an authentic tradition on account of those abuses and violations perpetrated by its counterfeit in its name. Not every act done in the name of religion is in fact true to its spirit. It is therefore necessary to distinguish between genuine religion and its counterfeit, between the "fundamentals" of a religion and the "fundamentalist" offences committed in its name.

The term "fundamentalism", however, is anomalous and its usage fraught with difficulty. Though one can speak of many types of "fundamentalism" (for example, political, economic or scientific), the term is primarily associated with religion. In the context of religion, the term was originally applied to an early 20th

---

[1] This essay was the Editorial for *Sacred Web*, Volume 7, published in July, 2001. It was anthologized in "The Betrayal of Tradition: Essays on the Spiritual Crisis of Modernity", ed. Harry Oldmeadow, World Wisdom, Indiana, 2005, p.101.

Century Christian revivalist group known as the "Fundamentalist Movement", whose views were characterized by religious rigidity and evangelism, but in recent years, particularly dating to the time of the Iranian Revolution in the late 1970s, the term has come to be extended to other religions, so that one now speaks, for example, of Sikh, Hindu, Buddhist, Christian or Muslim "fundamentalists". The term has come to be laden with connotations of political and religious extremism or militancy, which the media frequently labels as "terrorism" (one is reminded here of the comment by Robert Fisk that terrorism is in fact "a political contrivance. 'Terrorists' are those who use violence against the side that is using the word."). This is particularly true in the case of Islam, which has been demonized in the aftermath of the Cold War and the fall of the Soviet Union, by being depicted as a threat to modern American civilization by writers within the dominant media, such as the influential Samuel P. Huntington for whom this portrayal was an important component to his thesis of the "clash of civilizations". The deconstruction of the media's portrayal of religious (particularly so-called Islamic) "fundamentalism" in the West by writers such as Edward Said has yielded important insights. The language employed by the dominant media reveals its own biases. It is selective to brand, for instance, a veiled Muslim woman as an "Islamic fundamentalist", falsely implying that she would condone violence carried out in the name of her religion, while avoiding the term altogether in the case of the Jewish settler who guns down worshipers in a mosque in Hebron, or a Catholic car-bomber in Belfast, or a Protestant extremist who detonates a bomb killing innocent civilians in Oklahoma. "Fundamentalism" is a term that disguises a host of complexities. It reflects the dominant culture's modernist bias towards secularism and individualism, which are largely rejected by the traditional cultures that it labels as "fundamentalist". And it ignores the nuances that reflect the complexities underlying what it labels as "fundamentalism". What, for instance, does the term reveal when applied equally to the Taliban's desacration of Buddhist artefacts and to the Iranian government who opposed that desacration? It is far too simplistic to understand the term to refer merely to the monolithic culture of religious violence that is commonly denoted by its use within the dominant media. One has to seek a deeper understanding of the term.

This essay proposes a definition of religious "fundamentalism" from the perspective of traditional metaphysics. There are two features that distinguish "fundamentalism" in this definition: in its inward aspect, though not synonymous with the formal, it is formalistic to the point where the "spirit" of religion is sacrificed to its "letter"; and in its outward aspect, though not synonymous with the exclusive, it is exclusivist to the point where it denies any religious pluralism premised on transcendent unity. Each of these aspects needs elaboration.

To understand how the inward aspect of authentic religion differs from that of "fundamentalism" as defined here, a starting point is perhaps to consider the object of religion. Faced with the mysteries of existence and death, humanity has sought throughout history to understand the nature of reality and existential meaning. All authentic religion, premised on the transcendental origin and end of reality, holds that human beings may, by the grace of revelation and intellection, discern the underlying unity and integrity of reality which is embedded within our very selves, and that such knowledge, where it permeates our being, is transformative, unitive and salvific. It is the spiritual ground of reality, realized in us, that imbues us with a sense of the sacred, transforming our perception of manifest reality into a theophany in which we participate, not as separate creatures but as the Divine Self, the Eternal Witness, the only Existent. This is the inward aspect of religion, its heart or core. Considered from this standpoint, the object of religion is an alchemical transformation that corresponds in all religious lexicons to an intrinsic beauty or virtue that radiates as compassionate piety. This piety expresses itself in a sacred relationship between humanity, as Trustee, and the theophanic creation, as Beneficiary, whose spiritual radiance we, as transcendent beings, are privileged to both witness and express. This notion of piety and its concomitant obligation of stewardship—in Koranic terminology, *Amanah* or the Divine Trust—are in fact far removed from the dry formalism of "fundamentalism". It is important to note, however, that this definition does not reduce fundamentalism to exoterism. In all authentic religions, form is a necessary component of tradition, celebrated in its scriptures, rituals and liturgies. It is not the adherence to these forms, but the loss of their kardial significance, that is indicative of fundamentalism. Formalism, in the sense of deracinated religion, is the inward gaze of fundamentalism.

To understand how the outward aspect of authentic religion differs from that of "fundamentalism" as defined here, we note that religion as such admits of two approaches to the Divine: as Truth and as Presence. The first stresses the transcendence of Absolute reality, the Supreme Principle, and approaches the Divine through Knowledge. The second stresses the immanence of Infinite reality, the manifest Self, and approaches the Divine through Love. Outwardly, these approaches may sometimes appear to clash, but inwardly they are perfectly compatible. Truth is the transcendent aspect of Presence, and Presence is the immanent aspect of Truth. These polarities are in fact complements of each other, and no religious conception of the Divine is complete without including both. In Islam, for example, this is one of the central meanings of the principle of *tawhid* ("The Doctrine of Divine Unity": Reality is the integra-tion of transcendence and immanence). While an authentic religious tradition may emphasize one approach to the Divine over another (for example, Judaism and Islam will generally favor Truth over Presence and are therefore iconoclastic in matters of artistic expression, while Hinduism, Buddhism and Christianity will generally favor Presence over Truth, and are therefore iconodulic), it will not do so at the expense of religious pluralism. The commitment to a particular religious tradition, while entailing subscription to its creed and submission to its forms of worship, does not mandate the rejection of other genuine religious approaches. The infinity of Divine expression, and the consequent diversity of religious typologies, are dictated by the very structure of reality itself, whose transcendent and esoteric unity are the underlying foundations of its pluralism. The rejection of such pluralism is the outward gaze of fundamentalism.

From this it can be seen that "fundamentalism", as the term is defined here, is a form of reductionism—the "spirit" reduced to the "letter", multiple expressions of Truth reduced to one. But, it may be objected, surely all orthodox doctrines are reductionist by virtue of their very orthodoxy. And here it becomes important to distinguish between "orthodoxy"—or "right thinking" according to the doctrines and principles of traditional metaphysics—and "fundamentalism". Where fundamentalism isolates or ignores aspects of reality, mistaking the part for the whole, orthodoxy, by contrast—though it may emphasize a particular part—views reality as a whole, embracing all its aspects. These aspects, though they may appear to be opposed, are reconciled and accommodated within the traditional "principle of complementarity", which regards reality as a synthesis of polarities, a *coincidentia oppositorum*. To claim that orthodoxy amounts to reductionism is to fail to perceive any distinction between dogma (the necessary component of doctrine—necessary as a corollary of transcendence) and dogmatism (the fallacy of doctrine, deriving from its reductionist tendency). This is one of the errors of post-modernist deconstructionism.

But traditional orthodoxy is not itself immune from a tendency to reductionism. There are many diverse expressions of Truth, which are potentially salvific or redemptive in content, though these may sometimes appear to be unorthodox from the point of view of a particular tradition, or even from within the same tradition. Thus, it is as erroneous to claim that "Pure Consciousness cannot say 'I'" (*Sri Ramana Maharshi*) as to claim "I am the Truth" (*al-Hallaj*). Either both these statements are true, or neither is. Not only "I am in the Father" but also "the Father is in me". Or again, not only *La illaha* but also *illa 'llah*. God cannot be reduced to an aspect of reality, though every aspect of reality is an aspect of God—because God is absolute reality. Similarly, orthodoxy cannot be reduced to a "zero-sum" view of reality. Truth, in the end, must embrace all gradations within reality, though these may be ordered hierarchically. Any expression of reality that falls short of the Absolute, Unconditioned, Supreme Principle is nonetheless an aspect of reality, on pain of denying that the Absolute is also

Infinite. Yet it is not Reality itself, on pain of denying that Reality is hierarchically transcendent. Orthodoxy cannot be so rigorous as to deny, in the name of Truth, the humanity of man—notwithstanding his potential divinity; just as it cannot reject that potential in the face of the imperfections of man. This then is the challenge of traditional orthodoxy: to avoid the tendency to reduce a particular doctrine—which may be an aspect of Truth—to Truth itself; or to reduce Truth to an abstraction that devalues or denies the experiential reality of Presence.

Reclaiming the Center[1]

Your hearts were hardened and became as rocks, or worse than
rocks, with hardness.
For indeed there are rocks out of which rivers gush forth,
and indeed there are rocks which split asunder so that water
flows from them.
And indeed there are rocks which fall down for fear of God.
And God is not unaware of what you do!
(*Koran*, 2, *Al-Baqarah*:74)

Let us anatomize them, see what breeds about their hearts.
Is there any cause in nature that makes these hard hearts?
(Shakespeare, *King Lear*, III.vi.77)

Amid the din of voices that has risen up in the wake of the
"September 11th attacks" and the "War against Terrorism", there is
emerging the sense of a voice that has been lost, a voice that needs
to be asserted from amid the cacophony of voices, a voice which
arises from "the Center within" and which needs to occupy "the
Center without," a voice whose message of compassionate wisdom
is more important for us to hear, now, than ever before, above the
shrill crossfire of rhetoric that seeks to drown it—a voice, in short,
that demands to be heard. In this time of strife, this voice speaks of
the existence of a Center that is a sanctuary, a place of peace and
stillness, an abode of vision and light.

Looking out from this Center, one perceives with both compassion and sorrow the blinding emotions that fuel flames of hatred
and misunderstanding on both sides of the current conflict, leaving
in their wake a charnel-house of wanton destruction. It takes an
infernal ingenuity to utilize pen-knives or box-cutters to com-
mandeer a plane full of living souls and slam it callously into an

---

[1] This essay is a revised version of the Editorial for *Sacred Web*, Volume 8, published in December, 2001. It was written in response to "the September 11th attacks" and the war of reprisal launched in its wake, at a time of heightened tensions
regarding Islam in the Western world.

occupied office building, and (though a stern response to this evil provocation was no doubt warranted), it takes a cruel insensitivity to "collaterally damage" or displace millions of innocent civilians in the pursuit of "enduring freedom," while arguing that the means, however vile, are justified by the ends. By demonizing the enemy, we risk dehumanizing ourselves.

The human mind inclines to simplification and there is within each of us a tendency that invites us to view the current conflict in reductive terms—but we must resist this tendency. The war that is being waged is not a "jihad" between Islam and the West (as one side would have you believe) nor a mission of "infinite justice" (the hubristic tag first selected by the Americans for their military operations—before it was pointed out to the U.S. administration that the appellation would be offensive to the Muslim allies, who regard Allah alone as infinitely just) or "enduring freedom", in a war waged between the forces of Freedom and Terrorism (as would the other). Instead, the war is better understood as a violent manifestation of the conflict between two reductive mind-sets: secular dogmatism and religious dogmatism—sometimes termed Modernism and Fundamentalism, respectively. It is instructive to consider these viewpoints in relation to the evolution of pre-modern societies.

In this post-modern world, Traditional (pre-modern) societies are considered an anachronism. They are constructed on the basis of a hierarchical order. The Sacerdotium (the spiritual kingdom, or the "kingdom within", which corresponds to the "Center within" referred to earlier) has dominion over the Regnum (the worldly kingdom, temporal realm of "Caesar"), which in turn has domin-ion over the Commons (the vassals or subjects; the ruled). In this schema, it is essential for the Temporal Power of Might to be wedded to the Spiritual Authority of Right, for it is only through this union that Justice (a manifestation of Order) will prevail. This schema, premised on an essentially faith-based and transcendent world-view, can only operate either within a closed society with a commonly accepted religious tradition, or within a civil society premised on metaphysical principles of religious pluralism. Closed societies are not sustainable in the face of the porosity of the glo-balized world. The processes of globalization and modernization, particularly through advances in technology and communication, have eroded the walls that nurtured traditional societies, and we can witness how modern societies open into each other at a pace that is often faster than their ability to accommodate the challenges of diversity. This diversity has not been easy for traditional societies to accommodate, particularly where modernization has been accompanied by a secular ethos.

As societies become secularized, religion becomes privatized, and this creates certain problems. Religions—which are not merely faiths but "ways of life"—will necessarily tend to resist secular-ization, which is premised on the notion of the privatization of religion. In Islam, for example, there is no opposition between *din* ("Faith" or the sacred dimension) and *dunya* ("World" or the secular dimension). The World cannot elude the sacred embrace of the Divine, which informs it and which it is privileged to repre-sent. However, modernist notions of secular space have tended to compartmentalize and institutionalize, falsely reducing the sacred to "Church" and the secular to "State". Secular ideologies may notionally approve of constitutions founded on divine trust, and may even provide for freedom of religion, but human governance within secularism excludes divine or religious interference. As such, secular ideologies—which are a hallmark of modernity—operate on the basis of a clear separation between Church and State, forcing religions to privatize, and barring their involvement in matters of human governance. By so doing, they deprive religions of a neces-sary public dimension in matters such as economic justice, social equity, the regulation of morality, environmental responsibility, and questions of peace and security. To the extent that secular societies make room for private religious expression, particularly through democratic participation in a "civil society" whereby reli-giously-influenced personal views can be given expression through the ballot box, the likelihood of confrontation between religion and secularism can be minimized. But where such expression is stifled, religion tends to become radicalized and its reaction to secularism takes the form of religious dogmatism, or fundamentalism.

The radicalization of Islam, in certain of its expressions, needs to be understood in this context. There is inherent within the very nature of any religious expression the danger of two reductive tendencies: of excessive formalism and of non-pluralistic exclusivism. These tendencies are heightened when the particular religion feels itself to be under attack. Islamic fundamentalism, in terms of its modern expression (a pre-modern expression also exists, as for instance in the literalism of the Kharijites who opposed 'Ali ibn Abi Talib's concession to the rebels at Siffin to arbitrate—a concession which offended the Kharijites' literalist reading of the Koran in which Allah alone could act as judge) can therefore be understood as a reaction to Islam's confrontation with the forces of modernity. The modern-day Taliban are one among many expressions of this reaction, which goes back in history to at least the early 1700s and the foundations of Wahhabism. With the ascendancy of Western civilization, Islam was confronted by the powerful forces of modernity: the technological, capitalistic and secularist transformations of society, which brought in their wake a transformation of personal and social values. Many of these values, which are individualistic and fragmentary, are offensive to traditional Muslims: corporate greed, mindless consumerism, concupiscence, the culture of "sex, drugs and rock and roll", the deterioration of the environment, the dismantling of traditional families, and the general privatization of values. In short, many traditional Muslims have felt threatened by the implications of modernization (though, clearly, the modernist ethos that embraces these seductive values of "the Flesh, the World and the Devil," has permeated the Muslim world—as has been made all too evident by recent events). As Muslim societies have globalized, they have become more porous, less impervious to the seductive and pervasive influences of Western culture. Left alone to determine their own response to the forces of modernity, Muslim societies in all likelihood would have had fewer incentives to radicalize. But the interference of Western foreign policy in the affairs of the Muslim world has in many instances undermined the efforts of Muslim modernists to attempt an integration between modernization and traditional Muslim values, and has in fact stoked the fires of fundamentalism.

The widespread bitterness (particularly among Muslims) against certain Western governments must be understood in the context of their foreign policies: the European exploitation of Egypt for economic interests at the time of the creation of the Suez Canal, the subsequent British military occupation of Egypt, and its interference in Egyptian elections on several occasions; British and American policies during the last century, of intervention in the internal affairs of Iran, largely for strategic and economic reasons, which contributed significantly to the polarization within Iranian society; the double-standard of American silence against then ally Saddam Hussein while he was using chemical weapons against the Kurds in Iraq, contrasted with American intervention when its oil interests were affected in Kuwait (the U.S. government character-ized its intervention in Kuwait in morally righteous terms, but no such moral indignation prompted its intervention to prevent geno-cidal atrocities in Rwanda or Bosnia, where American economic interests were not threatened); the forced economic embargo against Iraq, which has merely punished an innocent civilian popu-lation by producing over one million deaths and no dislodgment yet of their tyrannical dictator (Saddam Hussein was eventually overthrown by the US-led coalition army, and was subsequently tried, convicted and executed for crimes against humanity. It is instructive in this regard to bear in mind Frithjof Schuon's caution against the rationalization of evil: "No doubt, 'the end justifies the means'; but only on condition that the means not vilify the end!"); the support of non-democratic or unpopular modern-day governments such as those in Egypt and Saudi Arabia; the imposi-tion by Western powers upon Palestinians of the State of Israel and the preferential treatment of that regime by the U.S. government, even in the face of Israel's condemnation by the United Nations for its oppressive treatment of Palestinians and its contravention of international law; and the disregard for the plight of post-Soviet Afghanistan, following American intervention through the arming of the *mujahedeen*. In the words of one commentator: "When the United States supports autocratic rulers, its proud assertion of democratic values has at best a hollow ring" (*Karen Armstrong*). None of this is intended to suggest that all "undemocratic" regimes are bad, nor that the "East" is devoid of blame in producing or tolerating "evil" regimes. The point we are emphasizing is merely that certain Western foreign policies (as well as the economic and cultural exploitation of the "developing world" by the forces of corporatism and globalization) have played a significant role in engendering resentment among large numbers of Muslims.

Caught between the frustrating effects of heavy-handed and cynical Western foreign policies, and the tyranny of autocratic governments that muzzle calls for a civil society and for democratic change, many Muslim societies have found the doors of dissent open only within the *masjids* (mosques) and *madrasas* (seminaries). In many instances, these environments have become receptive to the proselytizing influence of radical groups, which have reverted to reductive readings of the Koran, *ahadith* and Sunna to support their radicalism. Here, it is important to clarify that much that is done in the name of radical Islam is impeachable by more centrist interpretations of the religion. The Holy Prophet of Islam admonished: "The time is near in which nothing will remain of Islam but its name, and of the Koran but its mere appearance, and the mosques of Muslims will be destitute of knowledge and worship; and the learned men will be the worst people under the heavens; and contention and strife will issue from them, and it will return upon themselves". Not every act that is touted as Islamic is true to the spirit of Islam—even if it emanates from the mouths of those who have long beards and wear pious robes crowned with turbans. (To digress briefly, it is as dangerous for non-Muslims to "profile" Muslims as "terrorists" simply because they have Muslim features, names, attire or lifestyles, as it is for Muslims to reduce faith to emblems of affiliation. The backlash against Muslims in America in the aftermath of the September attacks on the basis of their badges of identity is as myopic as fundamentalism's emphasis on the same external indicia as an indicator of faith. It is this myopic mentality that is unable to look beyond these indicia to perceive underlying nuances, and therefore reduces the conflict to simplistic slogans that conform to the confuted "clash of civilizations" thesis).

It is important, now more than ever, for Muslims to reclaim the Center by articulating the true spirit of their religion. To begin, it is necessary to debunk certain views and images of Islam that are commonly held in the West: the "religion of the sword", the intolerance of other religions, the barbarism of Islamic law, and its oppression of women. These views and images are to some extent a product of a distorted "orientalist" mind-set reinforced by radical elements within Islam.

It is instructive to remember certain facts: the total world population of Muslims is over one billion; of these only about one-fifth are Arab; the largest Muslim states (Indonesia, Pakistan, Bangladesh and India) are not in the Middle East. Islam is not a monolith; it embraces a wide cultural diversity as well as diverse modes of religious expression. It was once the dominant civilization in the world, creating a bridge between the Ancient world and the Modern West. It has produced some of the greatest rulers, scientists and artists in the history of human civilization. Its influence has largely spread without the compulsion of violence ("there is no compulsion in religion" is a cardinal Koranic principle; Q: 2:256), and, with few exceptions, it has a humane record for religious tolerance and pluralism, protecting minorities throughout its history, extending its protection even to those outside the Abrahamic faiths.

The image of the Muslim warrior is particularly in vogue in the modern-day context of radical Islam, but much of the image-making derives from Western views of Muslims dating back to at least the time of the Crusades. It is true that the Holy Prophet of Islam engaged in battles, but it is a historical distortion to represent this compassionate Messenger as a military aggressor. The battles that were fought were undertaken as part of the preservation of the Muslim community in the desperate time of its initial establishment, and the Holy Prophet's preference for mediation and compromise was well-known even within his own lifetime.

The notion of *jihad* is much misunderstood. Contrary to Western misperceptions, *jihad* is not one of the Pillars of Islam. In a *Hadith* well-known to Muslims, the Holy Prophet commented after the Battle of Badr: "We have returned from the lesser *jihad* to the greater *jihad*" (*al-jihad al-akbar*), signifying the true sense of *jihad* as spiritual struggle. "If one considers that the end of a just war is true peace, one will understand the function of the 'holy war' (*jihad*) of the soul: the interior 'war' is simply the abolition of another war, that which the earthly passions wage against the immortal soul or pure intellect" (*Titus Burckhardt*). The notion of "holy war" must thus be understood as "the constant inner war against all that veils man from the Truth and destroys his inner equilibrium" (*Seyyed Hossein Nasr*). It is the physical, moral, intellectual and spiritual effort to embody sanctity within oneself and to manifest the sense of the sacred within society. This requires the Muslim to be politically committed to create a just and decent society, and to "struggle in the way of God" to achieve that end. However, violence is inimical to the ethos of Islam, and therefore interpreters of the Koranic invitation to *jihad* have generally been careful to stress that this concept is not intended to sanction aggression. The motive of *jihad* cannot be anger or any other wanton passion (in a famous episode 'Ali ibn Abi Talib stopped himself from delivering a lethal blow to his opponent after the opponent had spat at him, because the blow would have been tainted by his anger). *Jihad* in this sense must be understood as the "sacrilization of combat" (*Abdullah Schleifer*).

Another misunderstood notion is that of the martyr or *shahid*. The term *shahid* is related to the word *shahadah*. The latter term signifies the Muslim "testament" and is related to the Koranic episode in which each human soul, before gaining entry into the world, is asked to bear witness that God is their Lord (Q: 7:172). That testament is inscribed upon the tablet of our primordial nature, or *fitra*, and each Muslim, or believer, bears witness to it again in the form of the *shahadah* or Testament of Divine Unity: *la ilaha illallah* ("There is no deity if not the Supreme Deity"). The term *shahid* therefore denotes "one who carries this witnessing to

45

a human summit" (*Gai Eaton*). In the current climate of suicide bombers being recruited by politicized Muslim militants to become martyrs, with the promise of a sensual paradise (understood by the recruits in literal terms, no doubt, rather than in terms of its spiritual symbolism), one has to be careful to distinguish between the martyrdom that represents a "noble death" for the cause of ennobling what is sacred within us all, and that which represents a delusion manipulated by the cynicism of skillful and ruthless political militants. In this connection it is instructive to remember the famous *Hadith*, "The ink of the scholar is more sacred than the blood of the martyr".

Contrary to its fundamentalist expressions, which have received inordinate coverage in the dominant Western media, Islam is a strongly pluralistic religion. Islam itself is conceived of as an expression of the *din al-fitra* or primordial religion inscribed within the hearts of all men (note the *Hadith*: "Every child is born in the *fitra*; it is his parents who make of him a Jew or a Christian or a Parsee"), and the Koran speaks of mankind as a primordial community or *ummah* (Q: 2:213) prior to the advent of divine revelations through the different prophets. Each message is an expression of a pre-existing heavenly tablet, the "Mother of Scripture" (Q: 13:39). Religious diversity is acknowledged as an intentional part of God's design (Q: 5:48). Islam is seen as one among many revelations, the particularity of each of which is accepted (Q: 10:47), and whose messengers are not necessarily limited to those of the Abrahamic faith (Q: 40:78). Salvation too is viewed in pluralistic terms. Thus the Koran promises salvation to "whoso believes in God and the Last Day and does righteous deeds" (Q: 2:62), a formula that is not exclusivist but depends only upon faith in spiritual verities and their realization through virtue.

The Koran's social reforms are motivated by a goal of an ethical, egalitarian social order, with strong prescriptions for the protection and welfare of the economically disadvantaged and the politically vulnerable. Muslim laws, as derived from the Koran, are best understood in the context of the distinction between the "spirit" and the "letter" of the law. Writers such as Fazlur Rahman have therefore advocated that the Koran should be regarded as the *"religious source of the law"* instead of strictly as "a lawbook". Its prescriptions for social order and human governance have to be contextualized in a socio-historical background, from which (utilizing the gift of the supra-rational divinely-guided Intellect) the *ratio legis* or universal principle can be derived. (Spiritual hermeneutics are a delicate matter, especially within Islam which views the Koran as the inviolable and sacred word of God. Intellection, in the divinely-inspired, supra-rational and metaphysical sense, is the interior pole of Revelation. Adamic man, who has been "taught the names of all things" can, by the grace of God and the guidance of spiritual authority, divine the inner sense or spirit of all texts, whether the Self, the Universe or the Scripture.) According to this interpretation, it is not the specific changes relevant to a particular time and place which are of universal application, but the underlying spirit or principle impelling the specific change. It is the spirit of Islam, contained in the centrality of the *shahadah* and the doctrine of *tawhid*, that gives rise to its ethos of compassion, subordinating the horizontal social concerns of the Koran to the vertical principles that motivate them. Viewed thus, the changes instituted by the Holy Prophet of Islam within the largely barbaric tribal world of seventh century Arabia (the pre-Islamic world of *jahiliyah*: the time of ignorance) were radical, and the principles that prompted those changes—not necessarily their specific expression—remain relevant today. It is in this context that the Koranic treatment of women is best understood.

One of the predominant and defining stereotypes of Islam is that of the veiled woman. The veil has come to be understood among Westerners and among many oppressed Muslim women as an emblem of their oppression. But the Koran introduced the *hijab* as a protocol for the nobility and modesty of the Holy Prophet's wives (Q: 33:53), not as a custom of seclusion—a foreign practice, which was later adopted by Muslim societies. "Veiling and seclusion had as their original intent the protection, honor, and distinction of women" (*John L. Esposito*). And it is important to remember that modesty is enjoined in the Koran on men and women alike

(Q: 24:30 and 31). Despite its current pejorative connotations, veiling was never intended as a condescension towards women, a fact that is recognized by many Muslim women today, who freely choose to wear the veil. "Thus many of the Muslim women who first took the veil saw it as a symbol of power and influence, not as a badge of male oppression...Today when some Muslim women resume their traditional dress, it is not always because they have been brainwashed by a chauvinist religion, but because they find that a return to their own cultural roots is profoundly satisfying. It is often a rejection of the Western imperialist attitude which claims to understand their traditions better than they do themselves" (*Karen Armstrong*).

Koranic passages are often cited as evidence of Islam's unfairness towards women (for example, "men are a degree higher" than women, a woman's testimony is worth half that of a man, and women can only inherit one-half of the inheritance of her male sibling); and fundamentalist Muslim societies have relied upon literalist readings of scriptural texts to sanction the control of women. Here, again, one needs to consider the original context of the scripture in order to decipher the intent. Men and women are considered to be created from a "single soul", and are equal before God in terms of their spiritual responsibilities (Q: 4:124, 40:40). Men are not considered inherently superior to women, though the Koran recognizes the privileges of men over women, in general, in terms of wealth or power, for example (Q: 4:34), but these privileges are to be understood in the context of their concomitant responsibilities. However, the differences in gender are not overlooked in favor of the modernist tendency to treat men and women as equal. The Koranic view instead stresses the complementarity of gender diversity, without suggesting any inherent inequality between the genders, despite distorted interpretations to the contrary. The genders are differentiated functionally, and though these functions would translate into traditional roles within traditionally structured societies, the scripture is not in its spirit so rigid as to strait-jacket men and women into inflexible roles. Women are recognized as nurturers and are respected for their role ("Paradise lies at the feet of the mothers", said the Holy Prophet), and men as providers and protectors. It is well recognized that Islam greatly improved the lot of women and enhanced their status in the predominantly male-dominated Arabian society of the seventh century. In a society which practiced female infanticide and treated women as a sub-species, like slaves, without any legal rights, the reforms that the Holy Prophet introduced were remarkable: the establishment of the legal status of women, the conferring upon them of property and inheritance rights, marriage and dowry rights, and, more than these, the creation of a respect for women and the corresponding responsibilities of men and social institutions towards them. These reforms were in some respects not offered Western women until the nineteenth century, and were truly extraordinary in the context of seventh century Arabia.

It is true that some modern-day societies have chosen, in the name of Islam, to ignore the spirit of these reforms and have reverted to oppressive, even barbaric, interpretations of the scripture in order to regulate women. But their interpretations, formalistic and heartless, do not represent for the vast majority of Muslims the true spirit of Islam. It is dangerous therefore to judge Muslims on the basis of media images that project this marginal, albeit dominant, impression of Islam.

Islam is best judged by what lies at its Center. This Center is metaphorically described in the Koran and *Hadith* traditions as the Heart, the sanctuary of the Divine Spirit within Man. Of this Heart it is said by the Holy Prophet in a *Hadith Qudsi*: "My heaven cannot contain Me, nor can My earth, but the Heart of the true believer can contain Me". This is the "Center within", the microcosm, which is in fact the locus of Compassion, both radiating and reintegrating, *Rahman* and *Rahim*. From this central vantage point, to which all things are radially connected, a sense of Justice and Order emerges, and in its bosom lies a sanctuary of Peace. From the Eye of the Heart, all things are seen in a sacred light, and Man is ennobled as a creature of divine purpose: as the Divine Trustee, under the Koranic doctrine of *Amanah* (Q: 33:72), the steward of creation, the vicegerant of God, accountable to God, his Origin and his Destination. The aim of Islam is to live in this Center: the inner Equilibrium of "the Center within," and the outer Order of "the Center without." This is the true spirit of the message of the Noble Koran—indeed of the scriptures of all the great religious traditions.

How far then have we strayed from this Center! The Koran speaks of "diseased" and "hardened" hearts in contrast to the tender hearts of those who have taken on the qualities of Mercy. In Shakespeare's play, *King Lear*, the distraught king enquires into the heartlessness of two of his daughters, and ponders this question about humanity's lack of conscience: "Is there any cause in nature that makes these hard hearts?" Shakespeare suggests that disorder (both inwardly within the mind, and outwardly within the state) is the result of the loss of a spiritually centered vision. In our reading of the tragedy, there is a link between "hard hearts" and the loss of spiritual insight ("I stumbled when I saw"). To overcome the madness that we can be brought to in "this great stage of fools" one must develop the spiritual insight of compassion ("O! I have ta'en too little care of this. Take physic, Pomp!") and the loving heart (represented in the play by Cordelia). We must look beyond the "sophisticated" aspects of the world to perceive our fellow humans in the way Lear perceives Poor Tom, as "unaccommodated man". This way of seeing the world through the eyes of love, rather than through the jaded eyes of "sophistication", is central to all faith traditions. In Traditional metaphysics, the veiling of the heart is inherent within the very process of creation which imposes over our hearts a "veil of heedlessness". Yet, viewed aright, that is to say, when things are seen in their Divine Similitude, through the "Eye of the Heart" or the Intellectual Center of our innermost selves, the Cosmic Veil is not seen as opaque, but as metaphysically transparent to transcendence. It is by opening ourselves to transcendent mystery that we are able to enliven our consciences. It is by remaining aware of our immanent spiritual nature and what is sacred within us that we can perceive the world as a sacred theophany. Conversely, it is by reducing the "Face of God" to the Cosmic Veil that we lose the sacred vision that is our Center. The outward opacity of vision corresponds to the inward calcification of our rusted hearts, and we then become forgetful of the tender compassion (the "gushing river") that lies at their Center. When one is cut off from this Center, there is no sense of Order, and therefore no hope of Justice; without Justice, of Security; and without Security, of Peace. Thus we see in Shakespeare's play how a spiritually insightful empathy is the foundation of true justice ("Expose thyself to feel what wretches feel, That thou mayst shake the superflux to them, And show the Heavens more just"). Such heart-centered empathy of the "Divine Vision" is precisely what we most need in these troubled times. It is by reclaiming the Center within each of us that we will finally be able to achieve the just and lasting Peace that is the promise of all faith traditions—a promise we must honor within ourselves, and which we owe to our communities, and to all of creation, to fulfill.

Understanding "Tradition"[1]

Tradition has nothing to do with any "ages", whether "dark", "primaeval", or otherwise. Tradition represents doctrines about first principles, which do not change.

(Ananda K. Coomaraswamy, *Correspondence*, 1946)

...there is nothing and can be nothing truly traditional that does not contain some element of a super-human order. This indeed is the essential point, containing as it were the very definition of tradition and all that appertains to it.

(René Guénon, *The Reign of Quantity*)

The terms "traditional" and "modern" suggest a distinction between the old and the new, the fixed and the changing, the hallowed way of the past and the progressive way of the future. The underlying polarity that it reflects is rooted in the metaphysical structure of reality, in the architecture of the Absolute inviolability of Substance and the Infinite possibility of Form. This underlying polarity is expressed in the dialectic of Necessity and Freedom. Necessity is the organizing principle of deployment, of projection and reintegration: all that exists emerges from and abides within the common ground of all reality, whose transcendental Substance is simultaneously both its Origin and its End, the criterion of all objectivity. Freedom is the creative principle of this deployment, expressing itself in an infinite variety of modes and modalities of Form and in the immanent potential of our own supra-personal subjectivity.

The terms "Tradition" and "Modernity", as used by traditionalists like Seyyed Hossein Nasr, are not derivatives of the conventional differentiation between the terms "traditional" and "modern", though the traditionalists' particular usage of those

[1] This essay is a revised version of the Editorial for *Sacred Web*, Volume 9, published in July, 2002.

terms is premised on the metaphysical structure described above. This can be confusing.

For Nasr, "Modernity" (or more accurately, the ethos of Modernism) is "that which is cut off from the Transcendent, from the immutable principles which in reality govern all things and which are made known to man through revelation in its most universal sense", while "Tradition", by contrast, designates those immutable principles, the *sophia perennis* or primordial wisdom, which are rooted in the Transcendent. According to this definition, the "modern" (when associated with the ethos of Modernism) is not necessarily synonymous with the contemporary (or focused on the future), nor is the "traditional" (understood in the light of "Tradition") necessarily indicative of the continuation of history (or focused on the past). Tradition, in this sense, is meta-historical: its only relation to the past resides in the linkage of a particular religious tradition to its original source, which is to say, the revelation that authenticates it, the foundational scripture and its expressive forms of worship transmitted through the protective medium of the particular tradition. But this relation between a particular tradition and its historical origins is in a sense merely incidental. The relation between Tradition as such and Revelation as such transcends history. Revelation "in its most universal sense" is not a historical event: it is based in the eternal present and is continuous. Its authentication is not reduced to one's ability to retrace it to any particular point in history, rather its authenticity is guaranteed by its ability to resonate as true within the sanctum of the Heart, whose discerning faculty is the supra-rational Intellect. Knowledge is thus a resonance of the spiritual Substance that pervades the whole of creation, and whose presence reverberates within the undefiled Heart. Knowledge is not merely a form of intellectual taxidermy, rather a way of inhabiting the creature itself. It is to be fully human.

In common parlance, the terms "traditional" and "modern" suggest two differing attitudes towards the negotiation of change, the former resisting it, the latter embracing it. But "Tradition", in the sense of primordial wisdom, is not necessarily resistant to change. The image of Shiva Nataraja embodies the ideas of both stillness (the fixed, or being) and movement (the changing, or becoming). "Tradition" is a combination of both these elements. It is at once static Equilibrium and dynamic Attraction, the classical realism of transcendence and the romantic idealism of immanence. Man is both a slave of change (being subject to the processes of time) and its master (being equipped to transcend it, spiritually). The quest for salvation is, at one level, a quest for peace, the freedom from change, but at another, it is a quest for creativity and freshness, the freedom from petrification. The term "traditional" can have a pejorative implication of excessive rigidity and formalism, while the term "modern" can mean that which is unprincipled or excessively individualistic. In these senses, both the traditional and the modern are opposed to "Tradition", which recognizes the mutual interdependence of the organizing and creative principles of reality. When creativity ceases to conform to the hierarchies inherent in a spiritually ordered universe, volition becomes satanic and profanes Freedom. And when the demands of conformity stifle genuine spiritual expression, the intellect becomes tyrannical and profanes Necessity. "Tradition" recognizes that Necessity (the intellectual discernment that creative expression has a necessary organizing principle) and Freedom (the transcendence of creative expression in conformity to that organizing principle) are tethered together, and that intellectual discernment has moral implications. The human ethos is thus a dimension of the sacred structure of reality.

"Modernity", in the sense understood by traditionalists, indicates a tendency to moral "hardness" and intellectual "opacity". When reality is no longer perceived as metaphysically "transparent to transcendence", there is no spiritual reality perceived that can resonate within the human soul, nothing to "melt" the heart into compassionate submission, the true and serene Freedom, whose tawdry counterfeit is a soul enslaved by passion, yielding to the momentary gratification of self-indulgence before its unsated appetites are drawn away by the next seduction.

It is in this sense that "Tradition" and "Modernity" are placed in opposition. The traditionalist is not necessarily opposed to the "modern" as conventionally understood, only to "Modernity" as the ethos of Modernism that is the converse of "Tradition" in the particular sense defined above. A traditionalist may be "modern" in the use of dress, language, modern amenities or technologies, and yet will necessarily be opposed to "Modernity" in the sense of its denial of transcendence or sense of the sacred. Correspondingly, not all that appears "traditional" accords with "Tradition". So, for instance, fundamentalism—though it may don traditional garb and use traditional language—is the very antithesis of "Tradition", which eschews fundamentalism's reduction of the spirit to the letter, evident in its excessive formalism and exclusivism. "By their fruits shall ye know them", not by their appearances.

Words and labels, in the end, often conceal reality by abstracting it. At their best, they act as symbols, arousing meaning that lies dormant within us. "Tradition" and "Modernity" are ultimately aspects of our selves: "Duo sunt in homine", taught St. Aquinas, a teaching that resounds throughout traditionalist discourse and within each human soul. There is in the end an element in each soul that must be overcome for the greater good. "Tradition" invites each of us to fulfill our full human potential, to perceive the outer world with the inner eye, with compassion, and to conform the will to the intellect, thereby overcoming the usurping tendencies of the Promethean self, integrating Truth, Goodness and Beauty in our lives in order to achieve Everlasting Life.

On Faith and Intellect[1]

The eye with which I see God
is the same eye with which God sees me:
my eye and God's eye are one eye,
one seeing, one knowing and one love.
(Meister Eckhart: *German Sermon 16*)

Faith, as distinguished from mere credulity, is both a gift from the All-Compassionate and an exercise of spiritual imagination that is rooted in transcendent reality. It is "the evidence of things not seen" (*Hebrews 11:1*), yet it is not blind, but is rather the intuited awareness and acceptance of the very ground of our being, our primordial nature, the heart through whose eye all is seen. Thus it embraces and engages the complete being. In a celebrated *Hadith*, the Prophet of Islam defined *iman* (faith) as "a knowledge in the heart, a voicing with the tongue, and an activity with the limbs". Faith is thus the foundation of all ontological growth, the rock upon which rests the ladder that ascends to heaven.

The intellect, as distinguished from mere rationality, is the "eye of the heart", the highest cognitive faculty in man, once the "doors of perception are cleansed". It is "Eckhart's eye", whose supra-rational cognition is visionary or *darshanic*, direct and experiential, the sacramental convergence of knowledge and being in love ("one seeing, one knowing and one love"). The intellect, however, is an aspect of faith, being like faith an exercise of spiritual imagination that is rooted in transcendent reality. Thus it is said that "spiritual knowledge is born from faith" (*St. Theodoros the Great Ascetic*). To put it differently, the birth of meaning is an act of faith.

Faith can also be understood as the mystery of intimacy, and intellect as the intimacy of mystery. This view derives from the traditional perspective in which reality is simultaneously manifest

[1] This essay is a revised version of the Editorial for *Sacred Web*, Volume 10, published in January, 2003.

and hidden, proximate and distant, immanent and transcendent, and is therefore both intimate and mysterious. Based on this duality, faith is the *yin* element that represents our receptivity to the mystery of transcendence, while the intellect is the *yang* element that represents our access to the intimacy of immanence. To pursue this symbolism, as in the traditional *yin-yang* symbol, where each element is present within the other, faith also contains an actively receptive element that links it to the intellect, while the intellect also contains a passively receptive element that resonates with revelation, in a universal sense. Mystery and intimacy are thereby intertwined.

Faith, in its inception, is an orientation, an openness to transcendence. It is a pining for the mysterious intimacy of the Divine Breath being blown into our Adamic clay (see *Koran 32:9*). It is the lament of the reed-flute for the reed-bed, in the famous opening lines from Rumi's *Mathnavi*:

> Listen to the story told by the reed, of being separated. 'Since I was torn from the reed-bed, I have made this plaintive sound. Anyone apart from someone he loves understands what I say. Anyone pulled from a source longs to go back...'

Only by becoming hollow (empty of self through submission to the Divine Will) can the reed-pipe sound its plaint of love as the Breath of its Maker (the Breath of Compassion, *nafas rahmani*) blows through it again, thereby re-creating its achingly beautiful melody of love in an act of mysterious intimacy. Through such sweet surrender, faith experiences Truth as Presence and develops the existential certitude that the transcendent essence of existence is nothing less than love. The intellect, by contrast, is the repository of the transcendent foreknowledge of this truth (*aletheia*, suggesting "not forgetting" or awareness), inscribed within our hearts and recollected—by grace—in moments of tranquility. This recollection (*anamnesis* or "re-minding") is the intimate access of our deepest perception into the mysterious heart of transcendence.

The relationship between faith and intellect can also be understood in terms of the relationship between communion and sacrament: the pining for mysterious intimacy through communion and the intimate recollection of mystery through sacrament. Faith proceeds from the intimate center or "heart" of being and is central to the rite of communion because there is no communion without the grace of self-surrender, while the intellect is the "eye of the heart", the receptor of the mysteries of revelation, and is central to the role of sacraments as the intellectual experiencing of the sacred. At its highest level, faith functions as the intellect through its openness to the intimacy of immanence. This openness to intimacy is the source of our awareness of our communion with the Divine, that the spiritual substance of our innermost heart is itself divine and is thereby the source of our certitude and felicity. Correspondingly, at its highest level, the intellect functions as faith through its openness to the mystery of transcendence. This openness to mystery is the source of our awareness of the sacramental nature of creation as a continual revelation, that each moment and every atom is a unique and sacred radiance of the Divine, "the Truth whose theophanies are never repeated" (*Nasr*).

The openness to both mystery and intimacy gives rise in various traditions to certain spiritual gestures or *mudras* by which faith and intellect can be depicted. Faith is the upward-facing open palm (turned toward heaven) that receives the blessings and bounties of Mercy. It is an attitude of readiness, not expectancy, for expectancy negates the privilege of grace. Its role is "to make a void for the passage of God". This corresponds to humanity's indigence in the face of the divine. Yet man is not merely *'abd* (slave or creature) in relation to the Creator but also *khalifa* (vicegerant or steward). Through the intellect, man is *pontifex*, the prototype of the divine, latently endowed with the wealth of sacred knowledge, a supernal gift which man is entrusted to use wisely (see *Koran 33:72* and *4:58*). The intellect, then, is the instrument by which this latent sacred knowledge can be accessed for the stewardship of all creatures. To continue the symbolism of spiritual gestures, the intellect is depicted as the downward-facing open palm (turned *bodhisattvically* toward the world) that becomes a sacred passage for the flow of the gifts of the Bounteous which It directs through Its innate sense of Justice and Mercy. Receiving and giving, humility and charity, submitting to the Divine Will and being the Trustee of the Divine—these are the *mudras* of faith and intellect.

Thus, in the Mevlevi Sufi tradition, the celebrated figure of the Whirling Dervish in the sacred *sama* embodies these same spiritual gestures in a re-creation of the never-ending dance of revelation, so that as the dancing figure whirls horizontally across the floor around the imaginary pole that symbolizes the projected heart (the solar ground of all being that is the metaphysical center of his orientation), the Dervish's upward-facing right palm and downward-facing left palm together signify the sacramental attitude of his heart, delicately poised as a channel of love in between the two worlds, open simultaneously both to transcendence and immanence, to mystery and intimacy, simultaneously receiving and giving, in stillness and movement, welling up and descending in a continuous flow, as mysterious and as intimate as the Divine Breath, a cascade of Mercy and Bounty from the abundant reservoirs of the Eternal Font, from the celestial realm above to the infinite ranks of the terrestrial below.

Umberto Eco, Fascism and Tradition[1]

It is the very heart of fascism to think that what matters is not
what is true, but what one holds to be true. What one holds to
be true is important because it can produce that resolute will
tuned to its own triumph.

(George Grant: from *'The Triumph of the Will'*)

Handle a large kingdom with as gentle a touch as if you were
cooking a small fish.

(*Tao Te Ching*, Stanza 60)

This is the freedom of the universe;
Unfolded still the more, more visible,
The more we know; and yet is reverenced least,
And least respected in the human Mind,
Its most apparent home.

(William Wordsworth: from *'The Excursion'*)

In an essay titled "Ur-Fascism" (or 'Primordial Fascism') in his
book, "Five Moral Pieces" (Harcourt, 2002), Umberto Eco casti-
gates "the cult of tradition" as one of the causes of fascism. As "the
truth has already been announced once and for all", there can be no
advancement of learning: "all we can do is continue interpreting its
obscure message". Eco notes that "Nazi gnosis" (an oxymoron, by
which he apparently means "Nazi ideology") "fed on traditionalist,
syncretic, and occult elements", and he cites the example of the
influence of Julius Evola and René Guénon on the new Italian right.
He also censures tradition for its rejection of the modern world,
finding in its disapproval of Enlightenment thought the seeds of
fascist irrationalism and the rejection of all critical thinking. Finally,
among the various other characteristics that he cites as typical of
fascism, Eco singles out its hierarchic "elitism" as "a typical aspect
of all reactionary ideologies, insofar as it is basically aristocratic",
promoting a "cult of heroism", where everyone is "impatient to

[1] This essay was the Editorial for *Sacred Web*, Volume 11, published in June, 2003.

die", death being seen by the convert as a passage to "supernatural happiness".

These criticisms of tradition and of certain elements of its thought highlight two important points: first, that distinctions within traditional thought are subtle, and its doctrines are therefore capable of being misunderstood, particularly by the superficial reader, to whom they will appear as obscure or, worse, perfidiously alluring; and second, that traditional doctrines, being nuanced and textured, are easily susceptible to manipulation and abuse. In fact, the history of religions down to the present day (with its many examples of economically-shunted and politically-driven fundamentalist misreadings of religious literature) has shown both these tendencies at work, with offenders all-too-often appearing from within the fold, thereby proving the adage about the devil's ability to "cite scripture for his own purpose".

At its core, the misunderstandings of traditional doctrine arise from a basic misreading, whether superficial or abusive, of the traditional view of reality. The authentic Self in tradition is spiritual, which is to say that it is one with the substance of all reality. All spiritual questing is at once a search for an Origin (to which one returns) and a Center (in which one reposes), which are in substance identical. These correspond to the Heart of oneself, the genuine Self which is in essence the One Spirit that subsists in all reality. It is this Atmanic Self that must be understood as the Ubermensch (the Nietzschean "Superman"), as Ananda K. Coomarswamy noted in his essay on Nietzsche, not the psychic or sensational self of common parlance or of the ill-termed "Nazi gnosis". The Nietzschean "Will to Power" or its Blakean equivalent of "Energy" (symbolized by the "Tyger" whose "immortal symmetry" cannot be framed) are thus to be understood strictly as faculties of the authentic Self or the "Inner Man", and not as the personal cravings or lower impulses of the "Outer Man". Mistake the source and it is easy then to misunderstand the impulse emanating from it. It is this misreading that informs the view of those who mistake licentiousness for freedom and amorality for virtue. Coomarswamy chose to interpret Nietzsche's Ubermensch as an embodiment of virtue, not as a proponent of "selfishness" but of being "true to Self", one who is "commanded from within", beyond the dictates of rules (like Blake's Jesus, who acted "from impulse, not from rules"), beyond good and evil. Thus he quotes Nietzsche's formula of virtue with approval:

> That ye might become weary of saying: 'that an action is good because it is unselfish.' Ah! My friends! That your very self be in your action, as the mother is in the child: let that be your formula of virtue.

Clearly, this endorsement of virtue as spontaneity is greatly susceptible to abuse by the hypertrophic self, whose political counterpart is either the elitism of fascism (as evidenced by the Nazis' philosophical endorsement of Nietzsche's "natural aristocracy" of the Ubermensch) or the atomization of anarchy (whose more extreme postmodernist versions deconstruct all rules as agenda-driven and imperialistic exploitations). This form of hypertrophy, as we have argued, is to misunderstand the traditional view of Self—a misunderstanding which plays out in terms of how authority is perceived.

According to its critics, tradition, like fascism, is premised on the authority of the 'elite'. It would appear to those who misread tradition that the traditionalist is like the fascist in that it is his world-view that must be imprinted on society. It is the program of the aristocracy, the patrician's view of the world that must be brought to the plebeians, with the hierarchic structure of society being necessary to maintain the graduated distinctions between the scornful elite and the weak masses. As Eco states: "In the course of history, all forms of aristocratic and militaristic elitism have implied scorn for the weak. Ur-Fascism cannot do without preaching a 'popular elitism'". This is reminiscent of the argument of the Grand Inquisitor to Jesus in the narrative from The Brothers Karamazov:

> We have corrected Your work and have founded it upon miracle, mystery and authority. And men rejoiced that they were again

led like sheep and that the terrible gift that had brought them such suffering was at last lifted from their hearts. Were we right in teaching them this? Speak! Did we not love mankind when so meekly acknowledging their feebleness, lovingly lighting their burden, and permitting their weak nature even sin with our sanction?

Eco's fascist and Dostoevsky's Grand Inquisitor both justify their elitism in terms of their superior knowledge of what is good for the masses. Their 'authority', unlike that of the traditionalist, is based in fact on their temporal power. They are in truth opposed to the spiritual liberation of the masses, whose existence serves to validate their role. The Grand Inquisitor would in fact deliberately mislead the masses to keep them happy.

By contrast, the traditional view of authority is based on the concept of hierarchical order, connecting nobility (the privilege of rank, an emblem of outer order) to profundity (compassionate wisdom or piety, an emblem of inner order). There is no outer order (or Beauty) without inner order (or Virtue), no legitimacy of hierarchy unless premised upon the spiritually-ordered structure of reality, which proceeds from the subtle to the gross, from spiritual substance to material form, in a "great chain of being" (to use Lovejoy's celebrated phrase). According to this view, reality is hierarchical because (as the etymology, *hiero-arche*, of divine origin, implies) it is spiritually ordered, that is to say, ranked according to the degree of its spiritual luminosity which manifests in our primordial natures as piety. It is this ordering that confers social cohesiveness and preserves natural order. And by "untuning that string", as Shakespeare observes, "hark! what discord follows" (*Triolus and Cressida*, Act 1, Scene 3). The degrees of reality are not to be understood in an outward or superficial sense as, for example, by equating rank with any external badge or emblem of affiliation such as race, temporal power or ideology. Instead, rank corresponds to inner states and spiritual stations, and the authority that rank confers is related to the spiritual sensibilities inherent in that rank. These sensibilities relate to the vertical dimension of reality that connects nobility to profundity, the need for freedom to the desire for union. This is the foundation of the key principle of "noblesse oblige", an aspect of the Islamic principle of *Amanah* or Trust. It is the subordination of human governance to the divine law that establishes the ruler's right to be obeyed. There is a reciprocity between governance and obedience, between authority and its due. Authority resonates as inner beauty or virtue, as sacred knowledge or "gnosis", and as the wisdom of compassion or love. This resonance is what enables the Intellect, the spiritual receptor within each of us, to authenticate genuine authority and to attune us to the intrinsic harmony and identity of the Immanent Subject and the Transcendent Object, that we identify as sacred. This respect for one's innate abilities (contrast Eco's suggestion that tradition implies critical stagnation or irrationalism) is implied in traditional scriptures that eschew coercion in matters of faith ("There is no compulsion in religion": *Koran: 2, 256*), but this is counterbalanced by a necessary appreciation of the legitimate role of spiritual authority ("He who has no *Shaykh* has *satan* for his guide": Bayazid Bistami). Here, tradition does not advocate a blind adherence to anyone claiming authority. True authority is to be recognized by intellectual discernment, and exudes its own perfume, of rigor and compassion, found in all the great spiritual messengers and teachers. If traditional doctrines can be easy to misinterpret, traditional practices can be even more difficult to implement appropriately, hence the necessity of a guide. While fascist misreadings of tradition tend to emphasize the role of blind adherence to authority and correspondingly to diminish the role of the intellect, tradition in fact teaches that the Intellect is the spiritual receptor which can perceive (in Frithjof Schuon's well-known phrase) "the metaphysical transparency of things". It is thus the criterion of discerning the sacred and of intuiting authority. In the traditional view, the Intellect is the lamp that lights our world, perceiving created reality as "charged with the grandeur of God", from whence it springs. The Intellect is akin to an eye which becomes aware of itself through its seeing. Knowledge is therefore experiential, not merely discursive. In the words of Antonio Machado: "The eye you see is not an eye because you see it. It is an eye because it sees you."

Eco's misunderstanding of traditional intellectualism is reinforced by his depiction of traditional culture as "syncretic", which he portrays as having to necessarily tolerate a combination of different forms of beliefs, practices and contradictions, because "all the original messages contain a grain of wisdom, and when they seem to be saying different or incompatible things, it is only because they all allude, allegorically, to some original truth". Eco argues that a consequence of this syncretism is the intellectual stagnation necessary for fascism. While it is true that traditional doctrine espouses Aristotle's dictum that "There is nothing new under the sun", it is wrong to conclude that this implies intellectual stagnation. To understand why this is so it is useful to examine why tradition in fact opposes syncretism. Tradition distinguishes between the principial level and the formal level of metaphysical reality. Truth, whatever its formal articulation, is principially transcendent, which is why one can speak in traditional terms of "the transcendent unity of religions". However, tradition is opposed to the reductionist tendency inherent in syncretism, of locating identity at merely the formal level. Each revealed religious tradition is unique in the forms of its revelation, symbols and practices, and each constitutes a unique, divinely-gifted and integrated spiritual pathway to the realization of universal Truth. The ability to benefit from the practices and spiritual means of a particular pathway requires an intellectual receptivity that allows its symbols and practices to work their alchemical transformation upon the practitioner. The "symbolist spirit" of this intellectual receptivity calls for a degree of awareness in the adept that is in marked contrast to the relatively superficial engagement called for in offerings of the New Age spirituality or syncretisms of their counterfeit "designer religions". Traditional thought advocates not a relativistic syncretism of forms but a principled pluralism premised on the metaphysical transcendence of Truth. This distinction implies a respect for other religious traditions, not because all formal differences must be tolerated in a society, but because formal differences are perceived to dissolve where their diverse forms point to the same underlying Truth.

Eco notes that tradition implies a rejection of the modern world. René Guénon's writings undoubtedly influenced Evola. Both were outspoken critics of modernity, but unlike Evola, Guénon never lost sight of the central criterion of his traditional heritage—the metaphysics that tethered transcendence to immanence, freedom to compassion, the divine order to the created world. It was not feasible, according to the traditional world-view to reject any aspect of the created order except to the extent that it rebelled against the divine order, that is to say, to the extent that it distanced itself from the sacred. Thus fascism, which was profane in its Promethean attempts to divinize the egoic self and in its wanton disregard for the sacred, as evidenced by the horrors that it bred based on the claim that the ends justified the means, could never take root in the soil of tradition. Fascism opposed modernity because it opposed creative thought, while tradition opposed the eclipse of the sacred, not of creative thought per se, but the deracinated rationalism of nominalist scientism and the grotesqueries of de-spiritualized imagination. In critiques of tradition, the kinds of criticism voiced by Eco of tradition's rejection of modernity are often accompanied by the statement that tradition is premised on a nostalgia for the glories of the past. The appeal of this in fascist ideology is clear: the fascist ideologue can seek to return society to its Golden Age, ruled by superior men. This is a message often found in messianic movements of fundamentalist revivalism. Eco alludes to this in a different work (*Belief or Nonbelief? A Dialogue between Umberto Eco and Cardinal Martini,* Arcade Publishing, NY, 1997), in which he decries the nostalgia for "a timeless and archaic Tradition" that is opposed both to "the world and history". However, here too we find a vital misreading of tradition. While it is true that some traditional doctrines speak of cycles of time, tradition itself is not opposed to the temporal or created realm. Rather, tradition advocates a "cleansing of perceptions" so that we can perceive creation theophanically as the sacred effusion of the divine. It is not a particular age that tradition opposes but a particular lack of receptivity. As Shakespeare notes in *The Merchant of Venice* (Act 5, Scene 1):

Such harmony is in immortal souls;
But whilst this muddy vesture of decay
Doth grossly close it in, we cannot hear it.

It is not the glories of the past that tradition pines for. Rather, its nostalgia is for the sense of the sacred.

This brings us to Eco's criticism regarding the "cult of heroism". Tradition seeks to sacralize man's perception through awakening within him the knowledge of his true Self, which is one with the spiritual substance of all reality. The traditional references to death (such as the *Hadith*, "Die before you die"; or the Biblical "Death is swallowed up in victory. O death, where is thy sting? O grave, where is thy victory?": *1 Corinthians, XV*) are not intended to create an impatience for martyrdom for an ideological cause or for escape from the physical world. They are intended rather to promote a transcendental consciousness of metaphysical reality, so that one can "be in the world, yet not of it". The heroic struggle is an inner struggle against the egoic self, culminating in the heroic death of detachment, whose counterpart is the heroic rebirth of compassion. Death and birth, detachment and compassion, nobility and profundity—these are the marks of the spiritual hero. We return again to the principle of "noblesse oblige", referred to earlier. The traditional hero *bodhisattvically* journeys back to the physical world, knowing that each blade of grass is sacred and worthy of salvation. The hero's sacrifice is based on the knowledge that it is only by planting deep roots within the soil of earth that the tree of life can hope to reach the heavens. Unlike Eco's example of the fascist hero who craves a heroic death as a means to attain "supernatural happiness", the traditional hero combines compassion with detachment and attains happiness by hearing the celestial harmonies in his immortal soul and by seeing the divine radiance in the sacredness that surrounds him. It is by dissolving into the sacred that the soul is born into eternal life.

Towards a Traditional Understanding of Sexuality[1]

> In primordial man sexual ecstasy coincides with spiritual ecstasy,
> it communicates to man an experience of mystical union, a
> "remembrance" of the Divine Love of which human love is a
> distant reflection.
>
> (*Frithjof Schuon*)

> And all shall be well and
> All manner of thing shall be well
> When the tongues of flame are in-folded
> Into the crowned knot of fire
> And the fire and the rose are one.
>
> (*T.S. Eliot*: from 'Little Gidding')

In traditional thought, sexuality—as is the case with all qualities of the human order—is a reflection of qualities that reside archetypally within the divine order, and its roots are therefore metaphysical. The first instance of a division into male and female, and the first procreative act, occur in the divine order, and these therefore constitute archetypes that are reflected within the human order. Thus, before one can begin to address sexuality and the particular issues that it raises within modernity, one must be prepared to view these issues as symptoms of the denial of transcendence, which characterizes modernism, and trace their causes back to their metaphysical origins.

Tradition teaches that reality unfolds through multiple levels, arranged hierarchically, commencing with a metacosmic Supreme Principle, which is transcendent in relation to these cosmic levels. The Supreme Principle or Self (Aristotle's "Motionless Mover," which is to be understood as being 'without any trace of the development of manifestation'; in Hinduism, for instance, It is termed *Paramatma* or *Brahma Nirguna*, the Quality beyond all

---

[1] This is a revised version of the Editorial for *Sacred Web*, Volume 12, published in December, 2003.

qualities) is transcendent in relation to the cosmic levels that proceed from It, and contains within Its Essence, androgynously, as it were—not as separate entities, but as aspects of "a conjoint principle" (Aquinas)—the archetypes of two cosmic principles, an active (male) element and a receptive (female) element. The male element (*purusha, yang*) is the Absolute pole of Divine Essence, qualitatively represented by attributes such as Majesty and Rigor. The female element (*prakriti, yin*) is the Infinite pole of Divine Substance, qualitatively represented by attributes such as Beauty or Compassion. These polarities, the archetypes *in divinis* of male and female qualities, constitute the metaphysical elements of the auto-genetic union which is the origin of all creation. They reside within the very heart of the Supreme Principle, which Itself transcends the products of their union.

All creation is an act of divine self-procreation, "an act of fecundation latent in eternity" (Eckhart). This generative act is the archetype *in divinis* of procreation, symbolized as the impregnation of darkness by light. Tradition emphasizes that the generative act occurs through a union of the polarities, based on the principle of their complementarity, not opposition. This principle is vital to an understanding of gender relations upon the lower plane, as we shall see.

Creation can also be understood as divine self-reflection, a series of mirrors within mirrors, in which the image always includes elements of the original reflectors, these being the metaphysical polarities described above. It follows therefore that there is nothing in creation that does not contain the germ of its opposite. Thus human beings, though divided into genders that exteriorize and reflect the metaphysical polarities within the Supreme Principle, each contain within themselves the possibility of their opposite, just as the interior contains within itself the possibility of the exterior, and vice versa. This is depicted in the Taoist symbol of *yin-yang*, in which each element includes an element of its opposite.

In traditional cosmology, order is predicated on the hierarchical unfolding of the universe from a transcendent Center through a progressive exteriorization of the archetypal possibilities latent within Itself—combinations of qualities, attributes and forms—through multiple levels of being. Just as water vapor liquefies into water and then crystallizes into ice, so the universe unfolds out of essence into form, through levels which correspond, both microcosmically—within mankind—and macrocosmically—within the greater universe—to the spiritual, the astral and the material realms. These dimensions, within mankind, correspond to the Heart (the spiritual or intellective center of man), and, in descending order thereafter, the soul (the animic or psychic dimension), and the body (the sensory realm of the physical world). This architecture implies an order based on hierarchy, in which the exterior derives from the interior, the material/sensory from the spiritual/intellective through the intermediate realm of the astral/psychic. Reality is masculine (or essential) before it is feminine (or substantial). It is in this sense that the Logotic principle of creation sunders the feminine soul from the masculine Spirit (see *Hebrews* 4, 12). It is only when the feminine soul (anima, *nafs*) surrenders to the masculine Spirit (Animus, *Ruh*)—when the exteriorized will of the Outer Man yields to the interior principle of the Inner Man—that the Spiritual Self is born. This spiritual birth is the métier of all religious questing.

It follows from this view that all creatures share a common spiritual patrimony, an Origin or Center from which, *qua* creature, they are separate both temporally and spatially (this is the dimension of transcendence, or exclusivity), but in which, *qua* Spirit, they live and move and have their being (this is the dimension of immanence, or of inclusivity). Value or worth, according to this view, lie in the ability to reconnect with the Origin or Center, which are identical in traditional cosmology, and are located in the Heart or spiritual core of one's being. Traditional morality is therefore ontological before being behavioral. Morality is thus the correspondence between metaphysical structure and ontological value. An action has greater or lesser value in the measure that it draws one ontologically closer to or farther from the Origin or Center. With this criterion of morality in mind, let us now examine its implications for sexuality.

Sexuality, like all creation, is within the Cosmic Veil of *Maya*, and therefore contains a certain ambiguity. The ambiguity lies in the fact that, unless things are metaphysically transparent, their allure is seductive and illusory. Thus beauty can be perceived as a sacred theophany or can be viewed as an end itself, and thereby profaned. Sexuality, as a response to beauty, must therefore be sacralized, lest it be profaned as lust ("the expense of spirit in a waste of shame", as Shakespeare described it). Thus, the sexual act is not in itself sinful, so long as its orientation is sacred and within the bounds of the Divine Law, but when it transgresses these bounds, it is considered sinful. This explains why the same tradition can contain two apparently contradictory perspectives (participative and penitential) regarding sexual conduct. For instance, the Pauline perspective within the Christian tradition emphasizes the blessing of conjugal procreation (because it is assumed to be a sacrament, and is within the prescribed bounds of matrimony), while the Augustinian perspective encourages abstinence (associating the sexual act primarily with carnal desires). Both these perspectives, despite their apparent contradiction, share the view that concupiscence is a profanation of the gift of sex. It places the flesh above the spirit, in an inversion of traditional morality (which places the spiritual above the material). The denial of transcendence—which characterizes modernism—throws open the gates of licentiousness in a parody of true liberty. To paraphrase Dostoevsky, "When God is dead, everything is permitted".

Tradition is an affirmation of transcendence, hence of the principle that sexuality is merely a reflection of the higher, spiritual order within the lower, psycho-physical realm. Thus the gift of sexuality is a means of experiencing the Divine Union of which it is a distant reflection, and thereby of sublimating the sexual experience to a higher purpose. Sublimation may take the form of chastity—as in the case of nuns or monks, or others who take the vow of chastity, and who thereby transcend their sexuality by the principle of extinctive infinitude into the realm of paradisal bliss that is symbolized by androgynal unity. But sublimation does not necessarily require sexual abstinence, merely detachment and complementarity, as affirmations respectively of transcendence and harmony. Modernistic conceptions of "free love" and sexual hedonism are a parody of the principle of extinctive infinitude referred to above, particularly in their lack of detachment. It is by detaching oneself in the horizontal dimension that one can become fully engaged in the vertical dimension.

It is in the context of modernism's denial of transcendence that we need to view its challenges to traditional morality. In terms of gender relations and sexuality, the two principal challenges that have emerged are the equalitarian view of gender relations advocated by the modern feminist movement, and the sexual exclusivism advocated by homosexuals. Both these alternatives are unacceptable from the traditional perspective because both perspectives violate the archetypal principle of gender complementarity, the first by a false engagement, the second by a disengagement. Let us review each in turn.

In traditional thought, transcendence is to be achieved through the metaphysical complementarity of polarities, not through their opposition. Translated to issues of gender, this requires the emphasizing of gender differentiation so that each gender reflects its own natural attributes, which in turn constitute the basis of a complementary attraction. This requires the feminization of women, and the virilization of men, based on the principle that "opposites attract," prefiguring a harmonious union that reflects on the human level the *unio mystica* which is inherent in archetypal androgyny and central to the human entelechy. The feminization of women and the virilization of men is always subject to the metaphysical principle that the feminine soul is subservient to the masculine Spirit—or darkness to light. In other words, humanity fully realizes itself only through transcendence, by being receptive (feminine, or passive) in relation to its guiding intellect (masculine, or active).

From the perspective of the Supreme Principle, the metaphysical polarities which It contains are complementary and united within the identity of the Self. This Universal Self (the Adam Kadmon of Judaism) is therefore metaphysically androgynous. This androgyny represents a paradisal beatitude that precedes the differentiation of humanity into its two genders, a differentiation represented by the Fall. It is the goal of genderized humanity to regain the lost paradisal innocence of the Adamic Self, the archetypal androgyne that symbolizes the primordial state of human perfection, transcending all polarities. This is the symbolism of the hermaphroditic Hindu deity, Ardhanarishvara, who represents the complementary union of Shiva (the masculine Principle and active pole of the Spirit, which is celestial and solar) and Shakti (the feminine Energy and receptive pole of the soul, which is terrestrial and lunar).

The implication for humanity is that the polarities represented by the different genders are to be transcended, not by a denial of forms, but through the principle of complementarity. In the words of Seyyed Hossein Nasr:

> Individual human beings are born as men and women, not accidentally but according to their destiny. They can fulfill their function in life, reach the perfection which alone can bestow felicity and even transcend all traces of separative existence and return unto the One, only in accepting their destiny and transcending from above the form into which they have been born, not by rebelling against it.

In traditional thought the antagonism between genders (which modernism terms "the gender wars") is considered a rebellion against divine destiny. Thus, for instance, it is stated in the Koran,

> O Mankind! Lo! We have created you male and female. The noblest among you, in the sight of God, is the best in conduct. (46:13)

The "best in conduct" contemplates a complementarity of gender relations in keeping with the entelechy of mankind. Complementarity is an aspect of hierarchy, because the lesser is subservient to the greater: the soul (or Outer Man) must "obey" the Spirit (or Inner Man). To restate this principle differently, that which vitalizes us must draw its energy from its true source: the feminine Energy (Shakti) must conform to the masculine Principle

(Shiva). Thus, all human attempts to harmonize diversity—including gender differences—must conform to the intellectual principle of an engaged detachment, whereby humanity can hope to regain a foretaste of paradisal bliss in the dimension of the vertical axis, while maintaining a social equilibrium through mutual gender respect and support in the dimension of the horizontal plane.

From the traditional perspective, gender equalization—in the sense of the homogenization of the sexes—conflicts with the principles of diversity and hierarchy inherent in traditional cosmology. Homogenization is a parody of the quest for paradisal androgyny, in that it consciously or unconsciously attempts to create, on a lower plane of differentiation and diversity, an equality that is intrinsic to humanity on a higher plane, namely the equality of pre-gendered humanity, symbolized by the Adamic Prototype. From the traditional perspective, such an attempt is bound to fail, and can yield only a disequilibrium on the lower plane. The paradisal bliss symbolized by "androgynous unity"—the need for equality or homogeneity on the human plane being in essence an adequation of Divine Unity—can only be achieved by the genders embracing their own sexuality in accordance with the forms given to them and by complementing, through mutual respect, the sexual difference that the opposite gender characterizes. Thus the Majesty and Rigor of the male archetype finds a complementary resonance within the Beauty and Compassion of the female archetype, and vice versa. By opposing or, through homogenization, denying this marriage or union of archetypes, the quest for paradisal bliss needs must fail.

One of the negative effects of the modern feminist movement has been precisely this reductive homogenization of genders by which men have become de-virilized and women de-feminized. This in turn has created a false opposition of the genders, basing gender relationships on the footing of competition rather than of mutual respect and support, qualities that reflect the virtues of detachment and generosity. We hasten to add that much of what the feminist movement has sought to legitimately redress has derived from abuses of male privileges, in which males have abrogated their traditional responsibilities towards women, substituting respect and support with abuse and exploitation. In the words of Nasr,

> The revolt of the female sex against the male did not precede but followed in the wake of the revolt of the male sex against Heaven.

The "revolt against Heaven" was bound to adversely impact human relationships in an earthly dimension, and thus we inevitably find, in the context of gender relationships, that this impact manifests principally as the loss of respect and mutuality among the genders, which has in turn contributed to the breakup of the family and the erosion of the social fabric. We note also that technological innovations, in particular, modern forms of contraception, have contributed to the changing relations between genders, but it should be borne in mind that it is one's underlying values that shape one's attitudes to the use of technology, and these values, outside the bulwarks of tradition, have become corrupted and lost all sense of objectivity and proportion.

The other alternative that has emerged in modernity as a challenge to gender complementarity is homosexuality, the exclusivism—or disengagement—of the genders in terms of their sexuality. Modernistic and secular societies are increasingly accepting homosexuality as a norm, to the point that some legal jurisdictions are now permitting "same sex marriages". These developments are unacceptable to tradition in as much as they contradict both the revealed Law and the metaphysical order that underlies it. Temporal courts have purported to legitimize homosexuality on the basis of "equal rights" (note the term "gay *rights* movement", which emphasizes the importance of predicating legitimacy on the basis of "rights"), but it should be borne in mind that "rights" are subordinate to "principles". Thus, for instance, no claim based on the argument of equal rights could justify an incestuous marriage between consenting adults (a mother and son, for example), because their "right" to such a marriage is subordinate to the "principle" that incest is wrong. It is useful to bear in mind that etymologically, the term "right" is derived from the root "*rt*" (as in "rite" or the Sanskrit word "*rti*") which denotes order. To claim a right therefore requires that one relate it to the metaphysical order of the universe. It is by virtue of such order that "principles" can be derived. Temporal courts that have purported to legitimize homosexuality and "same sex marriage" on the basis of equal rights, have missed the mark. Social acceptability cannot be the criterion for deriving principles. Truth cannot be sacrificed to the malleable views of the masses. Morality is more than mere pragmatism. Human norms (that is, standards that are merely of the human order and not derived from principles that are rooted in metaphysical structures) are not objective, but merely preferences, and are therefore no substitute for an objective morality rooted in transcendence. Objectivity implies transcendence: no system can validate itself from within. Thus, as we have argued earlier, traditional morality is based on the correspondence between metaphysical structure and ontological value.

Applying this criterion of morality to homosexuality, we see that homosexuality is, by its very nature, opposed to the principle of sexual complementarity which is vital to the traditional worldview. It constitutes the profanation of form by disassociating it from its eternal archetype. Further, it constitutes the isolation of one aspect of the archetypal polarities by its ignoring of, or, worse, opposition of the other. In the words of Whitall N. Perry,

> The homosexual error is, among other things, that of isolating one pole of a binary cognate and treating it as an absolute, which does violence to the imperatives of the cosmic order.

To speak of the "homosexual error" should not be construed as a condoning various forms of societal discrimination or abuse, which have given rise to legitimate expressions of grievance by homosexuals, and which in themselves constitute an abrogation of tradition. However, though tradition demands tolerance, understanding and respect of the human margin, rooted in compassion, metaphysical truths are not subordinate to contingent needs or the circumscriptions of "political correctness". "There is no right greater than that of Truth". What is at stake here is the very foundation of traditional order—of harmony. The imperatives of the cosmic order mandate an equilibrium which results from the complementarity and union of the polarities inherent in the Supreme Principle. To violate those imperatives is thereby to invoke the disequilibrium that we are now experiencing in the modern world. Equilibrium within the lower order can only be achieved by reference to the higher order, which is the sole source of objectivity. We must take care not to subvert our spiritual purpose, for its effects reverberate not only here-below but throughout eternity.

Gender differences are part of the diversity of created forms, and tradition teaches us that such diversity can only be harmonized, not by homogenizing, opposing or denying forms, but by accepting them and transcending them. The journey of transcendence is a process of interiorization into "the crowned knot of fire", the sanctum of the Heart, our spiritual and regal Center. Tradition teaches us also that reality is the harmonious combination of archetypes, the essentializing fire that represents the pole of the Absolute, and the multifoliate rose that represents the pole of the Infinite. To be true to ourselves requires us to manifest the divine archetypes complementarily: to integrate the True, the Good and the Beautiful. "And all shall be well and/ All manner of thing shall be well" when we have made the journey to our transcendent Self, and have thereby attained the Truth that manifests inwardly as Goodness and outwardly as Beauty. It is by combining these virtues within ourselves that we can regain the paradisal bliss prefigured in sexual ecstasy.

On Translation[1]

Quince: Bless thee, Bottom! bless thee! thou art translated.
(William Shakespeare: *A Midsummer Night's Dream*, iii.1)

All that exists, whatever its modality, necessarily participates in universal principles... all things, however contingent they are in themselves, translate or represent these principles in their manner and according to their order of existence, for otherwise they would purely and simply be nothing.
(René Guénon: *Spiritual Authority and Temporal Power*)

A translation presupposes an 'original' or prototype, and the art of the translator implies faithfulness to that prototype. In traditional thought, the 'original' refers to the Origin, which is to say, Absolute reality, which is both the source of phenomenal reality (and therefore 'above' it, as it were) and its imprint (and therefore 'within' it). Thus, all that exists owes its origin to the Absolute, of which it is an expression.

The term "existence" (etymologically, "to stand out", from *ex-stare*) implies a projection from a norm, which is the Absolute. The Absolute expresses Itself in existence in two ways: through uniqueness and through universality. Uniqueness is the relativization of the Absolute through its extrinsic differentiation, by virtue of the Absolute being free to express its infinitude, while universality is the intrinsic sameness of this differentiation, by virtue of the Absolute being necessarily One. The uniqueness of existence, however, is not contradictory to the unicity of the Absolute, just as the universality of existence is not contradictory to the unity of the Absolute—this lack of contradiction being explained by the fact that the Absolute exhibits different attributes on different planes.

The Absolute, though transcendent, deploys through multiple levels of being in which it participates, as immanent. These lower planes unfold sequentially from the higher in a continuum from the

---

[1] This essay was the Editorial for *Sacred Web*, Volume 13, published in July, 2004.

subtle to the gross, from pure essence through increasingly graduated crystallizations or veils of form. In this process of deployment,
the higher is translated to the lower through symbol, by which the
lower participates within the higher.

Existence is a palimpsest. Each life and each generation represents a different text, but written upon the same Tablet, as it were,
and with ink from the same Pen. Though each individual history is
unique, history as such is the same: it is the expression of the same
passage—of prefiguration, projection and return. Though time
expresses this passage uniquely for each of us, the geography of this
passage is intrinsically the same: it occurs within the space of the
Sole-subsistent, the Divine Being of the Absolute. Each individual
history is therefore a translation of history as such.

"Life aims at pattern" (*Plotinus*) because the Oneness of the
Absolute forges life through pattern. The Infinite translates the
Absolute, and existence translates the Infinite. We are translations
of each other's lives. We each bear within our selves the imprint
of the Absolute, the potential for perfection. It is the same Center
that connects us all. To lose sight of this intrinsic connection and
of our perfectibility, is to lose the pattern of order and therefore
to succumb to chaos. It is only from the Center that order can be
perceived.

To translate is to convey meaning. Meaning is an epiphany,
the manifestation of the sublime. Man is in essence questing for
the sublime. Words themselves are inadequate to convey what one
seeks, because the object of human questing lies beyond the horizon of mere concept. It lies in the outermost reaches of our deepest
selves and in the innermost reaches of nature. However one may
strive to utter it, one is bound to fail because what one seeks to
utter is ultimately ineffable, compelling only silence, the silence of
ecstasy. In that silence is more than mere knowing, more even than
mere being: in that silence, the self can feel its soul aflame with
beauty, ablaze with the wondrous intimacy of all that lives, and
with whom it has its deepest connection. This is the sublime state
of the blissful awareness of Truth as Presence (the *satchitananda* of

Vedantism), the compassionate state of oneness or communion that all religious traditions refer to as the realm of the spirit.

Tradition teaches us that we are not who we seem: we are spirits, endowed with bodies, "trailing clouds of glory", as Wordsworth has written. Though the human can in reality never be separated from the fabric of the divine, nevertheless existence is a "discontinuous continuity", a "Cosmic Veil" of forgetfulness and so, unless we are spiritually vigilant, the world will tend to corrode our souls: "Shades of the prison-house begin to close/ Upon the growing boy" (*Wordsworth*). Tradition discerns the mundane as a translation of the spiritual, and the aim of religion, which binds the human to the divine, is therefore to awaken us to the presence of the spirit from a world that is "too much with us". "For man has closed himself up, till he sees all things thro' narrow chinks of his cavern," as Blake has noted, recognizing that human perception tends to opacity, reducing the spirit to matter, the Intellect to mere reason, the Heart to the ego, and the transcendent and wondrous source of vital existence to the mere mechanistic workings of the universe. This separative human vision is spiritually moribund:

> Whatever is here, that is there.
> What is there, that again is here.
> He obtains death after death
> Who seems to see a difference here.
> (*Katha Upanishad*, 4:10)

It compels the will to carnality, the intelligence to hubris, and it infernalizes the soul.

By contrast, the unitive vision of the Intellect, rooted in the Absolute, is salvific: it functions through the interpretive eye that reconnects the image to the prototype, the human to the divine. The eye of the Intellect perceives Truth as Presence, "the drop in the Ocean, and the Ocean in the drop". Its vision is transformative because "when the Rose blooms, the Garden is everywhere". To know is thus to see, but spiritual vision is not merely subjective (limited to the experiential vantage of the observer) nor merely objective (reduced to concept or abstraction) but is participative, fusing both subject and object in a unitary and engaged vision: "The eye with which I see God is the same eye with which God sees me" (*Eckhart*). Spiritual knowledge (gnosis) is therefore ontological. It is inscribed in and resonates within the depths of one's being. Thus it is said that "metaphysic affirms the fundamental identity of knowing and being" (*Guénon*).

Tradition teaches that the Absolute has translated Itself into the spiritual Center of man, and therefore "to know oneself is to know Reality". Metaphysical truths are ontologically evident. This is because "the Kingdom of God is within": "the Heart of the faithful contains God". The Heart, which is one's spiritual Center, is also the Center that is everywhere. To perceive is to metaphysically participate in what one perceives. This involves the engagement of the Heart in what one perceives. Therefore, to know is also to love. It is the integration of knowing and loving within the Heart that identifies the Heart with the Absolute. There is therefore a sacramental quality to being "enlightened": existence is metaphysically transparent and invokes the Presence of the Divine Self, which is none other than the Absolute Self which resides within the pure Heart of the faithful.

In metaphysical terms, translation can be understood as the passage from knowing into being, through love, and the transmutation of being into the Presence of Truth through symbol. In the words of Frithjof Schuon: "*love* is that which enables *understanding* to pass into *being*, or that which attaches us ontologically to Truth and thus opens us to the transforming magic of *Symbol*". There are two points about this statement that we wish to emphasize.

First, in metaphysics, the ontological is logically prior to the cognitive. Being precedes knowing, to which knowing returns. Knowledge is an attribute (not necessarily, but sufficiently) of being, not inversely as in the case of the Cartesian formula ('cogito ergo sum') which, understood in this inverse sense, is one of the great errors of modernist philosophy. In other words, the implicit Cartesian dichotomy of mind and matter is discarded in traditional thought by a view in which the material is a translation of the spiritual, so that the mind participates in matter through symbol, which renders matter as metaphysically transparent or translatable into spiritual terms.

Second, the interpretive art of the translator is not representational but symbolic: to represent is merely to depict, while to symbolize is to transport. The aim is not to portray but to convey. Translation, understood metaphysically, imports an ontological dimension of participation in the subject that goes beyond the mere act of depiction or imitation. Because a translation functions as a bridge between the Origin and our distance from it, a faithful translation can be understood as the elimination of that distance or as the telescoping of space into freedom: thus, paradoxically, to transcend space is to open up another dimension of space, which is unbounded and free. This is one meaning of the *Hadith*: "In my community are people who will enter Paradise with souls like the souls of birds."

The trajectories of gnosis are simultaneously the ascent through knowledge to Truth (the objective pole of reality, represented by the Absolute), and the descent through being to Presence (the subjective pole of reality, represented by the Universal Man). The Universal Man (or holiness), is therefore a translation of the Absolute (or the divine), just as Truth is the prototype of Presence. The translator's faithfulness to the prototype is a function of the translator's receptivity to the original text. To the extent that the text speaks to, or resonates within, the translator, one can say that the translator participates in the text through the act of translation. What is involved on the part of the translator is at the same time an exercise of one's own faculties (the search for meaning and expression) and an act of surrender (an openness to the Muse of translation). This dialectic of effort and grace corresponds to the trajectories of ascent through knowledge (or the igniting of the Intellect into illumination) and descent through being (or the vitalization of the spirit into holiness), referred to earlier. Without this participation, there can be no faithfulness in the translation. Like a seed buried under the snowy sands of winter, Truth lies embedded within the frozen heart of man. Tradition therefore teaches that spiritual knowledge is a process of intuiting what has been buried, of discovering what has been covered, recollecting what has been dispersed, of remembering what has been dismembered. It involves both the effort of receptivity (opening the eyelid of the Heart) and the grace of light (the sustaining light of divine Presence: "a light shining in itself in silent stillness", as Eckhart writes).

There are two errors to be avoided in the translator's art: one is to abstract the meaning of the text so as to deprive it of any quality of resonance, while the other is to ignore its meaning by sacrificing it to the desire for novelty in the name of creative expression. Metaphysically, these correspond to reducing reality to the objective and subjective poles, respectively. By isolating the objective pole, reality is abstracted or reduced to fantasy. The abstraction of reality creates the monster of false utopias, in which the resonance of the sacred theophany is merely an "externality" that is readily sacrificed to the utopian or fantasized ideal. In tradition, therefore, the ideal is not a mere abstraction (or illusion) but rather the ontological reality of the divine prototype, which is to be understood simultaneously as Truth and Presence. Thus Frithjof Schuon has noted:

> Nothing is more false than the conventional opposition between "idealism" and "realism", which insinuates in general that the "ideal" is not "real", and inversely; as if an ideal situated outside reality had the smallest value, and as if reality were always situated on a lower level than what may be called an "ideal". Anyone who holds this view is thinking in a quantitative and not a qualitative mode.

The second error is a form of hypertrophy. By isolating the subjective pole, reality is disconnected from its foundational Principle. It is to idolize the shoe by mistaking it for the ground on which it stands. Disconnected from its spiritual roots, reality becomes subjective, sacrificing moral and cognitive meaning for personal preference that defaults, in the absence of its spiritual Origin and Center, to materialism. The materialist forgets that there can be no originality (or creative value) outside of its connection to the Origin, and no order (or meaning) outside of its connection to the Center.

Translation, in the end, is the art of self-interpretation. It is to identify the well-spring of all creativity with the Origin and to locate it within the spiritual Center of one's Self. This spiritual Center of our self, to and by which all that exists is connected, as it were by a "sacred web", is the Heart. Thus one can say that there is no faithfulness in translation unless it springs from the Heart. This is the criterion of authenticity: it is to avoid the false attribution of originality to other than the Origin, by recognizing its identity with the most profound depth of oneself, that boundless and inexhaustible Spirit which forever pours Itself into Itself in an expression of constant and infinite mercy.

The Principle of Verticality[1]

The spiritual man is one who transcends himself and loves to transcend himself; the worldly man remains horizontal and detests the vertical dimension.

(*Frithjof Schuon*)

The principle of verticality, which is a fundamental principle of traditional wisdom, is based on the affirmation of transcendence as an aspect of Reality—that is, of a comprehensive and integrated reality that is Absolute. According to this understanding, Reality has both a transcendent Origin and an immanent Center, which are one, rather than being reduced to the merely horizontal dimension of its existential or quantitative elements. Verticality implies both Heaven and Earth, a worldview in which meaning and purpose are defined principally by both height and depth, and secondarily by breadth—that is, principally by man's relationship to God, who is simultaneously 'above' and 'within' creation, and who therefore governs all creaturely relationships—rather than by breadth alone—that is, solely in terms of the relationship between the subject and the world. It also implies that the horizontal is subordinate to the vertical, that is to say, the relationship between man and the world is premised on the primary relationship between God and man: to restate this in Christian terms, love of the neighbor is premised on the love of God.

According to the traditional worldview, existence is transcended by a supreme reality, which, whether expressed in theistic or non-theistic terms, is Absolute, and which, without derogating from its unity, is simultaneously (at the level of the primary hypostasis) expressed by the horizontal ternary, Truth or the Solely Subsistent Reality, Goodness or the Perfection and Font of all Qualities, and Beauty or Abiding Serenity and the Source of its Radiant Effulgence: in Platonic terms, the True, the Good and

---

[1] This essay was the Editorial for *Sacred Web*, Volume 14, published in December, 2004.

the Beautiful; and in its Vedantic approximation, *sat-chit-ananda*. All creation is prefigured in this Supreme Reality, which projects existence out of its own Substance into a world of form (hence etymologically, *ex-stare*, to stand out of, or to subsist from, as the formal world of existence stands out of, and subsists from, the Divine Substance) through a vertical ternary comprising, first, the Essential or Principial Absolute (which is Beyond-Being), second, the Relative-Absolute Source of Archetypes (which is the primary hypostasis of Being), and third, the realm of Manifestation (which is Existence). The world itself, and its creatures, including man, as such, are therefore of derivative significance and are accidental in relation to the Supreme Reality, which alone is substantial. The world is transient, ephemeral and illusory. The Divine Substance alone is permanent and real. This view of the transcendent, supreme and substantial reality of the Absolute (which, according to the principle of verticality, is described in terms of its elevation or perfection in relation to creation) finds its expression in all religious traditions:

> O Arjuna! There is nothing higher than Me; all is strung upon Me like pearls on a string.
> (*Bhagavad Gita*, vii. 7)

> It may be considered the mother of the universe.
> I do not know its name; I call it Tao.
> If forced to give it a name, I shall call it Great.
> (*Tao-te-Ching*, xxv)

> His greatness is unsearchable.
> (*Psalm*, cxlv. 3)

> In the world, inclusive of its gods, substance is seen in what is insubstantial. They are tied to their psychophysical beings and so they think that there is some substance, some reality in them. But whatever be the phenomenon through which they think of seeking their self-identity, it turns out to be transitory. It becomes false, for what lasts for a moment is deceptive. The state that is not deceptive is *Nirvana*: that is what the men of worth know as being real. With this insight into reality their hunger ends: cessation, total calm.
> (*Sutta Nipata*, 756-58)

All flesh is grass, and all its beauty is like the flower of the field. The grass withers, the flower fades, when the breath of the Lord blows upon it...The grass withers, the flower fades, but the word of our God will stand forever.
(*Isaiah*, xl. 6-8)

Therefore you must be perfect, as your heavenly Father is perfect.
(*Matthew*, v. 48)

Glory to God, the Lord of the Throne; high is He above what they attribute to Him!
(*Koran*, xxi. 22)

All that is on the earth will perish: But the face of thy Lord will abide forever—full of Majesty, Bounty, and Honor.
(*Koran*, lv. 26-27).

The principle of verticality implies hierarchy, and consequently a radically different view of space and time than that which exists outside tradition. The conventional view is based on a horizontal perspective in which man, as such, and the elements which comprise the universe, are perceived merely as quanta that relate to each other within the dimensions of space and time. Space is, as it were, the dimension of the locus of interactions, whose boundaries are defined by physical laws and subjective choices, and time is, as it were, the dimension of the sequencing of these interactions, in a linear trajectory, from the past through the present to the future. By contrast, the cosmological worldview of traditional wisdom is based on a perspective in which space is metaphysical before it is physical, so that it is perceived as the realm of Infinite Possibility, of the unfoldment of the spiritual substance into the material world through a continuum that is vertically integrated, with each level (or horizontal dimension) being qualitatively incommensurable or discontinuous in relation to the preceding level from which it emerges. In spatial terms, man's proximity to transcendent Reality is proportionate to his proximity to his immanent spiritual Center, and inversely so. In temporal terms, existence (in the etymological sense of emergence from the Divine Substance) is simultaneously a descent from a point of Origin and an ascent to a point of Return. The Center is meta-spatial, and corresponds to the Origin, which is meta-temporal. This view of space and time as dimensions of transcendental reality is found in all religious traditions:

> Creation is only the projection into form of that which already exists.
> (*Bhagavad Gita*, iii.2)

> Whatever happens, in any form or at any time or place, is but a variation of the One Self-existent Reality
> (*Yoga-Vasishtha*)

> I being one become many, and being many become one.
> (*Sutta-Pitaka*, Buddhist Pali canon)

> I am Alpha and Omega, the First and the Last, the Beginning and the End.
> (*Revelation*, xxii.13)

> He is The First and The Last, The Outward and The Inward; He is The Knower of All Things.
> (*Koran*, lvii.3).

Traditional cosmology, being predicated on verticality, also implies a hierarchy of faculties. The supreme faculty which resides in the spiritual Center or Heart of man—within the transcendent Self (in Vedantic terms, *Atman*)—is the cognitive faculty of the discerning Intellect, the Eye of the Heart, which is known in different religious traditions under the names *nous, buddhi,* or *al-'aql al-kulli.* This guiding faculty alone is capable of discerning what is real and distinguishing it from what is transient, ephemeral or illusory, and the Intellect therefore has precedence over the reasoning mind and the senses, both of which are capable of only a partial discernment of reality, and are thus subject to its beguilements. Under the traditional schema, the will is therefore subservient to the intellect, but if this role is reversed, man can become enslaved by his passions, the untamed will being then capable of impressing even the reasoning mind to its own causes, to justify its own desires. This hierarchy of faculties is common to all religious traditions. One of the best known images of this hierarchy is found in Hinduism:

> Know the Self as lord of the chariot, the body as the chariot itself, the discriminating intellect as charioteer, and the mind as reins. The senses, say the wise, are the horses; selfish desires are the roads they travel... When a man lacks discrimination and his mind is uncontrolled, his senses are unmanageable, like the restive horses of a charioteer. But when a man has discrimination and his mind is controlled, his senses, like the well-broken horses of a charioteer, lightly obey the rein."
> (*Katha Upanishad*, 1.iii.3-6).

The epistemological implication of this view is that knowledge is rooted in being, and therefore ontological knowledge is the basis of all true cognition of reality: this is the most profound and penetrating knowledge that traditionalists term "*gnosis*". Man therefore has the ability, through his innermost self, the transcendent Intellect, to divine that which is real: in Platonic terms, knowledge is simply recollection. It is the art of diver who stands at the precipice of himself and plummets within himself, to his innermost center, drowning in the ocean of transcendence. Such knowledge is transformative precisely because it penetrates to the very core of reality. It is therefore not mere 'mental' knowledge, but knowledge that also acts and feels: gnosis is thus to fully participate in the Presence of the Divine. All other forms of knowledge are partial, valid only within their own limited dimensions of competence. Thus each sense has its own appointed mode of perception, so too does the reasoning mind, but these faculties cannot fathom the heart of the Real. It is only through the Center that the circle is known, only through journeying to the Heart that the Inner Eye of the Intellect can be fully opened. An epistemology that denies verticality thereby limits perception to the outer senses and the reasoning mind, which then usurp the role of the higher faculty, pretending thereby to be competent beyond their limits. Thus the Biblical prophet laments: "O foolish people, and without understanding; which have eyes, and see not; which have ears, and hear not" (*Jeremiah*, v. 21).

In addition to the hierarchy of faculties, verticality entails a hierarchy of knowledge and therefore an authority based on knowledge. Truth is the prerogative of the wise, and the fragrance of wisdom is the virtue of the wakeful heart. Truth is 'wholeness', which is embodied as wisdom, that is, 'holiness' or sanctity. This is the foundation of all genuine authority. All other constructions of authority are merely formulations of the mind premised on an absence of verticality. Pseudo-spirituality, which may profess to affirm transcendence, betrays transcendence by mistaking the occult or purely psychic realm for the spiritual. Its so-called 'holy men' may be invested with authority by their believers, but this is no different to the secular authority conferred by the masses on their 'false prophets', the politicians, rulers, celebrities, experts, or other 'idols', in the sense that the authority claimed or conferred in each of these instances never transcends the horizontal dimension of psycho-physical existence, and cannot therefore be considered vertical in the metaphysical sense understood by tradition. Thus in all faith traditions, genuine authority is recognized as holiness (virtue) and right thinking (orthodoxy), and is established on the basis of voluntary obedience and discipline rather than through outer compulsion, and on outer forms of observance that are coupled with initiatory rights that provide bulwarks against deviation and error, while encouraging and promoting inner search, detachment and compassion.

By affirming transcendence, man affirms his exile from the Origin, and his commitment to a point of Return. By affirming immanence, man affirms his immersion within the sacred theophany, and his commitment to the Center. The purpose of human existence is thus understood in terms of the above commitments to the Origin and Center—to reintegration and sanctity, which are essentially the same goals. To return to the Origin is to return to the Center. It is to detach from contingency (which implies horizontality) while attaching oneself to the Divine Substance (which implies verticality). The teleological, soteriological and eschatological implications of this are common to all faith traditions: transcendence is the meaning of existence. Because the Center is everywhere (Divine Subjectivity being distinct from the atomized or egoic subjectivity), existence is the effulgent theophany of transcendence; it is the sacred radiance of the Divine:

> The center which is here, but which we know is really everywhere, is *Wakan-Tanka*.
> (*Black Elk*).

Verticality thus entails a shift in perception, rendering reality as metaphysically transparent: it is to perceive the sacred Center in all things:

> God's center is everywhere, His circumference nowhere.
> (*St. Bonaventura*).

On the basis of this perception, man is a steward to all that is sacred ("a vicegerent on earth": *Koran*, ii.30), bound to strive to subordinate his passions in view of his reverence of the sacred:

> Paradise lies in the shadow of swords.
> (*Hadith Qudsi*)

Thus man is thereby accountable for his transgressions, for deeds redound upon their doer:

> According to what deeds are done
> Do their resulting consequences come to be;
> Yet the doer has no existence:
> This is the Buddha's teaching.
> (*Garland Sutra* 10).

Vincit omnia veritas! It is through Truth that the round of existence and suffering is transcended, by dying to one's egoic self and realizing the Truth that lies within, in the innermost Self that is our transcendent and immanent Center. Truth is simplicity, and salvation therefore is purity. It is a return to innocence, to the primordial nature of one's kardial Origin and Center:

> Blessed are the pure in heart, for they shall see God.
> (*Matthew*, v.8)

My earth and My heaven contain me not, but the heart of my
faithful servant containeth Me.
(*Hadith Qudsi*)

While traditional man roots meaning in transcendence, the
worldly man perceives meaning in predominantly materialistic
ways. He compensates for his lack of verticality by an excessive
horizontality. Lacking quality, he searches for meaning in predominantly quantitative terms. What he lacks in depth, he strives to
express in intensity. What he lacks in wisdom, he makes up for in
cleverness. What he lacks of love, he pursues in power. What he
lacks in compassion, he compensates for in sentimentality. What he
lacks in nobility, he strives to express in tawdry celebrity. What he
lacks of beauty, he seeks in graphic realism or garish sensationalism.
What he lacks in wonder and reverence, he strives to express in
idolatry. What he lacks in vision, he compensates for in curiosity.
What he lacks of reality, he seeks in the abstract or the surreal.
What he lacks of spirituality, he seeks in hallucinatory experiences
or in the occult psychology of pseudo-spiritualism. What he lacks
of religion, he pursues in false creeds and utopias, in progressivism,
materialism and scientism.

As the world devolves, its beguilements increase, demanding greater understanding and resolve to resist its snares. Without
the guidance of the Intellect and its sense of a transcendent and
all-embracing Reality, which are implicit in verticality, traditional
doctrines and sacraments are leeched of their inwardness and
interpreted in a predominantly outer dimension, which is formalistic, literal, and therefore exclusivist. Reduced to their horizontal
elements, traditional precepts are liable to be misconstrued. For
instance, the "Golden Mean" is susceptible to interpretation by the
modernist as a license to experiment all things in moderation, that
is, an invitation to try everything at least once, regardless of whether or not the conduct is harmful or otherwise taboo. This is contrary to the traditional understanding of the precept, expressed for
instance in Aristotle's admonition that certain actions are immoral
and have no mean, and in Confucius' view that the avoidance of

excess is directed to the development of perfect virtue or *Jen*. The avoidance of certain types of conduct is necessary to the affirmation of transcendence. It acknowledges that the world is subordinate to God. It is for this reason, in part, that each religion, in its own way, proscribes certain conduct (for example, dietary restrictions, or rules against defilement). Equilibrium is rooted in verticality. It balances the material and the spiritual through the realization that the material, per se, has no intrinsic reality, but its value lies in its sacred quality as an aspect of the Divine theophany. But equilibrium is not merely a matter of adjusting the lenses we wear when we view the world, but of locating the Center in our innermost depths. It is by the effort and grace of recollecting who we fundamentally are that we can begin to approach the One Reality that dwells in the Heart of each of us. It is by invoking the Real, not merely through the Holy Names of our respective traditions, but by embodying the Eternal Word within ourselves, that we can realize Its Truth as Presence. It is by transcending ourselves in conformity with the principle of verticality that we can realize our full existential potential, thereby affirming the reality that "the world is charged with the grandeur of God" and that we are spiritual beings, endowed with bodies, and must therefore experience our deepest, highest, and all-embracing Reality by being *in* the world but not *of* it, *ad majorem Dei gloriam*, for the greater glory of God.

The Quest for Moral Certainty[1]

A good man, though his striving be obscure,
Remains aware that there is one right way.
(Goethe: *Faust*, Prologue in Heaven, 328)

One of the basic questions confronting mankind is how to live a moral life. The two principal solutions that present themselves as answers to this question are the absolutist morality of religious dogmatism and the constructed morality of secular dogmatism. Neither of these alternatives is appealing. Neither meets the criterion of "objectivity", or conformity to the nature of things, on which any morality must ultimately rest. It is this objectivity which provides the moral certainty that is centered in our own primordial nature and is premised on the transcendent Intellect of an engaged conscience which discerns and conforms to the nature of things, as opposed to the "certainty of folly" that is blind to it. It is through objectivity alone that one can achieve true serenity in the face of moral dilemmas, as opposed to what Frithjof Schuon has termed the "false serenity which becomes the accomplice of evil" and which is no more than the blind indifference of a disengaged conscience, not premised on the kardial vision of objectivity.

The absolutist morality of religious dogmatism is sclerotic. Its certainty is a form of righteous folly based on the simplistic assumption that moral laws are absolute and of universal application, appropriate to every situation, regardless of circumstance. Now, it is meet that there be moral laws, such as those of the Decalogue, that there be institutional guardians of such laws, and that one should strive to obey these, but always subject to the guidance of genuine authority rooted in the transcendent Spirit or Intellect. For laws, rules and codes address generalities and not particulars, and are expressions of underlying principles from which they are derived, principles which are both revealed and accessible

---

[1] This essay was the Editorial for *Sacred Web*, Volume 15, published in June, 2005.

to the awakened Intellect. Moral dilemmas are situational, therefore demanding more than a simplistic application of moral laws: they demand instead a morally engaged conscience, rooted in a particular soil, but reaching with every branch to the heavens above. In other words, morality is not so much a search for a code of laws that is absolute and applied indifferently to every context, as much as a quest for objectivity that is rooted in the particular details and differing contexts of each moral dilemma.

The problem with the secular alternative is that secularization disconnects morality from its metaphysical foundation, that is to say, from any transcendent principles that inform rights and responsibilities. Secularism, whether it absolutizes tyranny (either as fascism or as communism) or absolutizes democracy (either as conservatism or as liberalism), seeks in the end to construct a reductive or relativized morality based on preferences, not on objective principles rooted in metaphysics. Its laws may set moral "trends" or follow moral "fashions", in each case employing reason to justify its changing norms, with rationalizations that range from pragmatism and utilitarianism, to "principles" of "laissez-faire" and a quantitative egalitarianism touted under the banner of "equal rights". But "rights", too, are subordinate to the principles from which they derive, and these principles are both transcendent (centered beyond particulars and contingencies) and objective (in conformity with reality). Morality cannot therefore be reduced to simply a matter of preferences, nor is it merely a matter of consensus. It is a quest for objective and transcendent principles. Its roots are metaphysical.

Traditional metaphysics teach us that there are two sources of morality, and these are, first, Revelation (i.e. that which is "above" us, corresponding to transcendence or "height"), and, second, the Intellect (i.e. that which is "within" us, corresponding to immanence or "depth"). These two function as "transmitter" and "receiver", respectively, and are the sources of all objectivity. "Revelation" here is to be understood in its most general sense, which includes not only the revealed laws of the scriptures or those conveyed by the teachings of traditional teachers, but also the natural symbols of the ever-renewing cosmic theophany. In other words, all that exists possesses a metaphysical transparency capable of transmitting to the receptive "Intellect" a reality that is "the Face of God", a Presence that is participatory, yet "out of the swing of the sea". The "Intellect" here is to be understood as the supra-rational Center of awareness within the Self, "the ear of my ear" and "the eye of my eye", the discerning heart which is the locus of spiritual insight and the seat of the conscience. It is the awakened Intellect, aware of its universal and participatory nature, that ignites virtue, engaging our conscience to enter into the heart of a moral dilemma, to not merely *ap*prehend the solution to a moral problem through reason or dogma, but to *com*prehend it by participating inwardly in its particulars through compassion (corresponding to love of the neighbor) and from a vantage that is centered in the transcendent Self (corresponding to love of God).

According to tradition, man exists in two dimensions, the vertical, which corresponds to his theomorphic, inner spiritual reality, and the horizontal, which corresponds to his psycho-physical, outer material existence; in simpler terms, the inward and the outward. These dimensions are inter-related, so that the vertical/inward pull of divine attraction (corresponding to the supreme commandment in its primary aspect, namely, to love God) entails the horizontal/outward conformity to cosmic equilibrium (corresponding to the supreme commandment in its secondary aspect, namely, to love one's neighbor). Similarly, and conversely, it is by conforming to the cosmic equilibrium that one is drawn to the divine. The two supreme commandments of traditional metaphysics, namely, love of God and love of the neighbor, thus correspond to the two dimensions of human existence, and constitute the essential and principial foundation of all morality, to which all religious laws are subordinate.

Moral dilemmas may not always appear amenable to absolute resolutions because they exist at the level of contingency. The created world offers moral dilemmas which at times appear impossible to resolve: a kind of "Sophie's Choice" that requires us to decide, for instance, whether to prefer one life over another. This kind of dilemma cannot be resolved simply by applying the commandment

"Thou shall not kill" or by recourse to the principle of the sanctity of life. A different level of engagement is required; a deeper level of understanding in which all physical life is seen as perishable, yielding to the transcendent Self, which alone survives. Moral objectivity is the immanent reflection of this transcendent Self, whose substance, in accordance with the metaphysical adage that identifies the True, the Good and the Beautiful, is virtue. Like Arjuna on the battlefield, we must do our duty (*dharma*), even if this exceptionally involves killing, abhorrent though this choice may be, so long as the duty is the expression of virtue and reflects our innermost Center. Like the Good Samaritan, we must open our hearts to discern our neighbor, to understand that the boundaries that separate each from the other are as ephemeral as the boundaries of space and time, that are constantly dissolving, and that, through the oneness of the divine Self in which all beings participate, we are ourselves the neighbor. "Inasmuch as ye have done it unto one of the least of these my brethren, ye have done it unto me... Inasmuch as ye did it not to one of the least of these, ye did it not to me" (*Matthew* 25:40 and 45).

If the allegory of Arjuna engaged in battle against the evil Kauravas represents the divine attribute of Rigor, then the parable of the Good Samaritan helping the man who fell among thieves represents the divine attribute of Mercy. In a certain sense, all morality can be viewed as an attempt to reconcile the divine attributes of Rigor and Mercy, but allowing always that "God's Compassion precedes His Wrath". That is to say that His Rigor is a part of His Mercy. It is important to keep this in mind because, while it is obvious that evil can be wrathful, it is less obvious that goodness may also involve rigor. Tradition teaches that outer burdens yield inner blessings. All spiritual practitioners know this when, for instance, they engage in spiritual disciplines such as fasting or penance, that involve renunciation or sacrifice. When judging the morality of a situation, one must have the wisdom and humility to judge, like Khidr in the famous story of his teaching to Musa (Moses) (see Koran, *Surat al-Kahf*, 18: 66-82), so that one sees with the eyes "of the spirit", not "of the flesh". As Khidr taught, one cannot make moral judgments based on appearances alone: divine mercy may indeed operate through rigor: "Sometimes He gives while depriving you, and sometimes He deprives you in giving" (*Ibn 'Ata'illah*). Let us recall that it was Christ, the preacher of the Gospel of Love, who overturned the tables of the moneychangers in the Temple (*Matthew* 21: 12-13), and who elsewhere exclaimed: "Think not that I am come to send peace on earth: I came not to send peace, but a sword" (*Matthew* 10: 34). Therefore, there will be situations which appear conventionally immoral, but are objectively moral or virtuous, and vice versa.

What, then, is the vantage from which moral judgments can be made? Moral objectivity, as stated earlier, lies neither in fickle convention nor in petrified moral codes, but in the living heart of a morally engaged conscience, guided by an Intellect that is receptive to the Presence of the divine. It is only by entering the kardial Center that one can perceive the nature of things, obtaining a sense of the cosmic equilibrium into which all disequilibriums are fated to dissolve. "Good doers leave no tracks" (*Tao-te-Ching*, 27). Moral objectivity, then, is conformity to the cosmic equilibrium. It is achieved by one's discernment of the metaphysical ordering of reality and by one's conformity to that order. Moral conduct, in this sense, is a reflection of our innate nature. Its roots are ontological, embedded in transcendence, flowering in the fragrant blossoms of virtue. Such conduct requires us to yield in some circumstances and to resist in others, conscious always of the sacred Presence of the divine operating through and around us, in our hearts and in all things. In the quest for moral certainty, one must possess the humility and patience equal to the knowledge that there are no easy or simple answers to some moral questions. Hence the admonition: "Judge not". But this admonition does not absolve one of moral responsibility. On the contrary, the quest for moral certainty is a necessary part of human existence, and calls on us to strive for moral objectivity, to abjure judgment "by the flesh" and instead to pray for the grace to judge "by the spirit". It is to eschew the morality of abstraction, that is, the moralism that elevates a "cause" above the sacred vision of the Presence in all creatures. It is to perceive that the "flesh" is ennobled by the "spirit", and yet transcended by it. Moral objectivity and the serenity it brings, lie in this dual vision. They lie, not in precepts, preferences or reasonings of the mind, but in the virtue that emanates as both a radiance and a fragrance from the wakeful heart, the innermost and innate center of our selves, that is compassionate, yet detached, gifted with the simultaneity of dual vision. For God is in the world, and therefore one must love one's neighbor; and yet God is above all creation, and therefore one must submit to His dominion.

On Cultivating Awareness[1]

How easily we forget that behind the technical membrane that
mediates our life-needs, there *is* ultimately a world not of our
making and upon which we must draw for sustenance.
(Theodore Roszak, *Where the Wasteland Ends*)

There is a power in sight which is superior to the eyes set in the
head and more far-reaching than the heavens and earth.
(*Meister Eckhart*)

In the Garden of the Sages, the Sun sheds its genial influence,
both morning and evening, day and night, unceasingly.
(*Nicholas Flamell*)

Awareness is the full engagement of the intelligence in respect of its
perception of reality. No doubt there exist multiple and therefore
lesser levels of awareness, corresponding to the multi-dimensional
nature of reality, but what distinguishes humanity from other
creatures that appear capable of experience or even appreciation,
which are both categories of awareness, is a quality of intelligence
that is commensurate with the divine. To the extent that there is
something transcendent within man, namely a portion of the divine
spirit, awareness, understood in its most amplified sense, corresponds to self-knowledge and pertains to the religious impulse in
man. And to the extent that the divine is immanent in nature and
radiates as a theophany, awareness corresponds to the sense of the
sacred, namely the attunement of the intelligence to the radiation
of the divine.

One way of characterizing modernism is by its atrophied intelligence, its diminished awareness, particularly evident in respect of
its dealings with nature. According to the traditionalist perspective,
the modernist has been condemned to experience nature with
gloves on: to combat and tame it, to plunder it of its resources, and

[1] This essay was the Editorial for *Sacred Web*, Volume 16, published in January,
2006.

also to insulate himself from it, thereby resigning himself to a world of artificiality, to a diminished experience of nature.

Artifice, understood thus as opacity or the anaesthetization of the inner perceptive senses, is that which disconnects man from nature, that is, from the divine norm which is his archetype. This desensitization of man in regard to nature is thus a symptom of a profound disconnection between man and his spiritual self, and is the product of our dominant post-Enlightenment culture, the secular culture of Reason (instrumental or discursive reasoning, not rooted in the spiritual or transpersonal intellect). This culture has invested its faith in Reason and the chief products of Reason, in scientific technology and in the post-industrial urbanized environment that is its corollary, but at the cost of both a diminished vision of reality and the degraded environment that emerges from this diminished vision. The resulting disconnection is a loss of awareness of spiritual Presence, a loss of a sense of the sacred.

There is a correspondence between awareness and our articulation of it, between the words we use and their meaning. One important indicator of our loss of the sense of the sacred is therefore our language. The profanation of language occurs in ways that are insidious and subtle. There are many examples: we speak of lumber, not trees; harvest, not fish; livestock, not cattle. "Produce" or "inventory", not the underlying natural creatures or substances they signify. Language itself becomes opaque, mirroring our own diminished awareness and thereby concealing the underlying significance and meaning of our words. What we cannot readily identify is easy to violate. This is the genesis of environmental degradation, mankind's loss of its linguistic heritage, of the Adamic gift to know the names of all things. To name a creature is in a way to identify its soul, to relate it to one's own. The modernist consciousness thinks of steak or beef, not of cows; ham or bacon, not of pigs; this is the language that produces the ethos of the battery hen, of canned and packaged foods known by brand names rather than by their natural contents. What we cannot readily identify is also easy to sell. Marketers of processed foods and pharmaceuticals, for example, know this all too well.

Language is also the first casualty in political exploitation. It exploits power through the confining of awareness. The manipulation of truth, of the narratives of history, is an abuse of political power. Words like "terrorist", "fundamentalist", "militant", "insurgent", often conceal other realities, disguising truth, packaging it into neat labels or stereotypes for mass consumption. In the age of "manufactured consent" and globalization, it is no coincidence that political powers and economic interests are coalescing, or that corporatist tentacles have extended into the domains of the media. The corporatist control of the dominant media obfuscates awareness. The reality we experience is the reality we are shown. Thus it becomes necessary to ask questions such as: To what extent are the so-called "free" media corrupted by political and corporatist agendas? To what extent do these agendas diminish our spiritual insight? Selectivity is a matter of agenda. A natural disaster or famine in parts of Asia or Africa, involving the death or displacement of thousands, is likely to receive far less attention in some "Western" media, for instance, than a celebrity scandal, entertainment gossip, or a popular sporting event. In the age of the Internet and of "instant communication", when the world has in some ways shrunk in size, it is a paradox that the "sanitized" worlds of the privileged few are apparently perceived to be so remote from the "contaminated" worlds of the underprivileged many.

There is a connection between imperialism and artifice that is relevant to our discussion here: what we subjugate or exploit denies something of itself to us, just as what we do not open ourselves to can never fully enter us. Reality, experienced in its most profound sense, thus requires a free exchange, the yielding receptivity of love, not the grasping urges of power. Receptivity or intellectual openness, as understood by traditionalism, is the means of cultivating awareness, and it requires qualities of both engagement and surrender. These qualities distinguish traditional epistemology from that of secular rationalism.

Engagement, for the traditionalist, is a facet of surrender, just as the intellect is a facet of faith. Where engagement implies effort, surrender implies grace. Both must occur simultaneously.

Receptivity involves attuning the intellect to the transmitted grace of the divine. All things, if intelligently perceived, point to the divine. Unlike the secularist's irrational faith in Reason, the traditionalist's intelligence is grounded in the certainty of spiritual being. This certitude resides in the self-knowledge of the transpersonal and supra-rational Intellect, which perceives the world as the spiritual ocean in which it swims, viewing the world through its inner eye, the "Eye of the Heart", the intuited and experiential Center of its spiritual self. It is through the surrender of the egoic self to the spiritual reality of which it is a mere refraction, that human vision becomes clarified, perceiving reality as metaphysically transparent to its transcendent and spiritual core, rather than as opaque and clouded by the passions of the ego. To be truly human is therefore to penetrate the Cosmic Veil, to perceive the underlying inner essence behind the diversity of outer forms, and to realize the reciprocal obligations of the inner and the outer that such knowledge implies. It is to rediscover the sacred Center in our midst, in the radiant embrace of the divine, whose Face is everywhere, and nowhere more so than in our deepest Self.

Art has a particular function in this epistemology. Unlike the "art" of secularism, which is individualistic and opaque, traditionalist art is universal and symbolic, and is open to transcendence, relying on traditionally hallowed symbols to arouse spiritual states and to evoke and be the means of invoking the presence of the sacred. Similarly, in its architecture, its crafts and artifacts, traditionalist art subordinates form to function in a way that differs from the utilitarian or individualist aestheticism of its secular counterparts, by resonating the sacred, and thereby evoking universal and timeless spiritual values such as integrity, dignity, nobility, humility, compassion and generosity.

In the milieu of such art, and in the context of a revitalized awareness of reality, nature regains its proper dimension as an extension of the creative tableau of which humanity is a part, the sacred canvass of the divine, the membrane that connects us all, the skin through which we sense each other and the tissue that binds us to a common fate. To perceive this is to appreciate the traditional bond between man and nature, the respect for the limits that this bond implies, and the special role for humanity of ecological stewardship that this entails.

As in the cautionary parable of Pandora's box, the "gifts" of scientific technology that we have unleashed in our midst are of mixed value and may prove beyond our ability to control. The effects of the Internet and the cell phone, for example, are not fully known, but it is clear that these and other similar technologies being developed for mass consumption, whatever their deleterious effects, are here to stay. And it is becoming increasingly clear that these technologies do have certain influences that impede our awareness of reality. They contribute to the insulation and isolation of man from nature, converting our innate creativity and appreciation of nature's wondrous mysteries to a culture of smug and mindless consumption, which has the hubris to presume human ingenuity to be independent of any divine origin or influence. Dependent on our machines, we become creatively impoverished and spiritually inert. Imprisoned by our technologies, we blindly believe that these constructs of dependency are setting us free. In fact, they are clipping our wings: "Feathers in the dust, lying lazily content, have forgotten their skies" (*Tagore*).

This impoverishment is one aspect of the "artificial" worldview of "progressivism" that values the quantitative over the qualitative. Another example of this is to be encountered in the field of medicine, where scientist technologies and remedies tend to reduce the body to its mechanical elements, thereby isolating these from their underlying spiritual elements. The ethos of modern medicine is therefore skeptical of traditional holistic approaches that it cannot fully comprehend, even where these latter appear to be of remedial value. Its mechanistic approach tends to reduce the patient to a laboratory, often compromising the quality of "care" in its administration of so-called "health care". And by presuming to prolong life at almost any cost, consistent with its emphasis on the quantitative value of longevity, it frequently compromises the dignity of dying and the quality of post-surgical life, whose values are rooted more in a spiritual dimension of awareness which transcends its own narrow worldview.

A further example of the folly of "progressivism" is to be found in the field of modern economics, where values are predominantly materialistic, and where non-materialistic content is either devalued or disregarded as an "externality". By measuring "progress" in primarily quantitative terms and with aggregated utilitarian goals, qualitative factors and spiritual responsibilities are largely ignored, with the result that enormous injustices in both human and ecological terms are meted out and justified in the name of economic reforms. The diversion of rivers (with its consequent displacement of traditional societies and ecological disruptions) to create hydroelectric dams to run industrial plants and factories, the urbanization of societies to feed cheap labor markets to work in those factories to manufacture products such as designer garments that can be sold to wealthier customers enticed to buy these products by skillfully beguiling advertising campaigns, and the general fuelling of consumption through the manufacture of need (by the conversion of wants into needs) in order to perpetuate a culture of economic supply and demand, are some of the examples of economic progressivism. The result is the monetization of values and the commodification of everything, even that which is sacred and should be treated as sacred.

Post-modern humanity has lost its moral compass. With diminished awareness of its underlying spiritual foundation, humankind is fast losing touch with the criterion of the divine Norm, innate within the transcendent Self that is the Origin and Center of all kardial consciousness, and must therefore attempt to construct a morality based on human subjectivities—a morality that is therefore doomed to be relativistic and variable according to the vagaries of those subjectivities. Without a metaphysical foundation of objectivity, the resulting moralities of post-modern man are vulnerable to an equalitarian rationalism (blind to metaphysical hierarchies) and to the usurping effects of the appetites of the will (unrestrained by the intellect, and subject only to the de-centered rationalizing of instrumental reason). The outcome of such moralities is evident in the degeneration of the moral fabric of society, in freedoms which slide into licentiousness, in rights which subvert responsibilities, and in the resulting backlash of a frequently excessive conservatism that, as political correctness, demands outer conformity without properly addressing inner principles.

The centrifugal influences of modern societies that are fast spinning out of control can only be countered by a centripetal influence, an inner stabilization that corresponds to the realignment of the human consciousness with its divine Center. As the world that we live in crowds in around us and imposes on us the demands of its frenetic pace, we need more than ever before to find within us the serenity that we crave—the transcendent peacefulness of the "still-point" within us. The need for this serenity appears to be evident to the masses in the modern world who, claiming not to practice any particular religion, nevertheless claim to be spiritual seekers in quest of therapies such as yoga and meditation. But the New Age packaging of traditional disciplines that are commercialized and offered without proper guidance or metaphysical foundation are of limited value and in fact potentially harmful. Among the common abuses of these practices are the teaching of spiritual disciplines as mere recreational therapies without their accompanying metaphysical foundation, the failure to properly distinguish the psyche from the spirit, thereby focusing on nebulous psychic feelings rather than on spiritually-intellected insights, the misrepresentation of the role of exoteric elements of spiritual practices, thereby delinking them from their inner significance, the emphasis on religious choice without sufficient regard to the elements of grace or discipline, and pandering to the pick-and-choose syncretisms of "designer religions".

In contrast to these New Age therapies, traditional methodologies are rooted in the orthodoxy of traditional doctrines. These doctrines guide the initiate to discern, through the transpersonal Intellect that is the core of spiritual epistemology, that Reality is Absolute, therefore One, Perfect, Infinite and Eternal, beyond our ordinary awareness (transcendent) and yet within our innermost self (immanent), our Origin and End, creating, sustaining and reintegrating the cosmos through Love. Where traditional doctrines, whether expressed in theistic or non-theistic terms, emphasize Unity, traditional methodologies emphasize Union, and in each case the motive for integration is the ontological awareness of the transcendental Oneness of Reality, an awareness that is the criterion of all spiritual morality and rooted (because transcendent) in detachment and (because immanent) in compassion. It is the métier of man to cultivate such awareness, an awareness of the Presence within and around and beyond us, a Presence that, fusing object and subject, knowledge and love, *is* what it sees. Such awareness is Light, and its cultivation is Prayer.

Prayer is the act of illuminating oneself by the Light of awareness. All that exists is the Face of God, and all is perishing save His Face. The Gardener has given us the good soil of our primordial natures in which to sow, with seeds of faith, expressed through Prayer, a bountiful garden that is a Garden of Light. The fruits of this Garden are our acts of piety and virtue on Earth, blessed by the infinite bounties of Heaven, and it is promised to us that as we shall sow, so shall we reap. We have been created in His Image, and so we too must be gardeners, and are brought on Earth to cultivate the Garden that, by His Grace and Mercy, will be our portion of Paradise.

What is Normal?[1]

Although the Logos is universal, most people act as though they
had a private understanding.

(*Heraclitus*, Fragments)

Man, by virtue of his own central position in the cosmos, is able
to exceed his specific norm; he is also able to betray it and sink
lower—*corruptio optimi pessima.*

(*Titus Burckhardt*)

To Blake, or to the Christian world, the measure of the human
norm is not the average man. It is Jesus Christ, who is the perfect
man, the unfallen man, the image of man as created by God in
the first chapter of *Genesis.*

(*Kathleen Raine*)

In traditional thought, the "normal" is that which accords with
one's primordial nature. The Divine Norm is the model of perfection imprinted by God in man as his primordial nature, and the
"normal" is that which tends or corresponds to the Divine Norm.
One of the primary definitions of "normal" is therefore that which
is "natural". The unnatural—even if it is commonplace—is not
normal. But according to the maxim "*duo sunt in homine*", man has
two natures—a primordial nature with which he is endowed before
his formal creation, and a "fallen" or created nature corrupted by
the privative effects of creation. Traditional thought emphasizes the
primacy of the primordial nature and its central role in the human
quest to ascend from Earth to Heaven. In Islam, for example, the
primordial nature is termed "*fitra*"—that is, the paradigm or norm
according to which God created man. The quintessence of this
norm is its receptivity to the "*ruh*" or uncreated Spirit (the Spiritus
vel Intellectus of Scholastic terminology, which Eckhart calls
"uncreated and uncreatable", whose locus is the Heart or spiritual

---

[1] This essay was the Editorial for *Sacred Web*, Volume 17, published in June, 2006.

Center of man), which God breathes into man at the time of his pre-formal creation in Heaven. It is when man is born formally on Earth as a creature and takes his first breath (in Arabic, "*nafas*") that he acquires his created nature (in Arabic, "*nafs*"), which, unlike the translucent and pristine *ruh*, is, as it were, a cloud-like substance that envelopes the uncreated Spirit. This cloud-like substance can be more or less subtle or dense, luminous or opaque, in each human being, its plasticity and luminosity varying according to the degree to which it is transparent to the spiritual Light of the Supernal Sun. Therefore, one encounters different levels of *nafs*: al-ammara, al-lawwama and al-mutma'inna, the former two corresponding to the dense and opaque nature of "fallen" man— "fallen" in view of the fact that the subtle and tender qualities of the spiritual nature (which make the soul pliable—yielding and "obedient" to the Spirit) become hardened, and the pristine perception of the spiritual vision becomes obscured, by the congealing and opaque influences of creation (the psychic clouds of the cosmic dust of creation, designated in traditional metaphysics as the Cosmic Veil—in Arabic, *hijab*, and in Sanskrit, *maya*)—in contrast to *al-nafs al-mutma'inna* which is the soul of the saint, united with its Source (as "light upon light") and utterly transparent to its own transcendent Spirit. This transcendent and pristine perception of nature is the ontological self-knowledge of the visionary Intellect— the Heart's knowledge of itself, akin to the eye's awareness of itself through the very act of seeing—and corresponds to the unitary and integrated Edenic knowledge signified by the Tree of Life, as distinct from the fragmentary and divisive knowledge signified by the Tree of the Knowledge of Good and Evil, in the Biblical account in *Genesis*.

By virtue of its archetypal quality, the "normal" can also be understood as that which is universal—though not everything that appears universal is necessarily normal. This is because the universal must correspond to the primordial nature of Adamic man in order to be truly universal. The truly universal is that which extends the Presence of the Heart radially—like Light, which is the universal symbol of "the True, the Good and the Beautiful" or of

Wisdom, Compassion, and Harmony—beyond the limitations of its own Center (which are its veiled and egoic selfhood), so that (to paraphrase St. Bonaventura) "the center is everywhere, and the circumference nowhere". This veil-rending, expanded and unitary realization of the Presence of Oneness—which "sees" everything in the light of its spiritual reality—is universal in the most profoundly "real" sense: it converts merely sensory seeing to spiritual feeling, cognition to re-cognition, perception to "tasting", self-driven passion to compassion, and opacity to translucence—or, as Henry Corbin has succinctly stated, it transmutes the idol into the icon. To be completely "normal" is therefore to aspire to the Divine Norm, to be fully spiritually awake—to look beyond the outer forms of things in order to experience their inner reality as a participatory Presence, compassionately, right down to their metaphysically transparent core. It is to possess a sense of the sacred—to perceive in all things "the fragrance of the Divine". It may be objected that such fully-awakened and open Hearts are rare, and that it is therefore a misnomer to reserve the word "normal" to describe such extraordinary souls, and that for the masses the "normal" is merely the ordinary. This is, in a conventional sense, true, but tradition reminds us that the criterion for any true norm must be rooted in Heaven (in transcendence) and not merely on Earth. That is why all normal aspirations incline Heavenward, possessing both height and depth and, through these, both breadth and symmetry—while merely mundane aspirations, if they do not aspire higher, eventually die into the ashes of their own flame.

Now, the normal cannot be merely subjective (the transcendent perspective of the Divine Subject corresponds to the Object of the Divine Norm), because it must be "typical", that is, adequate to an objective archetype. This archetype is the Divine Norm, or Logos, which corresponds to the spiritual nature of man, and mirrors the Absolute Perfection of God. It is in view of man's theomorphic nature that one can conceive of the Human as Divine Logos or as the Universal Man (*al-insan al-kamil*, in Islam)—as typifying the Divine. However, this view of normalcy differs from the common understanding, which, having lost the criterion of an objective archetype of transcendent Perfection mirrored immanently in the *fitra*, compensates for this loss by reducing objectivity to an approximation denoted by the consensual aggregation of subjectivities, conflating the typical and the commonplace—in other words, gauging normalcy by external and quantitative criteria instead of on the basis of inner and qualitative factors. This conflation, however, has a metaphysical basis. Since the divine spark within man is a fragment of the Absolute, it therefore partakes in its attribute of Infinitude. The spiritual nature is therefore universal, and this universality engenders in man an innate sense of a norm that is universal. In the case of the spiritually awakened man, the norm is identified with the universality of the divine archetype—to which the receptive soul becomes attached, thereby rooting itself in transcendence and verticality. But in the case of the spiritually dormant soul, the vestigial influence of the intellect—operating as reason or instinct—projects the quest for normalcy outwards and horizontally, seeking it in the average, in the universality of consensus, in the apparent objectivity of "community standards". In the truly profane, however, the norm is inverted and identified with the purely subjective ego as the criterion of all objectivity, oblivious to the distinction between mere subjectivity and spiritual vision.

In traditional societies, where there is a general attunement to the transcendent, consensus is often regarded as a reliable criterion of objectivity and value ("in the multitude of counselors there is safety", *Proverbs*, 11:14). Consensual reliance (*ijma'* in Muslim jurisprudence) derives not only from such attunement but also from the inherent pluralistic inclusiveness implied by the unitary vision of tradition. However, in deracinated modernist societies, where traditional principles have eroded—and along with them, the sense of the sacred, there is a danger in relying too readily on consensus as a criterion of objectivity and value. Knowledge that is cut off from its metaphysical roots—from a metaphysically hierarchic order—relies on consensus as the criterion of objectivity and value, and undermines true intellectual authority. It mistakes the average for the genuine norm. In the words of 'Ali ibn abi Talib, "The triumph of mediocre men brings down the elite". In the common understanding, the "normal" has lost its traditional linkage to a criterion that is transcendentally interior and is reduced instead to the commonplace, to the merely external recognition that a view or practice has gained general acceptance over time and become customary, thereby causing most people to acknowledge it as "normal". The problem with such a merely external criterion of normalcy is that any consensus or apparent consensus of norms may be manufactured, as postmodern historians such as Michel Foucault have demonstrated, or may have been influenced by external factors such as cultural influences or changing fashions, and critics are therefore rightfully skeptical of the motives underlying the identification and the labeling of norms. But in all this, one should not lose sight of the fact that the real impetus behind the quest for normalcy lies in the metaphysical certitude that Truth is objective and therefore universal, and not in any intrinsic value associated with consensus itself.

While those postmodernists who are skeptical of the processes of normativity have made a valuable contribution in pointing out the motives behind normatization, their skepticism can lead to error—especially if taken to the point of denying all normativity. Their criticisms, when pressed too far, open the descent into relativism, and thence into the abyss of a nihilistic denial of all norms. [The nihilism underlying absolute deconstruction was evident to Jacques Derrida who, later in life, tried to equate deconstruction and justice, trying to tether the former to the latter but in the process raising a host of questions about the definition of "justice" itself.] It is a false logic that would deny the very basis of order in denying the basis of disorder. In metaphysical terms, while it is true that "there is nothing like unto Him", it is one thing to apophatically affirm the ineffability of the transcendent reality of the Divine Nature (i.e., to say that one cannot describe Perfection because its transcendent quality beggars all description)—all religions do this— but it is quite another, on this same basis, to deny the reality of the Divine Nature as the Divine Norm (i.e., to argue that Perfection cannot be a "norm" because any norm would imply a limitation and therefore an imperfection). If—for instance, as all traditional religions affirm—it is in the nature of God to be intrinsically Good, then it can be objected by skeptics of normativity that to attribute to God a norm (here, of Goodness) is to limit the Divine Nature. This is to profoundly misconstrue reality: it is to fail to realize that, while the contingent order may change, the Universal order is not subject to change. This is because freedom has not just physical but also metaphysical limits: necessity is inherent within freedom, and its boundaries—which define our very being—reside within our innermost natures, which thereby constitute our "norm". In this, we resemble God, the source of our being. For, while God is absolutely free, He would not choose to exercise His freedom so as to deny His Divine Nature—thereby, paradoxically, one might say that God, while absolutely free, is not—by His Divine Nature—free to be other than Himself: that would be to abrogate the very nature of His Divinity—and, in this sense and to that extent, the Divine Nature is normative.

To state this differently, it is normative to aspire to transcendence because, even if the transcendent is beyond our grasp, it is not beyond our aspiration, on the basis that man was not made for other than God, and therefore the spiritual nature of man is adequate to the Divine. Mankind can intuit the Divine, and—though limited as creature—is intrinsically free, but with a freedom whose very nature aspires to perfection, even as God in Heaven is Perfect. This natural aspiration has become veiled by the polarization of its perception into dualities through the very act of creation. And it is precisely by an exercise of our freedom to avert our wandering eyes from the periphery and to focus instead on the Center, to forgo the beguilements of the flesh for the rewards of the spirit, that we merit the grace to inherit the kingdom of Heaven. It is by reorienting ourselves towards the Divine—by turning our gaze inward, from the restless periphery of the clamorous world and of our insatiable appetites to the still and quenching Center of the Heart (a turning that is called *metanoia* or "repentance")—that we can begin to regain the unitary vision of Heaven and thereby perceive everywhere and in all things the sacred Countenance of the Divine. Such aspiration and orientation are the quintessence of what traditional teaching defines as "normal", and the locus of such aspiration and orientation is the transcendent Heart.

Modernism, in its denial of the transcendent, is predisposed to deny any normativity based on transcendence—and therefore based on the criterion of the Heart. The consequences of this denial are serious and profound. The "new normal"—more accurately, the "abnormal", because it is no longer rooted in immutable, timeless, and transcendent principles embodied within our innermost self—is now subject to the vagaries of time. Though these changing norms are being continually redefined according to the governing influences and contingencies of the times, some disturbing trends can nevertheless be discerned. These include three interlacing trends that are central to the modernist ethos and underlie all modernist definitions of normativity. These are materialism, secularism, and scientism.

The first of the three modernist trends we have identified is materialism, that is, the reduction of reality to the merely sensible order, of the immeasurable to the measurable, of quality to quantity. The effects of the materialist ethos (the "Reign of Quantity", as René Guénon famously termed it) are pervasive: they range from the monetization of values to the consumerist conflation of wants and needs, from the profanation of the soul to the degradation of the natural environment.

The second trend we have identified is secularism, that is, the desacrilization of the public sphere. The effects of the secularist ethos can be seen in the privatization of values and its paradoxical counterpart, the erosion of conscience—reflecting the reduction of morality to mere pragmatism and utilitarianism, instead of rooting it in the soil of piety and virtue. Secularization also brings in its wake a more horizontalized worldview, an individualistic rebellion against authority, and a greater respect for egalitarian rights than for hierarchic duties. Finally, secularization marginalizes formal religion, undermining the legitimate role of the forms of worship, and thereby paradoxically de-spiritualizing religion. This contributes to the rise of religious fundamentalism and of pseudo-religions, characterized by their syncretisms and their insidious reduction of the spirit to the psyche.

The third modernist trend we are emphasizing here is scientism, that is, the scientific ethos that confines its study to the world of matter but arrogantly claims that its methodology applies to understanding reality as a whole. In its denial of supra-rational intellection, the ethos of scientism reduces all epistemology to empirical rationalism. The effects of this ethos can be seen in the sundering of knowing from being, in the evolutionist and materialistic myth of progress, and in the loss of wonder and the erosion of genuine creativity that accompanies the technification of society. In all this, it can be observed that modernism is that which separates man from the core of his being—from his true Center.

The crisis of modernism is thus a crisis of disconnection, of disorder. Abnormality, in the traditional view, is the loss of one's Center (hence the notion of the "eccentric" who is abnormal precisely because he is "ex-centric"—removed from the Center), and therefore of order itself. Because order and harmony emerge only from the Center, the loss of centrality or transcendence also generates a crisis of aesthetics—of chaos, disharmony, and vulgarity—and of its inward aspect, virtue. Virtue is an aspect of piety or holiness. To be "holy" is, in a metaphysical and etymological sense, to be "hale" (healthy or, significantly, "hearty") and "whole". It is to possess the primordial conscience of one's innate nature, which is our own self-regulator and criterion of sanity. Hence, Frithjof Schuon notes: "That which really judges us is our own norm that we carry within ourselves and which is at once an image of the whole Cosmos and of the divine Spirit shining at its center." This is the essence of being normal.

The loss of transcendence is therefore a loss of integrity and is invariably accompanied by an outer and inner disintegration of cosmic order. The degenerative effects of modernism are a reflection of this disintegration, and have given rise to what has been termed "the malaise of modernity". This malaise is at root a spiritual disorder. While it may be true that "human kind cannot bear very much reality", it is also true that no human being can remain sane without the sense of a center.

In the case of de-spiritualized or "fallen" man, where the awareness of the Heart, the true Center, has been lost—where "the falcon cannot hear the falconer"—there develops a compensatory sense of a center that, in traditional teachings, is associated with the egoic self. This false awareness of the center is a pathological subjectivity that no amount of conventional psychoanalysis can cure—because it seeks the cure merely in the psyche, and does not perceive that the problem lies in the psyche's inability to transcend itself. By absolutizing itself as the locus and the limit of the known, the egoic perception reduces reality to its merely psycho-physical aspects, thereby veiling itself from the Infinite. But, as Titus Burckhardt has noted, "The soul, like any other compartment of reality, can only be truly known by that which exceeds it." The pathology of "fallen" man lies therefore in his reductive tendencies, in his inability to extend his imagination beyond the limitations of the Cosmic Veil. It is only through an act of faith—of genuine spiritual vision—that the usurping influences of the deluded ego can be overcome.

In an age-old and universal motif, the mythic Hero's task is to slay the Usurper so that the throne might be restored to the rightful King. Through this task—which represents the defining métier of man—order and sanity are restored within the cosmos. But first, the usurping ego must yield to what Nikitas Stithatos (the disciple and biographer of St. Symeon) describes as "our endemic divine and spiritual consciousness"—the intuitive and intellective self-awareness of the Divine Heart—the human portal into transcendence, the Kingdom of Heaven, which is, as Stithatos reminds us, 'within us' (see *Luke*, XXVII:21). It is the Divine Spirit that is the rightful King and our true Norm. Thus it is said, "Blessed be the King that cometh in the name of the Lord" (*Luke*, XIX, 38). Unless the usurping tyrant of the ego is overthrown, no peace can reign in the Kingdom of the Heart. It is the restoration of spiritual order that is the condition for the restoration of cosmic order, for all things within the circle of creation are held in existence by their immutable Center: "Like pearls on a thread, the entire universe is strung in Me" (*Bhagavad Gita*, VII,7). Severed from this spiritual order, "the center cannot hold". This is the pathology of the abnormal and the insane. Thus, Kathleen Raine has noted: "There is a norm, there is a human perfection, from which we are all deviants in one way or another, and the nearer a human being approaches to that Divine Humanity, as Blake said, the more one could call him sane, even though the average would call him mad insofar as he departed from the average."

To be truly human is, in the end, to transcend oneself. It is to rise beyond the mundane perception of one's humanity and to ascend to the norm of the Divine Humanity—the archetype that exists in the realm of the spiritual imagination, the realm of faith that is open to the eyes of the spirit. For it is only by faith—by the inner eye of the Intellect that discerns the Light of the Supernal Sun and longs to be consumed within its Presence—that the illusion of the Cosmic Veil can be overcome. To be "normal" in this sense is to be spiritually sane, to have awakened from the Cosmic Dream, to see—in the words of Ibn 'Arabi—that "the whole of existence is imagination within imagination, while true Being is God alone."

The Problem of Evil[1]

Without evil the All would be incomplete.

(*Plotinus*)

It must needs be that offences come; but woe to that man by whom the offence cometh!

(*Matthew.* 18, 7)

In order to overcome evil one must stand wholly outside it, on the firm solid ground of unadulterated Good.

(*Mahatma Gandhi*)

The problem of evil challenges the conception of a deity that combines the attributes of Omnipotence and Goodness: to possess only one of these attributes provides no guarantee that the deity will act in conformity with the other, and is thereby no safeguard against the existence of evil; the combination of both attributes in action is what is required to stamp out evil. And yet, despite the fact that it is precisely this combination of attributes that is claimed of the monotheistic God of the Abrahamic religions, evil nevertheless exists, giving rise thereby to the conundrum of evil and the problem of theodicy or justifying the ways of God to man.

To approach this problem one can begin by examining what one means by the term "evil". On closer inspection it will be found that the term refers to two categories of experience: the afflictions that are suffered either by virtue of the "conditions of existence" or of the "abuses of free will". The conditions of existence: privation, transience, imperfection. The abuses of free will: pride, vanity, hard-heartedness. From these factors comes what we call "evil". One could refer to these as "suffering" and "sinfulness", respectively. It is for this reason that religions consider evil either as illusion and ignorance—for example, in the case of Hinduism or Buddhism,

---

[1] This essay is a revised version of the Editorial for *Sacred Web*, Volume 18, published in January, 2007.

which focus on its manifestation as suffering from the conditions of existence—or as transgression and rebellion—for example, the Abrahamic religions, which focus on its manifestation as the sinful abuses of free will.

"The world is afflicted with death and decay, therefore the wise do not grieve, knowing the terms of the world" (*Buddhaghosa*). There are two questions this raises: first, are the "terms of the world" (or, in other words, the "conditions of existence") evidence of the lack of the Omnipotence and Goodness of God; and, second, how can the afflictions they cause be transcended?

The answer to the first question is that creation, if perceived as a theophany, is good ("And God saw everything that he had made, and, behold it was very good"—*Genesis*: 1, 31), and this goodness inheres within the Divine Attributes. But from the perspective of the relatively real, the world is an admixture of good and evil. Thus creation does not appear as good (or theophanic) when perceived as *samsara* (or *maya* in its lower sense), that is, when experienced in an illusory mode by a purely human perspective that is ensnared within the limiting conditions of existence. Paradisal vision is unitive and integral: it perceives the whole of creation as an aspect of the divine fabric, the Tree of Life. Nevertheless, when mankind heeds the serpentine temptation to "be as gods, knowing good and evil" (*Genesis*: 3, 5), its vision became separative, no longer part of the divine fabric but atomized in a manner that is represented by the Tree of Knowledge of Good and Evil. The fact of existence—though it entails "death and decay"—does not therefore, in and of itself, entail suffering at any level other than that of the relatively real because the privative conditions of existence can in fact be transcended by the detachment from illusion that pertains to knowledge.

Evil is metaphysically necessary, because existence is relatively real insofar as it is perceived as separation from the Origin. Frithjof Schuon explains: "The question: 'Why does evil exist?' really comes down to the question of knowing why there is existence: the serpent is found in Paradise because Paradise exists. Paradise without the serpent would be God." Thus, according to a *Hadith* of the Holy Prophet of Islam: "There is no sin greater than that of existence itself"—by which is meant that "to exist means to be other than God, and so to be bad" (*Schuon*). To exist is to be a creature, distinct from the creator, and in this disjunction lies the privative distance (or "ontological distance", as Schuon terms it) that we experience as suffering.

Existence—insofar as it pertains to the quality of All-Possibility inherent within the Infinite nature of God—is an aspect of God's Omnipotence, and—insofar as it pertains to the universality of the Divine Substance inherent within the Absolute nature of God—is an aspect of God's Goodness. As spiritual beings—insofar as we are created in the image of God, and thereby reflect both His Omnipotence and His Goodness—we possess both the paradisal vision or intellect to transcend our ignorance and to perceive creation in unitive terms as a theophany—as good, and also the free will to be detached from the imperfections of existence and to thereby open ourselves to the goodness inherent within our own spiritual substance.

The answer to the second question is that, though death and decay are the conditions of existence—and the suffering we feel as creatures is undoubtedly experienced by us, at its own level, as 'real', nevertheless the suffering caused by these conditions can be transcended through spiritual growth. To live in the world is to experience misfortune, suffering and death; yet one's response to these is not dependent on the conditions of existence. For some, an outwardly minor misfortune may be experienced inwardly as calamitous, while for others an apparently major affliction may be borne with ease. Much depends on one's attitude and this in turn depends on one's perspective. A deprivation is only experienced as a suffering to the extent that it reflects an attachment and is felt as such. Schuon writes:

> Man is the author of his misfortune insofar as it is felt as a suffering; the world is the author of it insofar as his misfortune endeavours to keep him in a cosmic illusion.

The illusoriness of existence reflects the illusoriness of the ego that experiences the cosmic illusion as real. From a metaphysical perspective, "the ego is both the one deluded and the illusion", and therefore to transcend suffering entails detachment from the ego. It is only by detachment from the ego that the Spirit can transcend the conditions of existence and the ego's own limited perceptions.

There are thus two components to detachment: first, detachment from the things of the world ("being in the world, not of it"), and, second, detachment from the egoic self ("no reality but the Real"). With regard to the first component, detachment lies in the awareness of the contingent aspect of creation (which accounts for its evanescence and imperfection), the realization that existence is a dreamlike state, "a glory that vanishes", and that wakefulness is the awareness of the Absolute Reality, "the glory that never vanishes" and that is Present within existence itself. With regard to the second component, detachment lies in the awareness that "I" am not, only God is. From this perspective, suffering—or *ascesis*—is a purification, a means of transcending the conditions of existence through spiritual growth. As Shakespeare reminds us:

> Sweet are the uses of adversity,
> Which like the toad, ugly and venemous,
> Wears yet a precious jewel in his head.

Spiritual trials are the means of detachment both from the privative conditions of existence that are experienced ordinarily as suffering, and from the egoic delusion that the individual self is Real. Some are tested by want, others by plenty. It is instructive also to recall the scriptural reminder that "Allah does not test a soul beyond its capacity" (*Koran*: 2, 286). This is another reason that "the wise do not grieve" for they have faith that trials are, in their own way, mercies, and that existence is a pathway to salvation: "Whom best I love I cross." Or, in the words of a *Hadith* attributed to 'Ali ibn Abi Talib: "Whom I love, him I slay. Whom I slay, him must I requite. Whom I must requite, Myself am his Requital". In each moment, the Sustainer remakes us, and each moment is thereby an opportunity for us to rededicate ourselves to Him. In each act of this rededication is a little death, where, by hazarding all that we have, we are reborn spiritually: "Look now, here is a bargain: give one life and receive a hundred!" (*Rumi*). Only by the annihilation of the egoic drop into the Ocean of the Real (*fana-fi-'Llah*) can the egoic mirage be replaced by the Spirit's perception of its Self-same Substance and Selfhood (*baqa-bi-'Llah*) as the theophanic Presence. Thus it is that by lighting the Lamp within our Heart, we can shine a Light upon the outer world. And it is by shining this Light—by perceiving the Divine Face as Present within existence—that our detachment from the relatively real is transmuted into compassion and love for the Presence of the Real.

Evil as sin: "Whatever of good befalleth thee, it is from Allah, and whatever of ill befalleth thee, it is from thyself" (*Koran*: 4, 79). We have already seen how this statement can be understood in terms of our limited perception of reality as suffering. But there is a second sense in which this statement can be understood, as alluded to earlier, and that is evil as the product of sin. This raises two questions that we will consider here: first, what is sin, particularly in relation to the gift of free will; and, second, what is the antidote to sinfulness?

"All sins are contained in this one category, that one turns away from things divine and truly enduring, and turns towards those which are mutable and uncertain" (*St. Augustine*). The "immutable Good" (transcending any dualistic concept of good and evil) is the Divine Spirit enduring within the Heart of man, which acts according to its spiritual nature, and not according to those changing precepts and norms of morality which imply a consciousness of post-paradisal distinctions of relative reality, of the "mutable and uncertain good" which exists only in a relational sense as part of the duality of good and evil. Sinfulness is thus rooted in disorientation. It is marked by the turning away, centrifugally, from the paradisal vision of the Divine Presence of the immutable Good towards the seductions of the world. "The man who has sinned has, in the first place, allowed himself to be seduced; and in the second place has ceased to be what he was before" (*Schuon*). In the extreme case, this turning away constitutes a mortal sin: "Mortal sin in metaphysics is the conviction or assertion of independent self-subsistence, as in Satan's case" (*Ananda K. Coomaraswamy*). But in more ordinary cases, sinfulness is the forgetfulness of one's spiritual nature in the face of the seductions of the world and the flesh. It is marked by the pursuit of worldly desires, the gratification of the passions, and attachment to the material world. The sinner in the ordinary sense is the one "who maketh his desire his god" (*Koran*: 45, 23), forgetting that desire exists only for the sake of Perfection, and that all contingent desires are insatiable because they do not seek to quench their thirst from the Fount of Perfection.

Is the transgressive character of human free will indicative of the lack of Divine Onmipotence and Goodness? We have read the scriptural admonition that evil cannot come from God, who is all Goodness, but comes from ourselves alone. Yet, it might be objected that God permits sinful transgressions and wickedness, and thereby belies His Benevolence, if not His Power. Man, of all His creatures, was endowed with free will as a mercy, to be able of his own volition to surrender himself to the mystery of his Maker in an act of absolute intimacy. Freedom is therefore the emptying of self-will so that whatever remains is good-will—that is, the grace of God acting through man. "All the activity of man in the works of self-denial has no good in itself, but is only to open an entrance for the one only Good, the light of God, to operate on us" (*William Law*). It is in this sense that all Good is from God alone, man's role being limited to surrendering to the operation of that Goodness by becoming "the void made for the passage of God" (*Schuon*).

As sinfulness is a turning away from God, so the antidote to sinfulness is a reorientation towards the Divine. This involves repentance or *metanoia*, the turning away from the mutable to the Immutable, from illusion to Reality, from the snares of the material world to the transcendent Face of the Divine Presence in all things. And this in turn requires the repentant to undergo rites of purification and prayer by which the spells and seductions of the illusory world can be broken and resisted, and the permanence of the Divine Presence can, by the grace of God, be summoned to abide within the faithful Heart through Invocation and Sacred Remembrance. "Resist the devil, and he will flee from you. Draw nigh to God, and He will draw nigh to you" (*James*: 4, 7-8). It is the desire for God that must replace all worldly desires, and by strengthening this desire through prayer, the eyes of faith are thereby opened, acquiring, by the grace of divine alchemy, the certainty of the vision of the spiritual Reality that underlies and transcends the whole of existence. For man was born to transcend his ordinary existence, the world of suffering and sin, and so to find Peace in the intimate embrace of Divine Mystery.

The Secular and the Sacred[1]

Secularization... implies the loss by man of his capacity of objectivation, of his power to distinguish illusion from reality, falsehood from truth, the relative from the absolute. The deepest objective of secularism is precisely to 'liberate' man from the order by which he is submissive to his Creator, to 'emancipate' him from his existential source, to 'change' the system of truth in which he lives into a factual and mental relativity. Thus an inevitable consequence is, not an accrued perspicuity in the imaginative life of man, but on the contrary an ever growing opacity.

(Tage Lindbom)

There is something in man that links him to the Eternal... If this immutable kernel in man cannot be directly grasped—anymore than can the dimensionless center of a circle—the approaches to it can nevertheless be known: they are like the radii which run towards the center of a circle. These approaches constitute the permanent element in every spiritual tradition and, as guidelines both for action and for those social forms that are directed towards the center, they constitute the real basis of every truly conservative attitude. For the wish to conserve certain social forms only has meaning—and the forms themselves can only last—if they depend on the timeless center of the human condition.

(Titus Burckhardt)

In its etymological sense, the term "secular" (derived from the Latin term "saeculum", denoting age or time) refers to the time-bound or worldly, while the term "sacred" (derived from the Latin term "sacer" and the old French "sacrer", denoting that which is holy) refers to the timeless or transcendent. The two terms are commonly believed to be in opposition, but this is in reality a false opposition. As Seyyed Hossein Nasr, and other Traditionalists following him, has stated, "There is nothing more timely than the timeless." From the perspective of Tradition, there is no discontinuity between the created order and its Origin

---

[1] This essay is a revised version of the Editorial for *Sacred Web*, Volume 19, published in June, 2007.

or Center. All that is created contains the trace of the divine and is, in view of its original nature, "good" or "holy", that is to say, "sacred". It is for this reason that the sacred can be defined as "the presence of the Center in the periphery"

(*Frithjof Schuon*)

Contemporary understandings of the term "secular" embrace two different versions: one that is neutral toward religion and asserts that religions should be largely free of political interference, and another that is hostile towards religion and seeks to exclude religions and religious influence from public expression, particularly from politics. It is with regard to the latter interpretation that the opposition between the secular and the sacred persists, and it does so as an aspect of the ethos of modernism, which is a worldview characterized by the denial of the transcendent and its concomitant loss of the sense of the sacred. To distinguish this fundamentalist interpretation from the moderate understanding of the "secular", we will refer to it as "secularism".

Modernism's secularist ideology, like all false ideologies, is rooted in a false epistemology—in this case, that associated with the worldview of the "Enlightenment"—derived from the theories of René Descartes. The Cartesian epistemology is popularly portrayed as a duality of "mind" and "matter", of the "knower" and the "known". This dualism is based on a particular reductionism in which intelligence—the "knower"—is reduced to the psycho-physical persona of the empirical mind (that is to say, the mind that is wedded to the scientific method of knowing by a process of sense-observation, objectively verifiable experimentation, and reasoning), while that which is knowable—the "known"—is reduced to the empirically verifiable, quantifiable and material world. This reductive dualism necessarily destroys the ontological foundations of knowledge and the basis for the cosmological correspondence within Tradition between microcosmic Man (the "knower") and the macrocosmic universe (the "known").

In Traditional epistemology, intelligence is the adequation of the Intellect to the Absolute, and is the faculty of the Intellect, enthroned in the Heart, whose substance is the Spirit "that knoweth all things". The Intellect is regarded as an Eye—the Inner Eye, the Eye of the Heart, the Third Eye—denoting that knowledge is vision. Intellection thus understood is akin to seeing, to witnessing the Presence of the Spirit within ourselves and in all things (in Koranic terms, to see "the Face of God"). It is this witnessing that informs the Intellect of its ontological connection with the universe. Through the mystery and intimacy of Spiritual witnessing, all is seen as one—that is, all domains are imbued with the Sacred in view of the fact that the Absolute embraces all things.

By contrast, the epistemology of modernism would deny intelligence the capability of knowing through any faculties superior to those of the senses and the reasoning mind—specifically, reducing all intellection to, at best, processes of reasoning. Without recourse to the Intellect, intelligence is devalued and removed from its very foundations. By curtailing the faculties of knowing in this fashion, the modernist view of knowledge limits its definition of what is knowable to merely the material realm to which its method of knowing applies. This results in a horizontalized and materialistic worldview, lacking any sense of verticality or transcendence, which René Guénon has labeled as "the Reign of Quantity". By creating a rupture between Man and his spiritual roots, modernism has severed the Golden Thread that connects him to the Absolute and thereby to his fellow creatures.

It is in this context that secularism needs to be considered—as an aspect of modernism. With its blind acceptance of scientism—the claim that all knowledge is subject to the criterion of the scientific method—modernism has created another false opposition, correlating to and paralleling that of the secular and the sacred: the opposition of science and religion. This is a false opposition because both "science" (derived from the Latin, *scire*, "to know") and "religion" (derived from the Latin, *ligare*, "to bind") are rooted in the wisdom of the Oneness of the Absolute—the integrity of knowledge and being. By confining knowledge to rational empiricism (and the scientific method whose philosophical counterpart is logical positivism), modernism has condemned it to alienation from its metaphysical foundations, and thereby from religion. For its part, religion, where it has become exteriorized and deracinated through the loss of its symbolist spirit and disconnection with its metaphysical roots, has thereby become incapable of reconciling the scientific realities of cosmology with its theological depictions. Deprived of their metaphysical underpinnings, the logical and mythological worldviews of science and religion have collided, and this conflict has tended to polarize both outlooks.

The desire to exclude religion from public discourse stems, in part, from its being viewed as irrelevant. If man can know by rational empirical faculties and without the need of grace, and if science (as conventionally understood—not the sacred science of Traditional metaphysics, the "*scientia sacra*") can potentially know all there is to be known, God will understandably be considered to be irrelevant in public affairs. This over-reaching science—or "scientism"—is one explanation for the current vogue in attacking God and religion. But these attacks and the impetus for secularism also spring from another, more insidious, cause: religious fundamentalism.

Religious fundamentalism is, in part, a reaction to modernism—which in itself is a form of fundamentalism. It shares fundamentalism's four major characteristics: that is to say, it is reactionary, conservative, literalistic, and (non-pluralistically) exclusivist. Religious fundamentalism is a reaction to the polarized worldview of modernism, which, by its denial of the transcendent, threatens the very basis of religion. It is also a reaction to the processes of modernization: as the world has become modernized through scientific technologies, it has become globalized and pluralized through more diverse encounters, and this pluralization and diversity has tended to relativize values. Religious fundamentalism is thus, in part, a reaction to this relativization, which has tended to erode traditional societies. And, finally, it is a politicized reaction to what can be termed the "political dimension of modernization". This refers, on the one hand, to the political exploitation of religious fault-lines—theological, cultural and sectarian—for political, economic, military or strategic interests, either by political dictators or by external imperialist or colonizing forces. [Examples include the Shi'a-Sunni conflict in Iraq, the Hindu-Muslim conflict in Kashmir, the Jewish-Muslim conflict in the Middle East, and, in recent history, the Catholic-Protestant conflict in Northern Ireland, to cite but a few instances where religious divisions have been exploited by politicians in the name of religion.] And, on the other hand, it refers to the muzzling of political dissent that is then given expression through the channels of organized religion. [Examples include the Islamic Revolution in Iran in 1979, and the growth of radicalized religious parties in countries like Egypt, Tunisia, and Algeria.]

In addition to being reactionary, religious fundamentalism is conservative: that is to say, it seeks to conserve 'fundamental' elements and values. The error of religious fundamentalism is to deny form its essential function. Instead of seeking to conserve elements and values that are "essential" to its worldview, it promotes elements and values that reflect a "formal" or externalized homogeneity—things such as the regulation of dress and outward behavior. This error springs from a conflation of formalism and orthodoxy, and is manifested by the two other features of fundamentalism cited earlier—literalism and non-pluralistic exclusivism. The reaction of religious fundamentalism to those forces that threaten to erode its fundamental values is to cling all the more forcefully to its outer forms. This approach results in a greater emphasis on the literal and formal aspects of religion, undermining its mythological aspects and rendering opaque its symbolic content. It also portrays a totalitarian tendency, which it displays by virtue of its claim to represent the Absolute. While Traditional metaphysics conceives of a supra-formal unity of religions, religious fundamentalism can conceive of no plurality in the modes of revelation, and therefore its religious exclusiveness is absolute.

When repugnant and heinous acts are undertaken in the name of religion, it is not always easy to distinguish those acts as abuses of religion. This distinction is even less apparent to those held in the thrall of modernism. Secularism feeds off religious fundamentalism (and vice versa). It is religion's betrayal of itself and its betrayal by those who commit abuses in its name that causes many—and particularly those who are disinclined to regard it as relevant—to regard it as abhorrent. It is all-too-easy, though simplistic, to deride religion in the wake of the events of 9/11—as do Dawkins, Harris, Hitchens, and others—or to proclaim a "Clash of Civilization" (the very phrase is an oxymoron: those who are civilized do not clash)—as do Lewis and Huntington. While it may appear politically compelling to respond to religious extremism by banning outer emblems of religious affiliation (such as *hijabs* worn by Muslim women, which have been banned from schools or public places in several countries) or to cling ever stronger to secularist ideals by privatizing religion and excluding it from any political expression, this is not the answer. What is needed is to revitalize the struggle—both within religion and outside it—for the heart of religion, to recover the sense of the sacred.

In the so-called secular world of politics, it is important to keep in mind the sacred order of things. There are two currents in political life: one is conservative, emphasizing group rights and individual responsibilities, while the other is liberal, emphasizing individual rights and freedoms. From the perspective of Traditional metaphysics, the error of the conservative strain lies in its tendency to absolutize values on the formal plane, without due regard to their essential or inner content. The error of the liberal strain lies in its tendency to absolutize freedom, without due regard to its concomitant responsibilities inherent in the structure of metaphysical order. Here again one finds a false opposition: the conservative goal is in reality to conserve the essential, while the liberal goal is in reality to seek liberation through transcendence. These goals are essentially one: from the transcendent perspective of Tradition, the conservative and liberal goals are reconciled when seen in terms of the Absolute: they are aspirations for conformity with the Absolute, for harmony with the sacred order of things.

From the perspective of Tradition, secularism is a false ideal. It cannot exclude religion because religion—in its Traditional sense as the quest for harmony with the sacred order of things—exists not merely in its outer elements but also in its inner or principial dimension. This dimension cannot be excluded because it transcends all formal expression. It exists in the hearts and minds of believers and embraces every dimension of human activity and endeavor. All aspects of politics, economics, societal relations, and all matters pertaining to the public sphere are engaged by religious thought. It is not only impossible to exclude religious views from politics, but it is also undesirable to do so. For religious views, in their depth, are seeded in the soil of the sacred. This endows them with an immense richness—the richness of the wisdom to find the alchemical connection that, despite our diversity, unites us all.

"Standing Unshakably in the True":
A Commentary on the
Teachings of Frithjof Schuon (1907-1998)[1]

Now as I write, I am ninety years old;
See, how time passes.
Passes—what does this mean? Nothing to him
Who stands unshakably in the True.
For real is that we are with the Most High—
It is indifferent why time passes away.
(Frithjof Schuon: World Wheel: Third Collection, VII)

Truth and virtue; beauty and love;
If these alone remained to me,
The world could sink into the waters—
Let me drink only from the beautiful and true.
(Frithjof Schuon: World Wheel: Fifth Collection, IX)

Precisely one century ago, the great metaphysician and proponent of the *religio perennis*, Frithjof Schuon, was born in Basel on the Rhine, near the area known as the Rhineland, home to many great mystics and sages. About his birthplace he writes in one of his poems: "I was born on the Rhine... The green Rhine is a symbol—it is the soul/ Moving toward the Limitless..." and in another poem he writes: "Ye think I was born on the green Rhine—/ Ye know not the place of my birth./ I myself knew it not—till one day/ The Most High spoke: be what thou truly art!" These two statements provide some vital clues to the understanding of the Schuonian worldview. The ontological roots of the soul's Origin (to "be what we truly are" is to discover our spiritual birthplace), and the soul's

[1] This essay was the Editorial for *Sacred Web*, Volume 20, published in November, 2007, as a special volume commemorating the birth centenary of Frithjof Schuon. All the quotations cited in this article are from the series of poems originally written by Frithjof Schuon in his native German, which have been translated into English, and published by World Wisdom Books in two volumes under the title "*World Wheel*" (Bloomington, Indiana, 2006) with an Introduction by William Stoddart and a Foreward by Annemarie Schimmel.

journey of Return (the soul flows inexorably into the Limitless Void, drawn by the oceanic pull of Mercy, symbolized here by the "green" hue of the soul's very substance)—these are the main themes of the Schuonian message. Reiterating this theme of the Return to the Origin, he explains elsewhere: "...what I have in mind in all my efforts/ Is a homeland, deep in God's Peace."

The centrality of this defining message is one of the keys to understanding Schuon, both as a teacher and as a man. Reflecting the viewpoint of all traditional teachers, Schuon emphasizes that the meaning of life is nothing less than the quest for the Face of God in the midst of life. It is the quest for the Truth that resides within each of us, for, as Schuon states: "We carry our homeland deep in our heart." It is the Return to this homeland, to the heart-consciousness of the Divine Presence, which constitutes the very essence of life. It is the lived reality of this consciousness that gives a human life its value. As Schuon notes: "Life is a Path from God to God—/ Otherwise it is nothing.../ Each day should be a Path from God to God." This Path requires man to transcend the human condition of "chatter all around" by seeking "God deep in the heart": "Blessed repose in the midst of human agitation./ The fate of man, and the life of the wise". It requires from us the effort to rise above the average: "What is the average man? Only late does he notice/ That life's to-and-fro cannot go on forever./ ... In reality, he has never been a human being." For, to be human means to have "consciousness of God" because "Man was created for eternity." "We are made/ For God, and for life beyond time." Schuon emphasizes: "Man's reason for existence is to be a mirror/ Of the Real, the Divine. Nothing takes/ Precedence over this." It is this "God-consciousness" or the spirit's mirroring of its eternal substance that constitutes mankind's nobility, the human ability to fulfill its existential purpose, for "Man is a door to Paradise", reflecting the teaching that the kingdom of Heaven is within our deepest Self. "Is not man the door/ To the meaning of existence, and so to bliss?/ God grant that the human condition lead us not astray./ God awaits us; be ye ready for Him."

*

*   *

Though Schuon was influenced in his life by various faith traditions—in particular, the spiritual worlds of the Vedas (which were the main influence of his metaphysical outlook), the Sufis (which, through the practice of *dhikr*, influenced his method of divine invocation), and the Native Indians (which influenced his views of harmony in nature and the created world)—and though he regarded all revealed faiths as united by a transcendent Truth comprising a Primordial Wisdom that alone, from the perspective of Truth, was orthodox, yet he was not a syncretist. He emphasized the validity of each orthodox faith tradition, stating: "There are diverse viewpoints in the Spirit's realm—/ The paths that God blesses are of equal value." Or again: "God's House has more than one door."

*

*   *

Pared down to its essentials, the quintessential Path for Schuon comprised a doctrine of Truth or Reality, and a method of Integration or Realization through Prayer leading to inner beauty or Virtue, or outer goodness or Beauty. This schematic of Truth-Prayer-Virtue-Beauty, and its variations, is reiterated throughout Schuon's writings. A few examples will suffice to illustrate this teaching:

> There are principles I constantly repeat,/ Because they belong to the sage who is without fault./ First comes the doctrine concerning God;/ Then the invocation of the Highest Name,/ Which purifies and liberates the heart;/ Then comes the beauty of all virtue, nobility of soul;/ And finally the sense of forms, inward and outward./ These are the four principles—/ God grant that they never be violated.

> Three things are sacred to me: firstly Truth;/ Then, in its wake, primordial prayer;/ And then virtue—nobility of soul which,/ In God, walks all the paths of beauty.

134

... truth, virtue and beauty;/ With these three, thou canst build a bridge—/ Only these three make life worth living.

Vedanta, and with it *japa*, are for me/ The quintessence of all religions.

*

*   *

Dealing with the first of the elements in the Schuonian schematic, namely Truth, Schuon writes: "Blessed is he who sees his path in the True./ ... Know thy Lord, and know what thou art." This concise comment contains several key messages. First, Truth can be known. Second, we are subservient to Truth, which (as our "Lord") is greater than us, and therefore transcendent. Third, Truth is also within us, therefore immanent, being what we are, and therefore our ontological substance.

Echoing traditional epistemological teachings through the ages, Schuon writes: "If thou knowest thy Lord, thou also knowest man;/ If thou knowest man, thou also knowest thy Lord." Recalling the Platonic teaching that knowledge of Truth is innate because it is inscribed within our very substance, Schuon writes: "Knowledge and certitude are inborn in thee." The source of certitude is our very spiritual substance, our Pure Being: "Certitude is Reality become Spirit—/ Whoever possesses it, has gained Pure Being." Intellectual knowledge is therefore ontological, and a process of Self-discovery. The journey of Self-discovery, however, entails faith, because Truth, though immanent, is also transcendent. Faith is receptivity to the inner Self, to our own spiritual substance and innate intelligence. Therefore, "in the realm of the wise:/ Faith and knowledge are the same./ In faith there is also this meaning:/ With love, I strive towards Thee." Schuon cautions, however: "Distinguish well between mere opinion/ And that which, through the Spirit, is the presence of the Lord—/ That which, beyond all doubt, is the seed of Pure Truth." The criterion for distinguishing Truth from its counterfeit is "the Pure Intellect"—that is, not merely the created intellect but the transcendent intelligence that corresponds to the spiritual substance of man: "In *tasawwuf* it is said that the Sufi/ Is not created; the Intellect proves this./ Both created and uncreated is the wise man's heart—/ As is the kingdom of Heaven." It is this "Pure Intellect" that is endowed with the ability to perceive Truth in all its manifold aspects: "To see things in God,/ To see God in things;/ To see things in themselves,/ To stand with God above them—/ This is the book of the world,/ There is no other;/ The reader is thy heart—/ There is no other light."

To know God (the "Lord") is to know the Absolute. Such knowledge is possible only to the extent that man transcends himself by looking with "the eye of the heart". Yet, the "Lord" cannot be reduced to merely that which is transcendent nor that which is immanent: "God is for us the highest Other;/ And within us, He is the deepest Self—/ Thus highest "Thou" and deepest "I"./ Both and neither is the Lord in Himself." He is both "Being" and "Self", the "highest Outward" and the "deepest Inward", the Supreme Reality that infuses and transcends existence. Too great for us to conceive ("Drink from the primordial source of the True—/ Do not force the True under your narrow bonnet."), the Absolute opens us into the realm of wonder and mystery: "Thou canst not put silence into words—/ Thou canst not speak of the inexpress-ible./ The soul would like to sing of that which has no limit—/ But thou must leave this song to the Most High." And yet the transcendent Intellect can know the ineffable, which is its own uncreated spiritual Substance: "Thou contemplatest the Impersonal in the Intellect;/ The Intellect, like What it sees, is uncreated—/ It knows, from the beginning, what thou knowest not." It is in this knowledge that resides the intimacy and nearness of God. For Truth is, by virtue of this knowledge, also Presence.

"The Lord is Reality and Presence." Schuon notes that God's Presence "dwells within thee" and "has its throne in thy heart's deepest chamber." The reality of the Divine Presence within us is the affirmative "yes" which is our highest purpose ("Our 'yes' to God in the kernal of our soul/ Is our path, and the star of our existence") and the source of our deepest happiness ("remain still in the proximity of the Most High—/ Thy happiness lies in the deepest folds of thy heart"). It is the means of transcending transient evanescence in the timelessness of Pure Being: "the stream of time/ Can do nothing against the kernel of eternity." The realization of the Divine Presence is also the affirmation of meaning, testifying to "the Highest Good"—"born of the yes alone"—and is, through such affirmation, the means of our liberation from the bonds of "psychic clutter". To affirm God means to die a psychic death: "If thou wishest to serve Truth, extinguish thyself—/ The ego has no right to blur the meaning of Pure Being." The Divine Presence is therefore both the embracing of nothingness in the 'vacare Deo' of psychic death (the Sufi 'fana') and simultaneously the blessing of spiritual plenitude that is its compensation (the Sufi 'baqa'): "*Vacare Deo*. Seemingly pure nothingness,/ Paired with the Highest Fullness."

*
*   *

As Schuon explains, the Path in any authentic faith tradition is more than a mere doctrine of Reality: it is also a method of Realization, of Integration, of Union. He writes: "Happy the man who does not find only half the Truth—/ Who unites it with the beauty of his soul." The purpose of religion, then, is Integration: man must transcend his humanity to be one in Spirit with the Divine Reality that infuses all Reality. The doctrine of Truth teaches us verticality, to "look Upwards"; the method of Realization teaches us transcendence, to "be Upright". This is the Path of Wisdom and Beauty, the "Path from God to God".

Two essential steps on the Path are commitment and prayer. Commitment is an act of "resignation" and "trust", sealed in a pact of "initiation"—to commit to God's Will and to one's inner Self. Schuon explains: "Initiation is a pact with God/ With a view to the Highest Reality: a promise/ That the initiate be faithful unto death,/ And betray not his word to the Most High—/ His word to himself. God never says 'no' to a soul,/ Except when this soul itself chooses to break its word."

137

*

* *

Prayer is the bridge between man and God. For Schuon, the "prayer of the heart" through the invocation of the Divine Name is the quintessential prayer. Thus he writes: "Doctrine, and prayer of the heart: the two poles/ Of the way to the goal." And again: "Firstly, the Name, which is the whole Truth,/ And which measures the values of earthly life;/ Then resignation and trust—/ May God build for thee the bridge." Prayer is the means of centering one-self in the Spirit, it is the cardinal virtue: "Remaining at the center should be thy virtue... / Flowing towards the Inward should be thy Path—/ There is no better bridge to Heaven." Sincere prayer is the effective means of invoking the Divine Presence, which is why Schuon can write: "The Name, O Lord, is Presence of God." Or again: "Where Thy Name is, there are Thy Truth and Presence./ There is nothing more in this world." In the quintessential prayer of the heart (which Schuon distinguishes from the canonical prayer and prayers of petition or thanksgiving), "God Himself speaks in the deepest folds of thy heart." Such prayer is "God-consciousness" or "God-remembrance"—in effect the Self-realization of Truth *as* Presence. This is the source of all certitude and serenity. Schuon writes: "What is God-remembrance? It is impassibility/ Within the din of the world, and trust in the Inward./ Serenity, certitude: thou shouldst remember them/ Wherever, whenever, and how-ever thou art." Schuon cautions against insincere invocation ("the one whose heart pronounces not Thy Name") but, in a verse that contains an echo of Tolstoy's story of "The Three Hermits", he portrays the miraculous powers of sincere prayer: "A woman from Senegal could hardly pray./ Arabic was too difficult for her. People thought/ She was too stupid even for religion; No wonder people laughed at her./ But one day—who could accompany her?/ She was seen singing, walking on the water."

*

* *

Prayer is the means of transcendence, that is, the mirroring of the Divine Reality through Virtue. To be virtuous is to offer oneself and one's actions to God: "The *a priori* of all activity/ Is *vacare Deo...* to be empty for the Most High." It is to accept "what pertains to the duty of thy function" with humility, gratitude, and generosity. "Truth demands virtue" because "God made the good in the world from Truth." Nobility is the crown of virtue because "Noble I-consciousness transcends itself." Schuon defines a noble man as "one who knows himself,/ And dominates himself." The character of virtue manifests in conduct that is rooted in spiritual-consciousness according to the principle of "noblesse oblige": "*Noblesse oblige.* The outward is good/ Only has meaning if the heart reposes in the Most High."

*
* *

The fourth element in the Schuonian schematic of Truth-Prayer-Virtue-Beauty proceeds directly from the metaphysical "sense of forms" and the conception of Virtue as nobility. Schuon explains: "What is the sense of forms? That one understand/ What the shape of everything means;/ Every form has something to say—/ The noble form wills to transmit light from Heaven./ Form and content: the latter justifies the former." Schuon often quoted the Platonic dictum that "Beauty is the splendor of the True," explaining that "Truth is the essence of the beautiful." As human beings are created of the Spirit, so beauty is a reflection of our inner Substance and therefore, he states: "Every spiritual consciousness/ Has an element of beauty, which we can feel." This sense of beauty is esoteric, pointing us to Heaven: "Beauty is esoteric: it enlightens/ Only those who can see beyond worldly pleasure./ Beauty's path is holy—for it will show thee/ How thy soul should ascend towards Heaven." Beauty is therefore also a means to transcendence, and a potentially efficacious means to experience Truth *as* Presence. In this sense, Beauty approaches Prayer as a bridge between man and God. Beauty is not only the radiance of the eternal within the translucence of form, but is also the reflection of "holy longing" for union—of love ("love follows from beauty"). For this reason, it tends towards integration, to purity and simplicity, which are hallmarks of the Sacred.

*

*   *

There are three specific themes that flow from Schuon's understanding of Beauty, and he touches on these time and again in his teachings: these are the themes of Art, Woman, and Nature. Art is that which expresses Beauty, which in turn reflects Truth. Artistic creativity and artistic interpretation begin with the attunement of the soul to the Spirit. In the case of creativity, the alignment is ontological: "What, in art, one has to offer,/ One must be." The point of art is to extinguish the self for the greater glory of God. While profane art may aim at "originality" (in the conventional sense of this term), sacred Art is a reminder of the Origin: "It is not originality that is decisive,/ But the value itself, whoever the creator may be./ ... The goal is not individual glory—but the Truth." It is Truth, not the individual norm or preference, which dictates the content and value of authentic Art: "Style is a God-willed norm." Both the expression and interpretation of Art must have recourse to symbols to point us to transcendence: "The soul must rise to the realm of symbols;/ Only then can art give joy to the spirit." Schuon distinguishes symbols from mere signs: "A symbol is not only a sign, it is the thing itself:/ It is an aspect of what it means." Symbols are the cosmological reflections of Truth, containing the "sparks of God's Presence". When these sparks ignite within the soul, they inspire us and fill us with joy. Thus Schuon explains: "Art exists to rejoice the soul—/ And above all to sow in our world seeds of the Divine."

Consistent with his conception of Beauty, Schuon regards the human form in symbolic terms and finds in Woman the quintessence of Beauty. Thus he states: "woman's beauty is a message/ That gilds all earthly things—/It is Heaven kissing the earth." One must be careful to place Schuon's remarks about Woman strictly

140

in the context of his symbolic conception of Beauty. Schuon extols the beauty of the female form and depicts Woman in her naked simplicity in his masterful paintings, but all this must be understood within the Schuonian framework of the metaphysical theory of forms. His love of Woman represents his love of the archetype of the "eternal feminine", which he is careful to distinguish from the profane "enjoyment of women". In one of his poems, for example, he clearly distinguishes between "two kinds of men: those who want to enjoy women, and those who love the eternal feminine", and in another he writes: "Beauty is one thing; procreating is another;/ Do not think that the second is the reason for the first." The archetype of the "eternal feminine", which informs Schuon's Marian tradition, is also a reflection of the connection between Beauty and Wisdom. Schuon cautions that beauty should be experienced symbolically and "should not remain outward or sensual" but should "show God's essential intention", testifying to the Highest Good and the True. This entails an ethical approach towards beauty: "What counts is not only that one should see the beautiful—/ But also that one should reject the ugly,/ Both outwardly and inwardly." One must strive to experience the inward dimension and inner meaning of beauty: "One can experience the beautiful like a thief;/ Nobly experienced beauty is the True!/ If thy soul does not strive towards the Inward,/ The most beautiful thing in the world will give thee nothing." Because "all beauty conveys profundity's meaning" and "praises the Lord", Beauty is the quintessential form of Wisdom: "In God wisdom and beauty are related./ That which testifies to the Highest Good is beautiful;/ In the beautiful, the spirit should see the True—/ Happy the man who sees the one within the other."

Related to his conception of Beauty is Schuon's teaching about the harmony of Nature and the regenerative power of the beauty of the natural world. The language of Nature is akin to that of Revelation, which is "a space/ Through which the Holy Ghost has passed." Therefore, he writes: "Beauty is first and foremost in nature—/ Everywhere thou seest the trace of the Creator." It is through the natural world that we are able to universally experience the proximity of Divine Presence and to be rejuvenated by its signs. Schuon writes of this experience, for example, in the following poem: "I praise the eagle and the swan,/ Lightning from Heaven and peace on the pond;/ By night, the owl, in early morn, the cock—/ The Creator has given us rich teachings here below./ .../ Heaven saw that I did not feel well—/ In the book of nature it allowed me to read." And he invites us to find uplift in our hearts from nature: "Learn from the song of the birds in the air,/ From the sound of the wind in the forest, from the fragrance of flowers;/ The languages God gave to nature,/ May they rejoice and uplift thee—/ Thou canst, O heart of man, learn from everything:/ From the flowers by day, from the stars by night."

*
*   *

Though Schuon emphasizes Truth, and therefore the path of knowledge, it would be a misconception to regard Schuon's approach as that of a "dry" metaphysician. On the contrary, it is integral to his conception that Truth entails "adherence to the True" through centering Prayer, which replenishes the Spirit, so that the True resonates within us and is reflected as Virtue and Beauty. Schuon reminds us that Truth is not a mere abstraction, but is the Supreme Reality of Pure Being, which is our Origin and "homeland"—the Limitless Ocean to which we are intrinsically drawn and to which we will inevitably and mercifully return. Schuon's message is that Truth *is* Presence—"Reality become Spirit": the firm ground on which we stand, and the unshakable Substance of our Being—and therefore knowledge is nothing if it is not also love—that is, the heart's deepest longing for union with the Divine Presence, for the "moist" immersion of the soul in the baptismal font of the Spirit.

"A Single Principle": On Faith and Pluralism[1]

Your creation, and your resurrection, is but as a single soul.
(Koran: Luqman, XXXI.28)

We live in that decadent age foretold of by the Prophet of Islam, where, according to a *Hadith*, "He that keepeth hold upon true faith will be as one that holdeth in his hand a coal of fire." In our times, orthodoxy is ridiculed as anachronistic when it is not being parodied or maligned. While atheism and radical secularism are on the rise, genuine religion is giving way to its two counterfeits: hard-hearted fundamentalism and mushy pseudo-spiritualism. We have, on the one hand, the hardening of hearts accompanied by the petrification of religion, and, on the other, a gullible thirsting for "spiritual experiences" accompanied by the growth of various diluted forms of quasi-religions—New Age trends, occult practices, and pseudo-spiritualist experimentation. Religion is not only at war with the dominant ethos of the modern world, it is also at war with its own parodies, and, in these wars, it is frequently exploited for political ends: religious groups, displaced from their principial bearings, are suspicious and intolerant of each others' ideologies and outward differences, and are easy prey for divisive manipulation, with the result that internecine and communalist strife is prevalent among religious groups in many parts of the world. Religious leaders are in greater need than ever to re-assert within their respective faith traditions those unifying and universal metaphysical principles that transcend the theological and exoteric differences that divide—principles that constitute the underlying universal "orthodoxy" of Tradition.

The Vedantic adage that "Truth is one, though sages call it by different names" is a timeless message whose import is of great urgency for our own strife-torn times. The recognition of this

---

[1] This essay was the Editorial for *Sacred Web*, Volume 21, published in June, 2008.

Traditional basis of orthodoxy is hampered in part by the post-modernist legacy which, by radical deconstruction, would oppose hierarchy and verticality in the name of equality, and, out of an anti-normative wariness of orthodoxy, would privilege relativist subjectivism in the name of freedom. This is one of the "philosophical" impulses behind radical secularism. The error of this approach is epistemological: by denying knowledge its ontologically objective roots, knowing lapses into the anchorless subjectivism of relativism.

In the face of these challenges, how, then, is modern man to construct a legitimate foundation for orthodoxy, and how are the faith traditions of the modern world to find a pluralistic approach consistent with the Traditional view that "Truth is one"? If pluralism is to be more than the relativistic subjectivism of "laissez-faire," or the tolerance of diversity for the sake of a homogenizing equality that panders to the "lowest common denominator," its true meaning must be sought in the objective archetype of the principial source of Reality—in the archetype of the "single soul" or Spirit, and in the metaphysical transparency of visionary faith that such an archetype epistemologically implies.

*

* *

An illustration of the meaning of visionary faith is found in the Koranic parable of the four birds (*Surah al-Baqarah*, II.260ff.). In this narrative, Abraham asks God: "Show me how Thou givest life unto the dead!", and God chides him with the question: "Hast thou, then, no faith?" Abraham responds: "Yes, but (show me the miracle) so that my heart may be at peace." And God then states the following parable: "Take, then, four birds and teach them to obey thee; then place them separately on every hill (around thee); then summon them: they will come flying to thee. And know that God is almighty, wise."

To interpret this passage, it is instructive to recall the Traditional doctrine that creation is a continuing process. Yet the ordinary consciousness of man is unaware of God's active Presence in this process—of how, in each moment, existence is remade anew. When Abraham asks God to demonstrate "how Thou givest life unto the dead", he is failing to perceive the ever-present and ceaseless miracle of creation (of how, in each moment, everything has to be remade so that the dead are indeed brought to life) and of God's active Presence in this process. Abraham, like Everyman, reflects the ordinary consciousness, and he wants ocular evidence of the miracle of creation—to witness with his outer eyes the dead being brought to life. God then questions Abraham's faith, thereby inviting him to perceive reality with the inner eye—the Eye of the Heart. When Abraham repeats his request for a miracle to calm his heart, God responds, not with the outer demonstration demanded of Him, but with the parable of the birds.

The winged creatures of the parable are free spirits—and are therefore like the soul of man, which they symbolize. However, just as one can train a bird to "incline to one," to heed its master's call and to fly to its master when summoned, so too there is in our soul something that can be trained to respond to God when summoned—something nascent in us that can "incline to the Spirit", and respond to the Call of Life so that what is dead within us can thereby be resurrected and brought to spiritual life. This element— faith, or spiritual vision—is the very faculty that God invites Abraham to employ in response to his heart's desire for certainty. Faith is "in-sight"—an inner receptivity to, and consciousness of, the "evidence of things not seen"—the potential to envision the invisible Reality or "Divine Face" that is present within us—and is everywhere. It is the "grain of mustard seed" that can grow into the parabolic tree of the "Kingdom of Heaven," whose broad-canopied Presence is everywhere. It is through faith that man sees God at work in the world, and can thereby respond to His calling. The Koranic parable ends with the words, "know that God is almighty, wise," signifying that faith, which is the natural predisposition of the soul to the spiritual Presence, is also the empowerment of the spiritual self through innate wisdom. For this knowledge is what enlivens us, binding us to God and thereby to our fellow creatures. It is by our awakening from our ordinary fragmentary consciousness into a unitive spiritual consciousness that our souls are "brought to life."

*

*   *

Faith, then, is the "insight" or spiritual consciousness of Presence. And once this higher consciousness is awakened and its light glimpsed, it must not be allowed to lapse back into the shadows of ordinary consciousness, but must be tenaciously cultivated through attentive invocation and prayer—and by integrating our lives with the higher Spirit that our faith has glimpsed. Through this process, a consciousness grounded in visionary faith can become the means of perceiving spiritual Presence at work in ourselves and all around us.

This theophanic awareness of Presence as a spiritual and intelligent unitive dimension of life has profound implications. The deep awareness of our ontological interconnectedness as spiritual beings—the sense of the sacred, of the spiritual fragrance in all things—is the very foundation of traditional morality. For "whatsoever ye do to the least of these, my brethren, ye do unto Me." Knowledge entails virtue for to know is ultimately to love, to be impelled to live in harmony with all things. The eyes of love look, beyond the outward and fleshly differences that can stale and draw us apart, to the abiding inner heart that we share with all things—the "dearest freshness deep down things" (*Hopkins*). To know deeply is therefore to perceive the core of our own being, and thereby to perceive its spiritual Presence within and around us. To be aware in this sense is to look into the mirror of love, and to be transformed by such love. Thus, according to a teaching of Meister Eckhart, "We love God with his own love; awareness of it deifies us." It is through faith, prayer, virtue, and love that the soul achieves its "resurrection" as the "single soul" or Spirit that alone, by the grace of God, can ascend to the Kingdom of Heaven.

*

*   *

The pluralistic implications of this esoteric approach to faith are obvious: the individual soul's ability to discern the universal Spirit ("He who has seen Me, has seen the Father"), and its predisposition to heed the summons of the Spirit by offering itself, in an act of egoic death and spiritual resurrection, as "a virgin soul into the embrace of transcendency," is not unique to any particular faith tradition, but is common to all such traditions. It is this foundational metaphysical principle of our common spiritual patrimony that radially connects us all—of whatever faith traditions—to the one and the same Spiritual Center. This is the true "orthodoxy of pluralism."

The authentic forms of a religion, which are the providential means of its expression through revelation, and of its transmission through tradition, are also the sacramental and efficacious vehicles of effecting, through grace, the spiritual transformation of its followers. It is therefore incumbent upon each follower to be faithful to his or her own religious forms and sacraments. One cannot journey from the circumference of our religious tradition to its universal Center without committing to a particular formal path. To this extent, the particular forms and sacraments of a religion, and their theological doctrines, are indispensable and are unique to each faith tradition, and constitute the orthodoxy of the particular faith tradition.

But the very outer forms and doctrines that distinguish a religion can also become the barriers by which they exclude others. It is therefore crucial to understand that, though each religion will differ in its particular doctrinal and practical expressions, including its forms and sacraments, these formal expressions need to be respected and celebrated by all religions as the providential, unique, and efficacious means for the universal journey that each religion seeks to make, though by different pathways, to the same spiritual Center—that is, the journey to the Divine Heart.

Rather than focusing exclusively on the "outer orthodoxy"— that is, the different formal expressions of Truth, and the apparently irreconcilable theological differences that set the different faith traditions apart, it is wiser instead to focus as well on the "inner orthodoxy"—that is, the universal metaphysical principles from which each religion stems, and to see how all religions share a common understanding of faith as the spiritual consciousness of the one Truth that is our Presence, in which we live and move and have our being.

Then, like the great Sufi mystic, Mansur al-Hallaj (d. 922), we might proclaim:

> I have meditated on the different religions, endeavoring to understand them, and I have found that they stem from a single principle with numerous ramifications. Do not therefore ask a man to adopt a particular religion (rather than another), for this would separate him from the fundamental principle; it is this principle itself which must come to seek him; in it are all the heights and all the meanings elucidated; then he will understand them.

Striving for "Wholeness" in the *Kali Yuga*[1]

> Man is a creature who has received the order to become God.
>
> (*St. Basil*)

To be fully human is not merely to exist. It is to exist in wholeness, to be reconnected with the very source of life. Existence (etymologically, from the Latin, "*ex*" and "*stare*", meaning "to stand out") presupposes an origin—a source from which one "stands out". This origin is also the innermost core (related to the French, "*coeur*", or "heart") of our being. As such, this meta-temporal Origin and metaphysical Center are referred to in traditional doctrine as the Heart. The Heart is the Inner Eye, the Self-reflecting Witness of Presence: "The eye through which I see God, and the eye through which God sees me, are the same eye" (*Eckhart*). All that exists is a "phenomenon", that is to say, a peripheral reflection of archetypes that manifest the Presence of the Absolute Reality which is the consciousness of the Heart. It is by the grace and compassion of this bounteous Reality that all phenomena derive their lesser existential reality, as finite expressions of Its Infinite Possibility, and as shadows of the Supernal Sun. Of all creatures, it is we, human beings, who have the privilege and capability of identifying with the Center of our being, of entering the sanctum of the Heart, of "knowing our Maker", and thereby of reconnecting with our source and Origin—the very "ground" of our being. In other words, we have the potential to be present in the Divine Presence, to *realize* the Real—to be "holy" or "whole". It is this realization that constitutes the human métier—one that is increasingly difficult to achieve, given the conditions of the modern world and the denial of transcendence which characterizes the modernist mentality.

According to traditional doctrines, we, who inhabit the modern world, are living within the last cycle of time—the *Kali Yuga*,

---

[1] This essay was the Editorial for *Sacred Web*, Volume 22, published in January, 2009.

or Iron Age, a period whose defining feature is its centrifugal influence—the flight from Reality. We experience this, in a general sense, as distortion and compression, through the closing-in of space and the acceleration of time. The disharmonies within space and time have reached the point where space is perceived more in terms of ephemeral matter than of substantive spirit, while time is an ever-receding fugitive from the "still point" that would unite it harmoniously with space. The world around us is increasingly opaque, presenting to us surfaces that appear more immediate and permanent than they really are. The veils of this world are increasingly alluring and seductive, rendering our vision less receptive to the "metaphysical transparency" of phenomena. Consequently, we are less able to "see a world in a grain of sand". Our experience of time has speeded up, so that while we cover greater distances than ever before, yet paradoxically our sense of space has shrunk and is getting smaller. We move at a pace that allows us little room for rest, little freedom for contemplation, little opportunity for gaining entry into the innermost sanctum of our souls. Consequently, we are less able to "hold eternity in an hour". Unable to surrender with ease to the natural gravity of the stillness that would draw us to our Heart and Center, we are subject to the centrifugal sweep of time, which draws our attention outward, to the captivating surface of things. There, movement is at war with stillness, time combats space, and "the center cannot hold." Time's vortex draws us from intimacy to solitude, from light to darkness, from the Center to the periphery. Increasingly, the world is becoming a distraction from God instead of the temple of His Presence, while the disoriented self—more and more disconnected and alienated from the world— is becoming its prisoner. We have lost our sense of the sacred—of the wholeness that is at the root of our being and which is our connection to the world.

Amid such conditions, what hope can there be for the encounter of man and his lost soul, for the longed-for return of the exile from the barren and alien wilderness? Seeking harmony without a spiritual compass, we alternate vainly between seeking it in the wrong place—by superficially immersing ourselves in the outer world instead of "looking within"—and seeking it in the wrong way—by seeking to control the world instead of "knowing ourselves". In the former case, we falsely idolize the world; in the latter, we vainly inflate our egoic self. Both these delusions diminish our humanity, because they materialize reality without ennobling the spirit; and they are unsustainable because "everything is perishing save His Face".

The crisis of the modernist mentality is at root a crisis of faith. We are skeptical of what we do not grasp through our material senses, and we are over-confident of the abilities of the scientific and psychic mind. By limiting our perceptions to the outer senses and the reasoning and occult mind, genuine spiritual intuitions are ignored or unrecognized, and the imaginal and spiritual realms are cut off from what we choose to recognize as "real". In the fragmented consciousness that remains, there is no "natural", spiritually organic connection with elements that lie outside the perceptual boundaries of the psycho-physical self, no sense of wholeness or of belonging to the Whole. Looking out through the "narrow chinks of our cavern", and lacking eyes of faith—both in the sense of the quality of attention that enables us to "see" the Divine Presence and the deeper connections we share with our fellow creatures, and in the sense of the conviction to respond to life in the comfort of this Presence and in the confidence of Its goodness—we encounter the world as "the other", as integrally separate from us, and as connected to us only in terms of the materialistic contexts that may bring about our encounters. But how, in the absence of a spiritual context, can we enliven the soul to feel the compassionate embrace of the Divine Presence? How can we explain love or reverence? To reduce these experiences to merely the emotional or sentimental is to impoverish the soul, for the Heart indeed has "eyes to see the invisible" and to heed and incline to the soft and sweet strains of Its silence. When the Inner Eye is opened, the world is no longer reduced to the unfeeling and impersonal aggregation of cogs and wheels of a heartless mechanism—which is how the world is experienced by the outer senses—but is instead experienced as the Divine Theophany remade anew in each moment, sustaining us, loving us, and which we in turn love and revere. It is the *summum bonum*, the highest pitch of all the qualities that it is our gift in life to experience—in fact, the very quintessence of our humanity, for we are the *imago Dei* or Divine Archetype *par excellence*, Adamic man, who has been taught the names of all things, whose arche-types reside within our innermost Self.

Along with the loss of faith, the modernist mentality has experienced a loss of "the symbolist spirit"—a loss of the ability to "interpret the Divine Names" or to perceive phenomena as the words of God. We have lost the ability to envision the spiritual con-nection between phenomena. Though all things are "signs of God", faithless man remains spiritually blind, resting content merely with the sign, never getting to the interior truth. This visionary impover-ishment has resulted in a corresponding aesthetic impoverishment that reflects humanity's loss of soul. Deprived of the fragrance of the sacred, there is no lasting satisfaction in the transient allurements of the world. For what we seek—whether we know it or not—is the Divine Countenance, for It alone is universal. The Beauty that we long for is found only in the Heart, which is its spiritual source and the font of all genuine Virtue. To seek it elsewhere, through purely sensory experiences or by escaping into psychic fantasies and self-deluding "virtual realities", is to seek it in vain. It is not found through acquisition, possession, or consumption, through intense feelings or numbness, through pleasure or mortifications, nor through merely outward forms of behavior. It is only by open-ing ourselves to the mystery and intimacy of the Heart that we can awaken the depths of our being—like a beautiful flower—to the immensely alive world around us and can respond to it with caring and compassion, and with justice seasoned with mercy, in the full-ness of our humanity and in the genuine submission of all in us that is merely human to the Will of God.

If the crisis of modernism is, as we have argued, a crisis of faith, then the "wholeness" that we seek is to be found through the res-titution of faith. This requires us to turn away from the superficial and corresponding to reorient ourselves to the Real, for "no man can serve two masters". At the individual level, the restitution of faith is the path of vanquishing the egoic self in order to gain entry to the inner sanctum of the Heart: "He must increase, but I must decrease" (*John*, 3, 30). It is through the path of self-annihilation or "decrease" that we can "increase" and, by the grace of God, achieve "wholeness". A corollary of faith is prayer. Because the "wholeness" we seek is so much greater than us, we can never attain it through our own individual efforts, but only through Its Grace. But we must merit this Grace for "God never changes the grace He has bestowed on any people until they first change that which is in their hearts" (*Koran*, 8, 53). This requires of us both the receptivity and the resolve of faithful prayer—of "remembrance" through contemplation and divine invocation, remaining confident in the divine promise, "Remember Me, and I will remember you" (*Koran*, 2, 152). And just as prayer or worship fulfils the vertical obligations of faith (of man, as such, in respect of God—or, in terms of the first great scriptural commandment, the duty to love God), so good works and virtue fulfil the horizontal obligations of faith (of man as his brother's keeper and as the steward of the world over which he is given dominion—or, in terms of the second great scriptural commandment, the duty to love one's "neighbour", in the broadest sense). Faith, worship, and a virtuous life: these elements constitute the Way—the Path to Wholeness.

The times are what they are, but each of us carries a responsibility to live to our fullest potential. This requires us to remember who we integrally are, and to reject firmly what we are not. In so doing, we must affirm our spiritual connection through humility, by detaching from the claims of the outer world, and through compassion, by acts of loving-kindness to all our fellow creatures. And, above all, we must strive in each moment to return to the Center—for "everything returns to Him"—and to rest in the Heart, surrendered to His Will and in the serenity of His Presence—content in the knowledge that nothing real can ever be lost, that God is Good, and that His Mercy encompasses everything.

The Secularization of Faith in the Modern World[1]

Be still, and know that I am God.

(Psalm 46:10)

how should tasting touching hearing seeing
breathing any—lifted from the no
of all nothing—human merely being
doubt unimaginable You?

(now the ears of my ears awake and
now the eyes of my eyes are opened)

(From, "i thank you God for this most amazing"
by e. e. cummings)

Faith, as distinct from mere belief, is an intellectual conviction. Faith is internally the active participation of the intelligence in the receptive mode of knowing, and outwardly the conforming of the will to its guiding intelligence. The intelligence is an active participant in faith by virtue of two factors: its mode of orientation and its quality of attention.

Mode of orientation: the intelligence must choose *where* it looks. In traditional metaphysics, faith is an epistemological orientation to the Truth. It requires a mode of orientation that extends through the full spectrum of reality, not merely outwardly but also inwardly, not merely across the horizontal dimension of reality but also beyond and within its vertical dimension. To have faith it is necessary to look to the "Orient," to the Source of Light, to the Divine Face that is everywhere. There is no faith without integrity.

Quality of attention: the intelligence must determine *how* it looks. In traditional metaphysics, faith requires an engaged openness to change, to the ever-renewing theophany, and to the transcendence that informs change. One must look not merely with the "eyes of the flesh" but also with the "eyes of the spirit." It is this mode of perception that enables the intelligence to perceive Truth as Presence. This quality of attention calls for a heightened "pres-

---

[1] This essay was the Editorial for *Sacred Web*, Volume 23, published in June, 2009.

ence of mind," for an interiority characterized by stillness. There is no faith without insight.

Faith, though receptive, is not passive. When the intelligence is passive in relation to its mode of orientation or its quality of attention, it experiences an epistemic closure that manifests either as engaged fanaticism or as disengaged credulity. The brainwashed ideologue can be as intellectually passive as his gullible subject. Fanaticism is not a sign of faith, any more than is credulity. Both are signs of intellectual passivity, and result from the disengagement of the guiding intelligence that directs the will.

Faith can also be understood as the receptivity of the intelligence to the Truth. It is the anamnesiac awareness of Presence, not only in its materially and psychically sensate aspects but also in its spiritual aspect as an ontological extension of the self as Being. Faith is the perception of Reality as diaphanous, not as opaque; and as the living and transcendent Subject of our looking, not as the impersonal Other that is distinct from our egoic vision. Faith is the mode of our attentiveness to those dimensions of reality, which, though they are beyond our active grasp, are not beyond our receptive reach. For, we have been given eyes to see the invisible.

In traditional metaphysics, the throne of faith is the "Heart", and the "Eye of the Heart" or "Inner Eye" of the Intellect is the seat of awareness. It is the witness of the ever-present and ever-changing theophany in which we participate. Faith, being open to transcendence, lends an extra sensibility (the sensibility of the drop's awareness of the Ocean) to each of our concrete senses, so that we see with the "eyes of our eyes" and hear with the "ears of our ears," knowing that each encounter is an encounter with embodied spirits, not merely with creatures but with ontologically connected beings. Faith heightens our awareness of beauty and of goodness, of those qualities that abide despite transience, impermanence and evanescence, and that reside in the depth of all things. This theophanic witnessing and heightened awareness, along with the wonder, gratitude, and praise, they evoke, are the deeper meaning of prayer. Faith is thus the foundation of prayer, and prayer is the strengthening of faith. This is the basis of the conviction that one associates with faith.

Insofar as faith is a mode of knowing (we have referred to it as "an epistemological orientation to the Truth"), it is also the source of certitude. Here we can usefully distinguish three forms of certainty: gnostic certainty, positivist certainty, and the certitude of folly. Gnostic certainty is the ontological awareness of Truth as Presence. It is rooted in verticality. Faith, as we have defined it, engages us to perceive beyond the horizontal dimension of one's measurable experiences and their rationalizations. Because verticality is experienced as interiority, it is difficult to test purely interiorized claims by outwardly empirical verification, but this is no basis to deny them. The reported experiences of sages in all civilizations universally support the truth of such claims, though one must continue to be skeptical of faith-based claims of knowledge that do not accord with one's intelligence. The positivist would deny any epistemological legitimacy to the gnostic's claims of certitude because the positivist restricts knowledge to the horizontal dimension. This categorical denial of verticality unduly restricts perception, and effectively limits the ambit of operation of the active intelligence. While the positivist's certainty is limited to rational empiricism pertaining to the horizontal dimension of reality, it is largely reliable within its own domain of operation. This claim cannot however be made for the certitude of folly which results from the practical suspension of the active intelligence, so that what passes for truth is any conviction that has been rationalized in order to pander to the will. In this case, one merely believes what one wants to, regardless of its truth.

Faith, insofar as it governs conduct, is the adhesion of the will to the Intellect. And because it perceives relations both principially and in terms of ontological connections, its worldview is both hierarchical and sympathetic. It is this innate intelligence that is the guiding force of faith and the basis of its ethics. The foundations of ethics are rooted in the very structures of reality and in the interiority of verticality. Practical ethics engages both principles and contexts, and an inner hermeneutics that interprets situations not in terms of rules but in terms of the spiritually concrete realities that engage us at our very core. This is the practical dimension of fidelity.

*

* *

One way to understand modernity is in regard to its "secularization of faith." This may seem at first a strange phrase. How can faith be secularized? If faith is understood to be "an epistemological orientation to the Truth," how can it be secularized at all, if we use the term "secularization" to mean "segregated and removed from public life"? Can the Truth be segregated, compartmentalized, dichotomized, banished from certain domains of life? This is non-sensical. But it makes perfect sense within the context of the modernist ethos that has come to define reality in truncated terms—as the external world of hard facts discernible only through the five senses (including the technological instruments that are their extension) and the rational mind, and as the internal world of the psyche that includes the rational mind. Within this horizontalized context, where the vertical dimensions of the outward Revelation or theophany and the inward Intellect or spirituality are denied, it would appear that faith can refer only to irrational convictions and superstitious beliefs. From the hard-line positivist perspective of modernism, gnostic claims of extra-sensory perception are as dubious as those of sightings of aliens from Mars.

The modernist ethos is largely skeptical of faith and authority. The movement from tradition to modernity is synonymous with the movement away from belief to reason, and from authority to self-reliance. In Western history, the traditional Age of Belief of the medieval world was eclipsed by the individualistic Renaissance of the 15th century to the 17th century, and the rationalistic Enlightenment of the 18th century—periods that ushered in the post-Enlightenment era of modernity. Advances in science and technology have brought us not only the industrial world but, in its wake, the post-industrial world of the internet and mass transportation, whose effects have been globalizing, extending beyond what we narrowly regard as the confines of Western society, and have led us into the present Information Age. These advances in the horizontal domain have almost blinded us to the corresponding losses that have accompanied them in the vertical domain—losses characterized by the diminishment of vision, or the loss of faith.

The denial of transcendence and verticality are based on a false metaphysics, and the effects of this denial have been catastrophic. The modern world has by and large transferred its faith in religion to faith in science. But science cannot answer all our questions about reality, and will never be able to. True, there are those who have an irrational faith in science, or rather in its ideology of scientism, and who claim that everything that seems a mystery today has a rational explanation that science can potentially discover tomorrow, that nothing is inviolate, that all things can be known by our own efforts. Yet, even the so-called "hard facts" of science are proving to be difficult to explain: "life" is much more than biology or chemistry can explain, and the foundations of those sciences rest on the science of physics that is bumping up against metaphysical dilemmas about the structures of the universe that are increasingly conjectural and abstract. Physics has shown that even "hard" matter is more porous than it seems. Modern psychology, for all its claims to understand the mind, can barely begin to comprehend "consciousness." It is becoming more probable, even by the evidence from science, that there is perhaps a continuum of reality that extends vertically, beyond the horizontal confines and the compartmentalizations of the modernist world view. Reason itself can teach us of its limitations. But there is no need to take the inner reality "on faith" in the pejorative sense of modernist positivism. In other words, there is no need to suspend one's critical faculties. On the contrary, faith, as understood by traditionalists, requires the active engagement of the critical Intellect, but in a receptive (rather than passive) mode. It requires us to be aware that the connections that we seek with the universe are within us, in the very depths of our Heart.

The secularization of faith in the modern world has meant, above all, a loss of vision. We no longer have the facility to view the world beyond its surfaces and skins. Our innate sympathetic consciousness that would allow us to engage with the world participatively, is in danger of being replaced by the vision of the world as a virtual reality. The beauty and majesty of Reality are becoming reduced to either a petrification or an abstraction, not a living Presence. As a corollary, we are increasingly losing our sense of the sacred and of our role in the world. This is a world where nature exists in opposition to man, for his domination. We have become in danger of losing our innate sense of cosmic harmony and trusteeship, barely responding to the environmental crisis that has already destroyed countless species and that could threaten our very existence. Our lives are becoming increasingly impersonal, our relationships increasingly compartmentalized and utilitarian. Lacking the vision to look beyond the exterior aspects of reality, we are increasingly seduced by its allurements, growing jaded or discontented in consequence of our blindness to the beauty and goodness that lies at the heart of things. And lacking true faith, we have no one to pray to, seeking instead the distractions of the outer world or an inner descent into the occult parodies of spirituality or the abyss of our surreal fantasies.

But despite this, faith is the token of our salvation and is a mercy from Heaven. We have only to raise our eyes a little to perceive the eternal sky that we all share. It is a sky that remains constant through all the changes it brings. And though our outward sojourn is here on the earth below, it is to that eternal sky that our souls will one day return, to be consumed by its Sun, that illumines our souls and lights up our world, and that can destroy all shadows if we but learn to become the bearers of its Light.

Of "Longing" and "Belonging"[1]

O wonder, all is wonder! How one flees Him from Whom
there can be no separation, to pursue that which can have no
duration.—'For verily it is not the eyes that grow blind, but it
is the hearts within the breasts that grow blind.' (*Koran*, 22:46)
(*Ibn 'Ata'illah*)

Verily, unto God do we belong and, verily, unto Him shall we
return.
(*Koran*, 2:156)

Each of us experiences in our own lives, and in our own way, a
fundamental tension between longing and belonging, between
fragmentation and integration, between the centrifugal forces of
discontinuity and the centripetal forces of continuity. This tension is grounded in the very structure of reality. All things emerge
from a Center and merge back into It. This Center—which is our
innermost core, and is described by most faith traditions as the
"Heart"—stands above the contingencies of transience and evanescence, of procession and recession. It is the Absolute matrix of all
things, paradoxically residing intimately within them ("the deepest
freshness deep down things") and at the same time mysteriously
beyond them ("out of the swing of the sea").

To the extent that we are graced to sense its Presence, we experience the Center as both intimacy and mystery. This is the intimacy and mystery of the "seeing" Eye, which is intimately connected
with all that it sees through its embracing vision, yet to Itself, it
remains a mystery: it sees not Itself except through Self-reflection,
proving its own existence through the very act of its seeing. It is by
delving into the Heart that we are able to engage in Self-reflection.
The Heart participates sympathetically in what it apprehends by

---

[1] This essay was the Editorial for Sacred Web, Volume 24, published in December,
2009.

virtue of its "imaginal" faculty. It is for this reason that the Heart is also often referred to, in its cognitive capacity, as the "Inner Eye", and that traditional sages are referred to as "seers".

It is our human need for the sacredness of intimacy that is the source of all desire—though this desire may become misdirected by reason of our outward disorientation that draws us to the periphery of things rather than inward to their Center. In the case of these peripheral attractions, the desires themselves are real but "they are veiled in unreality" (*Chandogya Upanishad,* viii.3.1) because they perceive the outer covering of things—their phenomenal and contingent aspects—as real. It is our human need to shield ourselves from the illusory and profane allurements of the outer world that is the source of our need for inwardness, for detachment and mystery. Our reverence for the "sacred" is rooted in both the intimacy and the mystery of the Real. At each moment, we stand at the threshold of the "sacred", awaiting the grace of its Presence. What we seek is infinitely "beyond" our capacity to grasp it, yet we are intimately "within" the compassionate womb (*"rahmah"*) of its embrace. In our deepest longing, then, resides the intimacy and mystery of sacredness.

By orienting ourselves to that innermost and sacred core of our being—we place ourselves more readily within its grace—though its grace is in no wise constrained by our own disorientation. Nor is the fact of our disorientation a refutation of its reality: the "sacred" does not cease to exist merely because we have averted our eyes from it. As Sri Ramakrishna explains, the outside world exists, even though the frog in the well knows it not. The world is "beautiful"—and creation is "good"—regardless of whether we care to see it as such, though it is only when our eyes are oriented to look beyond the phenomenal aspects of reality—and perceive in them the radiance of its noumenal core—that we may merit the grace and requital of the "beatific vision".

"Belonging" is the inner grace of our deepest "longing". Just as the fire dies into the ashes of its own flame, so our deepest desires immolate themselves within their own pyre, dying into the intimacy of the Presence that abides within us and is everywhere.

This is the essence of what the Sufis term *"fana"* (egoic annihilation), which is—from another aspect—the state of *"baqa"* (Self-subsistence). It is when desire comes to rest in Itself and discovers its own Center that it is able finally to transmute its longing into the grace of belonging, perceiving Itself in all things as omni-Present, in a pleromic state that transcends its privative conditions and the unrequited longing of its self-exile.

All desire is premised on separation. In this sense, all longing is itself an aspect of disorientation—even the longing of the "lover" for the "Beloved"—for it is based on the veiling of the self from the Self. Our deepest longing—though its gaze be directed to the Center—belies its peripheral point of view. What it lacks is an ontological re-alignment. That which veils our longing from our belonging is not merely the allurements of the outer world, but more profoundly it is our outer self that is a veil over our inner Self. Thus, Niffari states: "Your veil is yourself, and it is the veil of veils." The veil of oneself cannot be lifted except by the grace of God, which is the blessing of Self-illumination. Niffari explains: "You will not come out of your veil except through My Light." This "Light" is none other than the grace of vision by the lifting of the eyelid of the Inner Eye. It is the illumination of "right being" that rises from annihilating the veils of existence—and of the egoic self—in the Presence of the Heart. To "belong" is therefore the Self-realization of Who one already is.

While longing is the desire for escape, belonging is the "enigma of arrival": it does not seek to flee to where it is not, but to be where it already is. The intuitive soul knows that its true home is within itself, that if it cannot find the joy that it seeks *within* itself, then it cannot find it anywhere, and that it must therefore (as Eliot stated in *Little Gidding*) "arrive where we started and know the place for the first time". The soul's salvation is close at hand. Those who seek it elsewhere are like the person "who, in the midst of water, cries in thirst" (*Hakuin*).

Belonging is thus a homecoming—again in the words of Eliot, it is "a condition of complete simplicity". This condition implies the integration of the inner and the outer, and therefore requires a quality of heightened awareness and Self-reflection that is adequate to the Presence it discerns. Hujwiri explains: "The Sufi is he whose thought keeps pace with his foot"[2], i.e. he is entirely present: his soul is where his body is, and his body is where his soul is, and his soul where his foot is, and his foot where his soul is. This is the sign of presence without absence.

To be fully present entails an ethic rooted in the recognition of the infinitely compassionate nature of our Maker—in the appreciation of the fact that what we most long for, has already been given us. Like the sky above us, it is ever-Present. It is present in the theophany of existence and within the deepest core of our being. Transcending the conditions of our existence, this gift—which abides deep within us and from which "there can be no separation"—can never escape us despite our own ignorance of it and thereby transcends even the limitations of our very cherishing: it is the "Hidden Treasure" that has been gifted us, and far surpasses our estimate of its worth. We can never measure its true value for it transcends us infinitely and is infinitely beyond our capacity for its longing. This immeasurable gift is our Spirit, our immanent Self, the Font of all things, whose grace is the continual giving of Itself to Itself, in a boundless outpouring of love. This is the essence of Divine Mercy, which by Its Grace transcends even our own undeserving.

As the receptacles of this most precious gift, our human debt to the Spirit is one of deepest gratitude: it is incumbent on us to appreciate and embody who We truly are and to witness the reflection of the Spirit within the mirror of the world. This is the essence of Prayer, of Virtue, and of Beauty—the three elements that constitute the "Way" in all faith traditions. Prayer: the grateful remembrance and witnessing of the Spirit within ourselves and in all things. Virtue: the inner reflection of our Spirit in relation to all things, which we embody in the ethic of our living. And Beauty: the outer reflection of the resplendent Spirit in the forms of existence.

---

[2] Citing Abu Muhammad Murta'ish.

These three elements—which are all aspects of the Divine Mercy that is the quintessence of the Heart—are the means vouchsafed us to requite our longing and to transmute its base metal into the alchemical gold of belonging.

Part Two:

Papers on Metaphysics

Excerpt from "The Metaphysics of Human Governance: Imam 'Ali, Truth and Justice"[1]

Implications for Modernity of the Teachings on Truth and Justice of 'Ali ibn Abi Talib[2]

A key question confronting humanity regarding Justice can be stated in these terms: "Who shall rule, God or man?" The answer for modern man—who denies or, at least, is skeptical of its transcendent origin and purpose—is to separate Church and State, which corresponds to the Augustinian separation between the City of God and the City of Man. In Islamic terms, this might be understood in terms of an attempt to separate *din* (religion or the spiritual realm) and *dunya* (politics or the temporal realm). For Imam 'Ali, the answer to the question that we have just formulated was clear: the ideals of human governance are rooted in a proper understanding of the metaphysical structure of reality, whose core and criterion is spiritual. As he reminded Governor Malik, "God is the supreme Lord over the Caliph".

Having concluded that government must be founded on a spiritual criterion of Truth and Justice, however, it is not at all clear

---

[1] This is an excerpt from a revised version of a paper that was submitted and delivered to the International Congress on Imam 'Ali and Justice, Unity and Security, held in Tehran, March 13 through 16, 2001, organized by the Institute for Humanities and Cultural Studies. It was awarded the First Prize for the best essay submitted in the English language at an award ceremony organized by the Institute in Iran in March 2002. The full text is published in *The Sacred Foundations of Justice in Islam: The Teachings of 'Ali ibn Abi Talib*, Essays by M. Ali Lakhani, Reza Shah-Kazemi and Leonard Lewisohn, Edited by M. Ali Lakhani, Introduction by Seyyed Hossein Nasr, (World Wisdom, Bloomington, Indiana, 2006).

[2] 'Ali ibn Abi Talib (c.600 - 661) was the son-in-law of Prophet Muhammad, and the Fourth Caliph of Sunni Islam. Shia Muslims venerate 'Ali as their first Imam, the political and spiritual successor of the Prophet. Imam 'Ali is generally venerated by all Muslims as one of the foremost sources of Islamic spirituality.

that Imam 'Ali advocated a theocracy as the only legitimate form of government, though a theocracy is the prototypical state in Islam.[3] At the very least, he appreciated that human governance might embrace diverse forms of government, some of which might be benevolent and just, and others inequitable—and that he favored the former. For instance, remarking on the Kharijites' slogan "There is no order and law but that of God", Imam 'Ali stated:

> Yes! There can be no law and no order but that of God; but they (the Seceders) infer that none should be king or ruler over mankind but God.
>
> How is it possible? Necessarily there ought to be some form of government of man over man. There ought to be human agency as a ruler, and this may be either (transpire to be) a pious and benevolent ruler or an ungodly government.
>
> A benevolent and godly government is necessary so that, under its kind rule, Muslims and non-Muslims alike may prosper...[4]

The notion of "kind rule" for the benefit of "Muslims and non-Muslims" alike suggests that Imam 'Ali may have had in mind a non-theocratic pluralistic government. Whether or not Imam 'Ali advocated theocratic rule, we may infer from his views that certain traditional bulwarks are necessary to enable a society to provide government consistent with the principles of Truth and Justice. Given the conditions of modernity—in particular, its much lamented loss of a sense of the sacred, there is no doubt a need

---

[3] Titus Burckhardt: "The prototypical Islamic state is theocratic, for in it spiritual power and temporal power are combined. Herein it differs from the traditional Christian state which, in Christ's words 'My kingdom is not of this world', can never be identified with the Church." (*Fez: City of Islam*, trans. by William Stoddart, Islamic Texts Society, Cambridge, 1992, p. 53).

[4] Sermon 45, *Nahjul-Balagha, Sermons, Letters and Sayings of Imam 'Ali*, trans. by Syed Mohammed Askari Jafery, Tahrike Tarsile Koran, New York, Second American Edition, 1981 (henceforth referred to as *Nahjul-Balagha*, Jafery). There are variant translations in English of Imam 'Ali's writings as rendered by Sharif ar-Radi. We will also refer to the translation by Sayed Ali Reza, Tahrike Tarsile Koran, New York, Fifth American Edition, 1986 (henceforth referred to as *Nahjul-Balagha*, Reza). This statement also appears as Sermon 40 in *Nahjul-Balagha*, Reza.

to establish structures within society that rest on these traditional bulwarks, but it is beyond the scope of this paper to examine this issue in detail; suffice it to say that the multiplicity of viewpoints and interests regarding most issues of social governance among humankind suggests a solution rooted in a notion of "principled pluralism"[5] grounded in an objective and universal metaphysical perspective that is consistent with, yet transcends theology.

It is clear that, in Imam 'Ali's view, human governance and social justice were predicated on principles of divine governance rooted in such a metaphysical perspective, and premised on an ontological understanding of *tawhid.* Based on this view, there is no dimension of a theophany—no matter how we choose, from a human perspective, to compartmentalize, atomize or marginalize it—that can elude the sacred embrace of the Divine. All things are rooted in the spiritual dimension and must be referred back to their spiritual foundation. Without this "verticality", what is genuine and salvific in religion will atrophy, dissolving the moral basis of civilization.[6] A corollary of this view is that there can be no

---

[5] The distinction between metaphysics and theology is that between the *din al-fitr* and the *din al-islam.* The exoteric component of any revealed tradition, while remaining vital to that tradition, is subordinated to its esoteric core, which is premised on a transcendent "principle" referred to, for example, in this passage from the *Divan: Muqatta'at* of Mansur al-Hallaj: "I have meditated on the different religions, endeavoring to understand them, and I have found that they stem from a single principle with numerous ramifications. Do not therefore ask a man to adopt a particular religion (rather than another), for this would separate him from the fundamental principle; it is this principle itself which must come to seek him; in it are all the heights and all the meanings elucidated; then he will understand them."

[6] Lamenting the loss of "verticality" in modernism, Gai Eaton remarks: "The horizontal depends upon the vertical, the outward depends upon the inward and, when the spiritual element is pushed into the background, then practical—down-to-earth—religious practice falls away. It no longer has any solid foundation in the transcendent reality which, by its very nature, gives all things under the sun their proper weight, no more and no less." (*Remembering God: Reflections on Islam,* Charles Le Gai Eaton, *Chicago,* ABC International Group, Inc., 2000, at pages 129-130). Martin Lings observes that if man "is cut off from the spiritual plane, he will find a 'god' to worship at some lower level, thus endowing something relative with what belongs only to the Absolute. Hence the existence today of

opposition in metaphysics between *din* and *dunya*. By contrast, the modernist worldview, though it often includes a constitutional reference to God, is secular, based increasingly upon the privatization of religion. In part, this secularism is paradoxically often attributed to the desire to uphold the freedom of religion within a pluralistic society and thereby to avoid a theocracy based upon one particular theology. But religious views cannot be absented from the public sphere, however one might attempt to compartmentalize society into realms of the sacred and the secular.

Imam 'Ali's teachings clearly endorse a qualitative, spiritually devolutionary and sacred view of the world, where value descends from above to the domains below. This is the foundation of hierarchy and moral authority, an acceptance of a divinely ordained world in which freedoms are bounded by moral imperatives and rights by spiritual standards. By contrast, the modernist worldview is quantitative, materially evolutionary and secular, which celebrates freedom and equality without anchoring these in the objective and transcendent criteria of spiritual reality[7]. Its "authority" operates from below, not from top down, and is founded on subjective preferences or rationalized principles rather than on universal, transcendent, metaphysical principles grounded in the very structures of reality. Without a proper spiritual underpinning, its "freedom" is degenerative and overreaching[8], leeching from the soul the enrich-

---

so many 'words to conjure with' like 'freedom', 'equality', 'literacy', 'science', 'civilization', words at the utterance of which a multitude of souls fall prostrate in sub-mental adoration." (*Ancient Beliefs and Modern Superstitions*, Martin Lings, Quinta Essentia, 1991, p. 45).

[7] Commenting on the modernist outlooks on freedom and equality, Martin Lings observes, "each in its own way is a revolt against hierarchy." (*Ancient Beliefs and Modern Superstitions*, Martin Lings, *supra*, p. 45). He notes, "The desire for freedom is above all the desire for God, Absolute Freedom being an essential aspect of Divinity" (*ibid.*, at pages 45 and 46), and "The need for equality, which is part of the nostalgia in the soul of fallen man, is above all the need to be 'adequate' once more to the Divine Presence" (*ibid.*, p. 48).

[8] Emphasizing a universal traditional viewpoint, Schuon observes that "freedom consists much more in satisfaction with our particular situation than in the total

ing and salvific elements of reverence, mystery and wonder which are required to sustain it, while its "equality" is homogenizing and weighed down by "political correctness", thereby inhibiting both legitimate authority and creative expression. The presumptive and laissez-faire modernist notions of "freedom" and the excessively rights-based modernist notions of "equality", which promote mediocrity by pandering to the 'lowest common denominator', are in marked contrast to Imam 'Ali's view that true knowledge (*irfan*) and piety (*ihsan*) are the foundations of moral authority, and are hierarchical and therefore elevating. Genuine freedom vertically transcends horizontal limitations through detachment, while genuine equality is the intrinsic adequacy of the soul to compassion. The egoic individualism of the modernist cannot but degrade the soul, in contrast to the compassionate detachment of the faithful seeker that is ennobling. The Imam's caution is sadly true for our times: "The triumph of mediocre men brings down the elite"[9].

---

absence of constraints, an absence scarcely realizable in the here-below, and which moreover is not always a guarantee of happiness" (*The Transfiguration of Man*, Frithjof Schuon, World Wisdom Books, Bloomington, Indiana, 1995, p. 52).

[9] Quoted by Whitall N. Perry in *A Treasury of Traditional Wisdom*, Whitall N. Perry (ed.), Second Edition, Middlesex, Perennial Books, 1981, p. 968. This criticism of mediocrity and by implication of the centrifugal influence of societies that are governed primarily or purely on the basis of consensus rather than Principle, is also a criticism of a certain kind of democracy. Thus, Muhammad Iqbal wrote: "Democracy is a certain form of government in which men are counted but not weighed." In her essay, "The Development of Political Philosophy" (Chapter 6 of the anthology, *Iqbal: Poet-Philosopher of Pakistan*, ed. Hafeez Malik, Columbia University Press, NY and London, 1971, at page 156), Riffat Hassan comments on this idea. She writes: "Iqbal's criticism that in a democracy persons are 'counted' not 'weighed' must be interpreted as an assertion that society takes note of 'individuality'—which is a material fact, but not of 'personality'—which is a spiritual fact." Though societies cannot always be governed by sages or "Philosopher-Kings" in the traditional utopian model outlined by Plato in his *Republic*, Imam 'Ali's cautionary words serve to remind us that all consensus (*ijma*) and personal striving for truth (*ijtihad*) have to be principled, that is, based on metaphysical principles (*usul*). Thus, certain kinds of democracies—namely, those that exclude any reference to the metaphysical roots of governance, that reflect rulership that is "sympathetic, humane and congenial" and tied to the principle of *noblesse oblige*—can in

No doubt, the domains of the secular and the sacred may be opposed from a certain theological viewpoint, but, as we have seen, there exist metaphysical principles—rooted in the very structure of reality—that transcend even theology. This points to a crucial distinction between metaphysics and theology, and the primacy of the former over the latter. It is on the basis of this distinction that the poet Jami could state:

> Be aware that justice and equity, not unbelief nor religion,
> Are needed for the maintenance of the kingdom.
> Justice without religion, for the next world,
> Is better than the tyranny of a religious Shah.[10]

It is, therefore, essential that the criterion for Justice be rooted in a sound metaphysical view of reality that admits of the transcendent and operates out of a sense of the sacred. We have argued earlier that the Divine Quintessence—which is the Origin of the sacred—corresponds to Compassion or Mercy, the life-blood of creation and the dialectic of the *Nafas Rahmani*. It is this Quality, whose spirit constitutes our innermost being or *fitra* that is the true criterion of Justice. It is of this transcendent quality that Shakespeare writes:

> ...mercy is above the sceptered sway,
> It is enthroned in the hearts of kings,
> It is an attribute to God himself;
> And earthly power doth then show likest God's
> When mercy seasons justice.[11]

---

fact erode social values and undermine the bonds of affinity and love between the government and society that are vital to the fabric of a healthy society.

[10] Quoted p. 2 of *A Dictionary of Oriental Quotations*, edited by Claude Field, Swan Sonnenschien & Co., London, 1911. The passage, translated by Rehatsek, reads:

> Adl wa insaf dan na kufr wa na din
> Anche dar hifz-i-mulk dar kar ast
> Adl be din nizam 'alam ra
> Bihtar az zulm-i-Shah dindar ast.

[11] Act IV, scene i, *The Merchant of Venice*, William Shakespeare.

True Justice, in this sense, as we have argued, is only attainable through the "middle-path" of Imam 'Ali—a path that corresponds to the "way-mark" of our innermost being[12].

And here we come to two errors that are central to modern conceptions of Justice: the first is the error of premising Justice on a secular dogmatism[13] that devalues the transcendent by its anthropocentrism (man's way, not God's); and the second is the error of premising it on a religious dogmatism that devalues the immanent by its deracination of religion (following the letter, not the spirit). In the first case, the error is prone to manifest in the form of relativism—for instance, in the post-modernist tendency to subjectivism and permissive liberalism within society. In the second case, the error is prone to manifest in the form of reductionism—for instance, in the fundamentalist[14] tendency to reduce the vitality of spirituality to a mere abstraction and to reduce the life-blood of

---

[12] "For every one of you, Islam has fixed an ideal. Strive to achieve it. For all of you, there is a way-mark; try to be guided by it. Islam has its aim for each of you to aspire and to attain it. God has imposed certain duties and obligations upon you; discharge those duties and comply with those commands."—Sermon 181, *Nahjul-Balagha*, Jafery. The "way-mark" (or "sign") referred to in this passage is the human ideal or archetype corresponding to our *fitra* or primordial nature.

[13] Tage Lindbom writes: "Secularization... implies the loss by man of his capacity of objectivation, of his power to distinguish illusion from reality, falsehood from truth, the relative from the absolute. The deepest objective of secularism is precisely to 'liberate' man from the order by which he is submissive to his Creator, to 'emancipate' him from his existential source, to 'change' the system of truth in which he lives into a factual and mental relativity. Thus an inevitable consequence is, not an accrued perspicuity in the imaginative life of man, but on the contrary an ever growing opacity." (*The Tares and the Good Grain*, by Tage Lindbom, trans. by Alvin Moore, Jr., Mercer University Press, 1983, p. 109).

[14] The term "fundamentalism" is a complex and nuanced term. We use this term to refer to the reductionist tendency in religions that sacrifices the "spirit" of religion to the "letter" (though, we emphasize that we do not thereby equate "fundamentalism" with the "exoteric") *and* is exclusivist to the point that it denies religious plurality premised in a transcendent unity (though, we emphasize that we do not thereby equate "fundamentalism" with the "exclusive"). For a discussion, see "'Fundamentalism': A Metaphysical Perspective", p.32.

religion to mere blind adherence to prescribed formulae.[15] Neither of these positions—relativism or reduction, secular dogmatism or fundamentalism—accords with Imam 'Ali's conception of the basis of a "just society". The Straight Path is the "middle path" that steers between these two errors. There is a lesson in this for modernity.

Ultimately, as Imam 'Ali teaches, Justice is based on Truth, and Truth is a matter of recognizing spiritual realities and conforming to them. The criterion of judgment, both in the sense of self-regulation and of human governance, lies within ourselves (our *fitra*) and not in any constructed worldview (whether utopian, consensual, rational, or pragmatic) derived from outward things. Though the voice of this message may be dimmed in the ambience of modernity, its relevance remains vital for the salvation of human beings and human societies. The truth of this message is universal, and we cite one example of its articulation, in a beautiful passage by Robert Browning, from the poem *Paracelsus*:

> Truth is within ourselves; it takes no rise
> From outward things, whate'er you may believe.
> There is an inmost center in us all,
> Where truth abides in fullness; and around,
> Wall upon wall, the gross flesh hems it in,
> This perfect, clear perception—which is Truth.
>
> A baffling and perverted carnal mesh
> Binds it, and makes all error: and to *know*
> Rather consists in opening out a way
> Whence the imprisoned splendor may escape,
> Than in effecting entry for a light
> Supposed to be without.

As the Imam taught, it is only by striving to know what we truly are, and to be what we truly know, that we can hope to fulfill the conditions of Justice. For Justice is an attribute of Truth. We end with Imam 'Ali's cautionary words:

---

[15] See "Pluralism and the Metaphysics of Morality", p.12.

Your cure is within you, but you do not know,
Your illness is from you, but you do not see.
You are the "Clarifying Book"
Through whose letters becomes manifest the hidden.

You suppose that you're a small body
But the greatest world unfolds within you.
You would not need what is outside yourself
If you would reflect on 'self', but you do not reflect.[16]

[16] Cited by Sadr al-din Qunawi (d. 1274), a disciple of Ibn al-'Arabi, in his book, *Mir'at al-arifin fi multamas Zayn al-Abidin.* The citation from Qunawi is translated by William C. Chittick and quoted in his book, *Sufism: A Short Introduction*, Oxford, Oneworld, 2000.

The Metaphysics of Poetic Expression

A Poet's affair is with God, to whom he is accountable, and of
whom is his reward.

(Robert Browning, in a letter to Ruskin)

One thing alone makes a Poet—Imagination, the Divine Vision.

(William Blake)

Section One: Traditional Metaphysics—
A Phenomenological Approach

This essay is intended as an outline for the philosophical understanding of "poetics," or the aesthetics of poetry. The primary
approach adopted in this essay will be to examine poetics, not in
terms of conventional literary theories, but in terms of a poetic
aesthetic grounded in the "first principles" of Traditional metaphysics—that is, based on the universal principles underlying and
informing the very structure of reality.

This principial treatment is based on a particular view of phenomenology that relates the outer manifestations or phenomenal
reality to their inner core or essential reality. The view of poetics
proposed here rests on a phenomenological view of the source of
meaning—in particular, aesthetic meaning—whereby the significance of phenomena[1] derives from a deeper, ontological dimension.
In an essay on "The Question of Comparative Philosophy," the late
Henry Corbin explained this view of phenomenological enquiry as
follows:

---

[1] "The word 'phenomena' always implies an 'of'; appearances, but 'of what?'
Any reality the phenomena have must derive from the reality of that 'of which'
the phenomena are appearances."—Ananda K. Coomaraswamy, *Selected Letters
of Ananda Coomaraswamy*, Alvin Moore, Jr., and Rama P. Coomaraswamy, eds.,
Oxford University Press, New Delhi, 1988, pp. 131-132.

Essentially it is connected with a motto of Greek science: *sozein ta phainomena*—preserve the phenomena (the appearances). And what does that mean? The phenomenon is what can be seen, what is apparent. In appearing it reveals something that can be seen in it only while simultaneously remaining hidden beneath its appearance. That is, something reveals itself in the phenomenon and can reveal itself there only by hiding. In philosophical and religious disciplines, the phenomenon is found in technical terms containing the Greek root *phany*: epiphany, theophany, hierophany, and so on. In Persia the phenomenon, *phainomenon*, is the *zahir*, the apparent, the exterior, the exoteric. The thing that reveals itself while hiding itself in the *zahir* is the *batin*, the interior, the esoteric. Phenomenology consists in "preserving the phenomenon," preserving the appearance, while disengaging or unveiling the hidden thing that reveals itself beneath the appearance. The *logos* of the phenomenon, the phenomenology, is therefore the hidden, the invisible thing beneath the visible. It allows the phenomenon to reveal itself as it does to the subject to whom it is revealing itself. Thus the phenomenological approach is entirely different from that of the history of philosophy, or historical criticism.[2]

This trans-historical approach is quintessentially metaphysical: it is what the Sufis call *"kashf al-mahjub"* or the unveiling of the mysterious, and is based on the spiritual hermeneutics of *"ta'wil"*, or retracing of meaning through metaphysical "first principles" to the *"awwal"* or Origin. As Corbin explains:

> *Ta'wil* is tracing a thing back to its source, to its archetype (*tchizi-ra be-asl-e khwod rasanidan*). Taking it back, we make it pass from level to level of being and in doing so bring out the structure of its essence...[3]

This retracing of meaning, through the realm of archetypal sources, connects it to the meta-historical or transcendental realm,

---

[2] Corbin, Henry, 'The Question of Comparative Philosophy: Convergences in Iranian and European Thought', *Spring: An Annual of Archetypal Psychology and Jungian Thought*, 1980, Spring Publications, Inc., Irving, Texas, USA, pp.1 to 20, at pp.2 and 3.

[3] *Ibid.*, p.3.

so that the phenomenal world is thereby seen, in terms of the unveiled "structure of its essence"—as spiritually radiant or as transparent to transcendence. It is in this sense that the "appearance is preserved," according to the Greek adage—through its radial reconnection with its noumenal and transcendent Center, which, as we shall see, is the intellectual and ontological heart of man.

The perspective adopted in this essay is that of "Traditional metaphysics"—or the timeless and universal principles about the structure of Reality, which Huston Smith has described as "this subterranean watertable which, pressurized by truth, as its adherents believe, gushes forth wherever and whenever the earth is scratched."[4] It is a perspective common to all the major religious traditions, in their scriptures and commentaries, and in sacred philosophies in all civilizations—and in the twentieth century, it is a perspective associated with a school of thinkers known as the "Traditionalists" whose pre-eminent exponents were René Guénon, Ananda K. Coomaraswamy, Frithjof Schuon, Titus Burckhardt, Martin Lings, and Seyyed Hossein Nasr. The term "Tradition" refers here to metaphysical truths, to knowledge of the Sacred Origin, Presence, and End of things, and its sapiential continuation or transmission through all faith traditions. It is "that whole body of canonical symbolic language in which such metaphysical knowledge is enshrined, and in which the prophets, theologians, poets, and artists have transmitted it through the ages."[5] The metaphysical truths and their symbolic expression are the province of the Imagination—or the faculty of the "imaginal" Intellect—and engage an aesthetic sensibility that is implicit in this faculty. As such, the term "Tradition" also encompasses the Imaginative Arts. Traditionalist ideas therefore resonate within a wide group of thinkers who are not always reckoned strictly of the Traditionalist School, such as Henry Corbin, Kathleen Raine, Philip

---

[4] Smith, Huston, *Nasr's Defence of the Perennial Philosophy*, Chapter 2 in Part Two of *The Philosophy of Seyyed Hossein Nasr*, Volume XXVIII of the Library of Living Philosophers, Open Court, 2001, at p.140.

[5] Raine, Kathleen, *Blake and Antiquity*, Bollingen, Princeton, 1963, p.101.

Sherrard, Harold Bloom, and Wendell Berry; and in poets and writers ranging from those of Antiquity (such as Homer and Virgil), of the Medieval world (Dante), the Renaissance (Shakespeare, Milton, and Metaphysical poets such as Donne, Herbert and Vaughan), the Romantics (Coleridge, Shelley, Blake), and the Moderns (Yeats, Hopkins, Whitman, Emerson), to many in the non-English writing traditions (Li Po, Rumi, Sa'adi, Attar, Hafiz, Shabistari, Kabir, Mirabai, Juan de Cruz, Rilke, Neruda, Jiménez), and many others we could name, as well as many inspired anonymous authors. The term "Sacred" denotes the trace of the Absolute transcendent core of Reality in all phenomenal things—in other words, of the Center in the periphery. The term "metaphysics" refers not to the branch of philosophy conventionally associated with Aristotle's *"Metaphysica"*, but to the *philosophia perennis*, or the universal substratum of all wisdom, whose universality is its intellectual Center and Origin[6], which is the spiritual core or "Heart" of man. In order to understand this kardial Center—which will be an essential feature of our argument regarding the metaphysics of poetic expression—it is necessary to contextualize it in the worldview of Traditional doctrine.

According to Traditional metaphysics, there are five descending levels of Reality[7]. These levels, while hierarchic, form a continuum of Reality, so that each higher level is, as it were, reflected in the next descending level, which is sourced from it. The first and highest is the supra-personal Absolute core and ultimate Source of all other levels: it is the Essence, which is Beyond-Being. The second is the archetypal realm of the uncreated Being or uncreated Logos, who as Supreme Creator, is the archetypal font of all created

---

[6] "(...) ubiquity is a product of perennialism's truth, not its criterion. Its criterion is the intellect." Smith, Huston, *Nasr's Defence of the Perennial Philosophy*, Chapter 2 in Part Two of *The Philosophy of Seyyed Hossein Nasr*, Volume XXVIII of the Library of Living Philosophers, Open Court, 2001, at p.142.

[7] For a summary, see William Stoddart, *Remembering in a World of Forgetting: Thoughts on Tradition and Post-Modernism*, World Wisdom, Bloomington, 2008, pp.61-62.

qualities and attributes that are manifest in the phenomenal world. These first two levels, though capable of conceptual differentiation, are intrinsically One, and are metacosmic, transcendent, and divine. The three lower levels, by contrast, are cosmic or human, pertaining to the created domain of "existence." They are, respectively, the Spirit/Intellect, the soul/psyche, and the body/matter. While the soul (*anima*) and body—respectively, the fourth and fifth levels—constitute the psycho-physical and "formal" existence of the individual, the Spirit (*animus*)—the third and "intermediate" level that connects the human to the divine—constitutes the supraformal level of the created Logos or "Intellect" (*intellectus, nous*)[8], the supraconscious awareness which resides in the "Heart" of man, his innermost being and ontological Center through which he can access the higher, transcendent levels of reality. This hierarchic structure of reality and the possibility of supra-human Intellectual awareness to ascend to higher levels of reality—in fact, to perceive Reality to its very core, "imaginally" and not through the "narrow chinks of his cavern"[9]—will be central to our argument.

There are two features of this Traditional worldview that we wish to emphasize: its epistemology, and its structure. With regard to the first feature, epistemology is an aspect of ontology[10].

---

[8] Aquinas: "To understand [*intelligere*] is to apprehend an intelligible truth simply; to reason [*ratiocinare*] is to proceed from one understanding to another. Ratiocination is compared to intellection as motion to rest, or as acquiring to having. One is a process; the other is an achievement." *St. Thomas Aquinas: Philosophical Texts*, trans. Thomas Gilby, London, Oxford University Press, 1951, entry 666 from *Summa Theologica*, IA, 78, 8.

[9] "If the doors of perception were cleansed/ every thing would appear to man as it is, infinite.

For man has closed himself up, till he sees/ all thing thro' narrow chinks of his cavern."

—end of Plate 14, "The Marriage of Heaven and Hell"—William Blake.

[10] In Scholastic terms, the Intellect is the translucent spiritual intelligence of man—the "*Spiritus vel Intellectus*" or "*animus*"—in contrast to the murky egoic and psychic soul—or the "*anima*"—that is the locus of the discursively reasoning mind or the "meddling intellect." In Traditional epistemology, knowing is an aspect of being, and so spiritual intelligence is ontological because it stems from the

Knowing is rooted in being, just as the Intellect is rooted in the Spirit. The corollary of this is that when knowledge is separated from its ontological foundation, it is cut adrift from its transcendent Source and is cast upon a perilous sea without any objective anchoring. To know is to be anchored in one's spiritual Center. It is to refocus one's awareness from the periphery to the Sacred Center or "Heart." It is to be intimately aware of the very substance of Reality, which is also one's selfsame substance—the core of one's being, which is the Spirit. Knowing, in this sense, is therefore a mode of "remembrance": to know is to be profoundly aware of who one is—of one's sacred Origin and its Presence everywhere. This remembrance is both a reorientation and a reintegration—the conscious redeployment of the faculties heavenwards, against the centrifugal forces that operate as a gravitational force of descent into the infernal world. Knowledge therefore implies integrity—to be "at one" with the Oneness of Reality, to sympathetically participate in what one knows—which is the foundation of all virtue and piety. Such knowledge is not abstract but is a *"theoria"*—a way of both "seeing" or witnessing Reality as Sacred Presence or theophany, and a way of "realizing the Real". This profound sympathetic "seeing" is, as we shall see, central to poetic vision, and is denoted by the term "Imagination".

The second feature of the Traditional worldview that is important for our argument relates to its structure from the perspective of man, who is, as it were its cosmic center. Because the human levels of reality are distinct from the higher divine levels—because the Absolute is Infinite and *beyond* the finite measure that bounds our limited human awareness and our merely human existence, reality is said to be *transcendent*; but, at the same time, because

unitive Being of the Divine Logos in which it "lives and moves and has its being", and which endows it with its objective nature. By contrast, ordinary consciousness—whether operating through the discernment of the outer senses or through the discursively reasoning mind—is dislocated from its ground of Being and is therefore fragmentary and merely subjective. It is this foundational or essential mode of knowing—which is ontological—that constitutes the objectivity of the Adamic Intellect.

nothing eludes the embrace of the Divine—because we live and move and have our being in a spiritual ocean that is *within* us, as it were, and whose Presence we can witness through our higher Intellect, reality is also said to be *immanent*. Transcendence engages us with the mystery of reality, while immanence engages us with its intimacy. The "Poetic Genius"—to borrow a phrase from William Blake—consists in the unity of vision that perceives reality as an interpenetration of the finite in the infinite ("a World in a Grain of Sand"), and of the temporal in the Eternal ("a Heaven in a Wild Flower"). It consists in perceiving both aspects of reality, the transcendent and the immanent, simultaneously—both as "the hills in the painting" and as "the painting in the hills"[11]—reflecting at once the mysterious and intimate soul of all things mirrored in the infinite immensity of the intimate Heart.

Thus, as will shall see, it is the poet's task to look beyond the miasmic limitations of ordinary perception, to search for the clarity of essential reality that lies beyond its obscure veil—beyond the mysterious curtain of transcendence—and to perceive its Presence immanently—within the intimate fabric of being: in the words of Corbin, quoted above, to "pass from level to level of being and in doing so bring out the structure of its essence."

Section Two: What is "Poetry"?

When Boswell asked Johnson to define poetry, the latter replied:

> Why, Sir, it is much easier to say what it is not. We all *know* what light is; but it is not easy to *tell* what it is.[12]

---

[11] Liweng, Li: "First we look at the hills in the painting,/ Then we look at the painting in the hills."

[12] Boswell, James, *Life of Samuel Johnson*, 1791, from an entry dated 12 April 1776.

Johnson's observation points to an aspect about poetry that we wish to emphasize: poetry encompasses a particular kind of sensibility rather than a particular kind of form[13]. Thus, with regard to its form, one can think of examples of verse that are not poetic, and of prose that are. Both are potential vehicles of Truth and meaning, while their forms of expression will not necessarily determine their nature.

There are no absolute distinctions between poetry and prose, for they are both, so far as they are intelligible, linguistic vehicles of the Truth. The specific aspect of words as written or spoken—in verse or prose—is an accidental feature; the essential distinction concerns words in whatever pattern or arrangement as manifestations of Truth.[14]

While the form of the poem may vary, the distinguishing feature of the poetic sensibility lies in its orientation and receptivity to the Truth—to the mysterious and ineffable essence of reality, and to the profoundly intimate connection between things. Poetry is, in the words of Wendell Berry, about "the proper human connection to the world"[15]—not merely a connection with the outer forms of things, nor with some abstract idea of their meaning, but with what George Steiner has called "Real Presences". A hallmark of this sensibility is its ability to envision transcendence in a manner that "preserves the phenomena"—to witness the essential connection between the phenomenal world of our ordinary perceptions and the noumenal world that radiates through it. It is to perceive Truth *as* Presence. Poetry, in this sense, partakes of the sacred and, at its

---

[13] As the reader will see, this is an aesthetic sensibility in which Beauty is an aspect of Being. As Brian Keeble has written, " ... in seeing beauty the mind acts and apprehends in the selfsame act Being Itself." *God and Work: Aspects of Art and Tradition*, by Brian Keeble (World Wisdom, Bloomington, Indiana, 2009), p.44.

[14] Livingston, Ray, *The Traditional Theory of Literature*, University of Minnesota Press, Minneapolis, 1962, p.77.

[15] "The Art of Living Right: An Interview with Wendell Berry" from *The Bloomsbury Review*, June-August 1983, pp.23-33.

highest level, poetic expressions have a translucence that can be regarded as the radiance of the divine.

Merely didactic or philosophical prose or verse is not necessarily poetic, even if it purports to deal with metaphysical matters. Poetry must be not merely objective in its content in order to be adequate to Truth, but to function as poetry it must also provide its audience with a transformative experience of its content: it must be *felt* as Truth, so that what is spoken of in the poem has a reality that is felt as Presence. Poetry must function as "revelation", in the most profound sense of the word. This requires a certain quality of vision and of expression on the part of the poet, as well as a certain pitch of attention on the part of the audience. We will have more to say later about the relationship between the poet and his audience, and also about the revelatory function of words, but the point we wish to emphasize for now is that there is a type of poetry with which we are concerned, which is both sapiential and experiential—and which, as we argue, is the quintessence of poetry.

Poetry has been called "*vinum daemonum*" or the "devil's wine" by St. Augustine—highlighting its ability to arouse the lower passions through "enchanting" or "entrancing" elements that can—like a drug—appeal primarily to the subjective emotions, without partaking through the intelligence in any objective connection with Truth[16]. Some "poetry" has a merely subjective aesthetic appeal unconnected with any objective or intellectual merit. These superficial forms of poetry (the idiosyncratically subjective "poetry of feeling" or the outwardly focused "poetry of surfaces") can clearly cast their spell and arouse the emotions, but they are essentially cut off from Truth. It is these forms of poetry that were criticized

---

[16] The poetic consciousness is not a flight from the real, but a flight from the prison of ordinary consciousness. Its ecstasy is marked by an underlying sobriety. See Ralph Waldo Emerson, *Essays, The Poet*: "Milton says, that the lyric poet may drink wine and live generously, but the epic poet, he who shall sing of the gods, and their descent unto men, must drink water out of a wooden bowl. For poetry is not 'Devil's wine,' but God's wine."

in traditional doctrines.[17] Thus, as we shall see, both Plato and the Koran, for example, cautioned the lovers of Truth, or those described as the "faithful," to distance themselves from the spells of such poetry.

From the outset, poetry has always been associated with higher powers, as an inspired gift from the gods, expressing on the human plane—either as speech or as music—something of the divine. For the Greeks, poetry was associated with the Muses, those primeval goddesses of the creative arts and inspiration. The poet was considered an inspired being or an "enthused" (god-inspired, from the Greek *"en theos"*) soul, and poetic expression was a means of articulating the more subtle or refined aspects of reality. It was a means of remaking into the concrete form of speech and sound the ineffable verities to which the poet was privy through inspiration. For Plato, the ordinary poetic inspiration was not connected to Truth in a universal sense, and the poetic art was merely imitative or "mimetic."

Plato alludes in his writings to the long-standing feud between the philosopher and the poet,[18] which is rooted in the distinction between "making" (the activity of the poet) and "contemplating" (the activity of the philosopher). While *"poeisis"* was associated with the activity of "making" through imitation (*"mimesis"*) and ignited only the lower emotions, contemplation was associated with the unitive vision (*"theoria"*) which was engaged through the "insight" of the higher Intellect (*"nous"*). Thus, "mimetic and dulcet" poetry[19] pertained to the imitative arts, which Plato regarded as

---

[17] For example, Aquinas referred to poetry as "inferior learning" (*infima doctrina*), stating that "poetic matters cannot be grasped by the human reason because they are deficient in truth" (*Summa Theologica*, I-II, 101, 2 ad 2). This is because "poeisis" or "making" was conventionally regarded as lesser than "contemplation" or pure consciousness. However, as is argued later in this essay, in its superior sense, "poeisis" is rooted in an ontological consciousness that is pure intellectual thought.

[18] Plato, *Republic*, X.607b.

[19] Plato, *Republic*, X.607c. Such poetry was banned from the ideal state.

merely the manufacture of images and "far removed from truth."[20]
These mimetic creations were merely phantasmal imitations, the
"beautiful words"[21] of those possessed by a "*daimon*" or a Muse, so
that even the worst of poets, bereft of his senses and under the spell
of his Muse, could sing the best of songs,[22] without knowing in the
least what they meant.[23] The creations of superficial poetry, the
"poetry of pleasure," merely appealed to the lower emotions. Plato
referred to these creations as "currying favor with the senseless element that cannot distinguish the greater from the less, but calls the
same thing now one, now the other."[24] Such poetry was not rooted
in Truth—in the reality of the archetypes—and therefore was not
sapiential but merely the inspired reproduction of phenomenal
reality, thrice-removed from its Origin.[25] Socrates taught that such
poetry, though outwardly charming, was not oriented to the Truth;
being merely mimetic, such poetry was to be banished from the
ideal state.[26]

However, Socrates allowed a place in the ideal state for "hymns
to the gods and the praises of good men,"[27] and to poetry that was
morally useful and conducive to Truth.[28] Such poetry he associated

---

[20] Plato, *Republic*, X.598b, 605a-b.

[21] Plato, *Ion*, 542a.

[22] Plato, *Ion*, 534e, 535.

[23] Plato, *Apology*, 22c. Also, *Meno*, 99c-d.

[24] Plato, *Republic*, X.605b-c.

[25] Existent things are once-removed in that they derive from an archetype; they
are twice-removed when we apprehend their appearance; they are thrice-removed
when the poet or painter copies or reproduces that appearance as an artistic creation. This argument is advanced by Plato in *Republic*, X.597e.

[26] Plato, *Republic*, 595a: "Of the many excellences which I perceive in the order
of our State, there is none which upon reflection pleases me better than the rule
about poetry: the rejection of imitative ["*mimetike*"] poetry, which certainly ought
not to be received." See also: *Laws*, 817a-e, and *Republic*, X.607a.

[27] Plato, *Republic*, X.607a.

[28] Plato, *Republic*, X.607c-d: "But nevertheless let it be declared that, if mimetic
and dulcet poetry can show any reason for her existence in a well-governed state,

with the contemplative practice of the turning of the soul away from the merely phenomenal world to the archetypal realities— "from the world of becoming into that of being."[29] This higher practice of poetry is linked to the Scholastic view of poetry as the imitation of the divine archetypes. Such poetry was not merely mimetic but "original," pointing to the ontological reality of our spiritual "Origin"—as referred to in Corbin's earlier description of *ta'wil*. Such a view of poetry is linked to a profound aesthetic that connects "making" to an ontological archetype. It is in this sense that one can justly speak of poetry as "creative". Patrick Laude remarks:

> The essence of art—and sanctity—is not mimetic but "original" in the sense that the artist is to discover within himself the very "origin" of his being as willed by God. Imitation must here be taken as the imitation of process and not the copying of a product. That process is actually a perpetuation of the process of Creation.[30]

"All true Traditional arts are imitative of the art of the Divine Artificer,"[31] and we will have more to say shortly about poetry as "a perpetuation of the process of Creation." For the present, what we wish to emphasize is the contrast between, on the one hand, mimetic poetry that appeals to the lower emotions and is related

we would gladly admit her, since we ourselves are very conscious of her spell. But all the same it would be impious to betray what we believe to be the truth... Then may she not justly return from this exile after she has pleaded her defense...? By all means. And we would allow her advocates who are not poets but lovers of poetry to plead her cause... and show that she is not only delightful but beneficial to orderly government and all the life of man... so we, owing to the love of this kind of poetry inbred in us by our education in these fine polities of ours, will gladly have the best possible case made out for her goodness and truth." See also: *Laws*, 817a-e.

[29] Plato, *Republic*, VII, 518d.

[30] Laude, Patrick, *Singing the Way: Insights in Poetry and Spiritual Transformation*, World Wisdom, Bloomington, 2005, p.167.

[31] Livingston, Ray, *The Traditional Theory of Literature*, University of Minnesota Press, Minneapolis, 1962, at p.29.

to a superficial imitation of phenomena and to an aesthetic of "beautiful words" or "surfaces" disconnected from any archetypal or ontological reality, and, on the other hand, a contemplative sense of poetry, appealing to the higher intelligence, that is truly "original" in that it reconnects us to our ontological source. It is this latter view of poetry that is hallowed in Tradition, and which is the subject of this essay.

It is noteworthy that while Plato emphasized the moral purpose of poetry, Aristotle focused on an aesthetic value associated with the unity of the artist's composition; and that while Plato denounced the merely emotive appeal of poetry, Aristotle allowed for its cathartic or cleansing values. Both, however, stressed the importance of a coherence founded on the ontological integrity of subject and object. For both Plato and Aristotle, the moral purpose of poetry (its inner Goodness, in the Platonic sense) "coheres" ontologically with its ordered and harmonious composition (its Beauty). This coherence is a reflection of Truth as the ontological substance of the Transpersonal Self, which, according to Tradition, is the source of "wholeness" or "holiness" associated with the sense of the sacred. Poetry, in this integrative sense, is therefore understood as the radial reconnection of circumferential man to his Origin and Center.

In this higher sense, the task of the poet is to remember, and arouse remembrance (in the audience of the poem) of, the eternal verities implanted in our very souls. To remember, in this sense, signifies an awakening to a higher and deeper apprehension of reality in which the ordinary things of the world are perceived luminously and sympathetically, in the light of their sacred translucence. The poem arouses in us a perception of the world in the light of its Divine Similitude, so that we see things theophanically, as the resonance of the eternal verities of the soul. The counterpart of this metaphysical recollection is the art of "naming," that is, expressing the qualities and attributes of things in the light of their theophanic radiance. The poet's art is to remember the Face whose Presence is everywhere, and to "name" what he perceives in the light of this recognition. The poet heaves this Presence out of the depths of his being to the surface of his tongue. This is the sense in which the term, "poem," is used by Octavio Paz in the following passage:

> ...the poem makes us remember that which we have forgotten: this that we really are.[32]

We shall have more to say later about poetry as remembrance. But we note in passing that this "remembering" is associated with the Platonic notion of learning as *"anamnesis"* or the remembering of innate truth, and also with the Koranic notion of *"dhikr"* in both its receptive (auditory) and expressive (invocatory) senses, which are discussed in later sections of this essay.

As in the case of Plato, a similar criticism of superficial poetry is found in the Koran:

> And as for the Poets,
> [they too are prone to deceive themselves and so]
> It is those who stray in error who would follow them.
> Seest thou not that they wander distracted in every valley?
> And that they so often utter things they do not practice?[33]

One of the hallmarks of Traditional criticisms of poetry focuses upon the poet's lack of orientation to Truth. In the Koranic passage cited above, this disorientation is signified by the expression "they wander distracted in every valley." Note here that the poet is wandering in a "valley" and is not resting at the peak, which would signify the abode of Truth. The last line in the quoted passage emphasizes that the poet's disorientation is ontological, and points to the need for integrity in the poetic consciousness—the connection between "who one is" and "what one creates." And so, the Koran continues with an exception of a type of poet that is exempt from the general criticism leveled at the poets:

> [Most poets are like this] except those who have faith and are virtuous,

---

[32] Paz, Octavio, *The Bow and the Lyre*, Austin, 1973, p.94.

[33] Koran, *Surat Ash-Shu'ara*, 26:224-226.

who remember God unceasingly...

As we shall see, the Koranic—and Socratic—exception reserves a privileged place in traditional society for the contemplative poet, for the integral and unitive poetic vision of the Good, which links poetic creativity to "remembrance" (*"dhikr"*)—that is to say, the witnessing of the creative act and thereby the poet's ontological rootedness in the most profound and abiding reality of the Presence of the Supreme Reality—the Truth, which is Good and Beautiful.

It would be appropriate at this point in our argument to comment on the relationship between poetry and religion—though the next part of this paper, which deals woth *"poeisis"* and *"logos,"* will elaborate further on the connection between poetic expression and the act of cosmic creation. For now, we will confine our remarks to the resemblance of poetic inspiration and religious contemplation. It should be remarked that, like Hermes, the contemplative poet is a crosser of boundaries. He is, as it were, an intermediary between the subtle world from which his inspirations are derived and the formal world of their expression. Like the mystic, the contemplative poet is a dweller at the isthmus (the *"barzakh"* in Arabic)—which corresponds metaphysically to the Logos, the juncture between the phenomenal and the noumenal worlds, represented by the third level of reality in the Traditional worldview described earlier. Thus the poet's power lies in being able to ascend, by the grace of inspiration, beyond the formal limitations of ordinary or outward consciousness to a transcendent realm. In the more gifted poets, there lies the potential, by grace, to "see the invisible" or to gain an ontological connection with deeper reality by being transported to "a higher state of being"—and then to clothe this witnessing or pre-verbal sensing of the transcendent realm with the formal cloth of the poem.

Commenting on this power, Freidrich Schlegel has remarked:

The life and power of poetry consists in its ability to step out of itself, tear off a fragment of religion, and then return into itself and absorb it.[34]

While in the common understanding of poetry, there is no necessary connection with religion in the sense used by Schlegel, the particular sense in which the term "poetry" is used in this essay connects it to a higher order, to the archetypal dimension from which it derives. George Steiner has argued that all poetry is religious in the sense that it refers to a transcendent dimension[35] and that works of art, certainly in the West, which are of central reference, have a 'gravity' and 'constancy' and 'meaningfulness' which are in essence all religious categories.[36] What is essential in

---

[34] Schlegel, Freidrich, *Philosophical Fragments*, Ideas 25.

[35] "Does this mean that all adult *poeisis*, that everything we recognize as being of compelling stature in literature, art, music is of a religious inspiration or reference? As a matter of history, of pragmatic inventory, the answer is almost unequivocal. Referral and self-referral to a transcendent dimension, to that which is felt to reside either explicitly—that is to say ritually, theologically, by force of revelation—or implicitly, outside immanent and purely secular reach, does underwrite created forms from Homer and the *Oresteia* to *The Brothers Karamazov* and Kafka."— Steiner, George, *Real Presences*, University of Chicago Press, 1989, p.216.

[36] "One asks: Can there be a secular poetics in the strict sense? Can there be an understanding of that which engenders 'texts' and which makes their reception possible which is not underwritten by a postulate of transcendence, by Plato's "aspiration to invisible reality?"... Can a logic of immanence account for the coming into being of the fact of meaningful form? A triple echo may be of help. The precept is in Augustine; the rephrasing is by Boehme; it is Coleridge who transcribes: 'I warn all Inquirers into this hard point to *wait*—not only to plunge forward before the Word is *given* to them, but not even to paw the ground with impatience. For in a deep stillness only can this truth be apprehended.' *Datur, non intelligitur.* There is no mysticism in this monition, only the elusive light of common sense. For it is a plain fact that, most certainly in the West, the writings, the works of art, musical compositions which are of central reference, comport that which is "grave and constant" (Joyce's epithets) in the mystery of our condition... I am arguing that the 'gravity' and the 'constancy' are, finally, religious. As is the category of meaningfulness."—Steiner, George, *Real Presences*, University of Chicago Press, 1989, pp.224-225.

the poetic sensibility is the openness to transcendence. Thus, D.H. Lawrence has written:

> I always feel as if I stood naked for the fire of Almighty God to go through me—and it's rather an awful feeling. One has to be so terribly religious to be an artist.[37]

It is in the sense of being deeply aware of the presence of things that the poetic consciousness resides. We are not suggesting that poetry must be consciously religious poetry. There may be a poetic quality to secular prose or verse (for example, much of Shakespeare's writing) as much as to religious prose or verse (for example, much of the Bible, especially the "Sermon on the Mount," or *The Book of Job*). It is not the overtly religious content that makes it poetic, but its ability to engage its audience with intimacy and mystery, to evoke sympathy and sublimity, to be open to transcendence. There is much consciously religious verse that does not function effectively as poetry because, though it may be sapiential, it does not rise above the level of the didactic or the prosaic: it does not engage the audience to an intimate participation with its subject. But the highest order of poetry will be consciously rooted in Truth and will have the capacity to evoke Presence—to alchemically transform the audience to experience the world intimately in the light of the eternal verities. Poetry of a high order will reflect the divine order by resonating archetypal realities rooted in that order. The poet's art is to reflect and remake on Earth a work whose prototype is in Heaven. Such poetry can be termed "the poetry of accomplishment." Other, lesser forms of poetry may aim—consciously or subconsciously—to express Truth, without authentically achieving such expression. These lesser forms might be termed "the poetry of good intentions." Below these forms lies what conventionally passes for poetry, some of which may incidentally express Truth, without intending it. Such poetry might

---

[37] *The Letters of D. H. Lawrence*, vol. V, ed. James T. Boulton and Lindeth Vasey, Cambridge UP, 1989, letter 550.

be termed "the poetry of surfaces." Remarking on the distinction between the poetry of good intentions and the poetry of accomplishment, T. S. Eliot has noted as follows:

> Above that level of attainment of the spiritual life, below which there is no desire to write religious verse, it becomes extremely difficult not to confuse accomplishment with intention, a condition at which one merely aims with the condition in which one actually lives, what one would be with what one is: and verse which represents only good intentions is worthless—on that plane, indeed, a betrayal.[38]

Similarly, Gao Xingjian has remarked on the necessity of the integrity between what one writes about and the life one lives, between art and ethics—or, in Platonic terms, between Beauty and Virtue, which are respectively the outer resplendence and the interiorization of Truth:

> Truth when the pen is taken up at the same time implies that one is sincere after one puts down the pen. Here truth is not simply an evaluation of literature but at the same time has ethical connotations... For the writer truth in literature approximates ethics, it is the ultimate ethics of literature.[39]

We have noted above how the Koran admonishes "they (who) so often utter things they do not practice," while insisting on the exceptional poetic qualifications of faith, virtue and "remembrance." Also, we have noted how Plato insists on the higher contemplative poetry that is rooted in logic, in Truth, and in the world of being. The mimetic arts that result in the superficial poetry of surfaces and of merely good intentions are "false sublimations" of the ordinary reality and derive from a metaphysical disorientation that lies at the heart of the modernist ethos, whose poetry is

---

[38] Eliot, T. S., *Spectator*, 12 March 1932, Vol. CXLVIII, p.361.

[39] Xingjian, Gao, *The Case for Literature*, Nobel Prize Acceptance Speech, anthologized in *Nobel Lectures From the Literature Laureates, 1986-2006*, The New Press, 2007, p.94.

characterized largely by subjectivist elements and sentimentalism.[40] For now, however, it is important to note that a Traditional poetic aesthetic requires poetry to be objectively intelligible and therefore oriented to Truth, through an openness to transcendence that is not merely abstract but concretized as Presence.

The sense of poetry that we wish to emphasize in this essay is not merely the poetry of surfaces that is "conceived and composed in the wits" but that which is, in the words of Matthew Arnold, "conceived and composed in the soul."[41] It must be both "true to the impact of external reality and...sensitive to the inner laws of the poet's being."[42] In other words, it must reflect the ontological truth of things. It is in this sense that Francis Bacon thought poesy "to have some participation in divineness," and Johnson (in words that were later echoed by Shelley[43]) could remark on the role of the poet "as the interpreter of nature, and the legislator of mankind."[44]

---

[40] Remarking on the nexus between "poetry" and "logic" and its roots in the objectivity of the Intellect, Seyyed Hossein Nasr, has noted (Nasr, Seyyed Hossein, *Islamic Art and Spirituality*, Albany, 1987, p.91):

> According to traditional doctrines, logic and poetry have a common source, the Intellect, and far from being contradictory, are essentially complementary. Logic becomes opposed to poetry only if respect for logic becomes transformed into rationalism, and poetry, rather than being a vehicle for the expression of a truly intellectual knowledge, becomes reduced to sentimentalism or a means of expressing individual idiosyncrasies and forms of subjectivism.
>
> Poetry must associate itself with a higher form of emotion than mere sentimentalism. This higher emotion—which Maritain links to "intuitive knowledge"—is, as we shall see, the transpersonal emotion of spiritual "sympathy." Poetic sensibility requires objectivity and therefore must retain the intellectual capacity that frees it from the idiosyncrasies of the merely subjective.

[41] Arnold, Matthew, *Essays in Criticism*, Second Series, 1888, 'Thomas Gray'.

[42] Heaney, Seamus, *Crediting Poetry*, Nobel Prize Acceptance Speech, anthologized in *Nobel Lectures From the Literature Laureates, 1986-2006*, The New Press, 2007, p.156-157.

[43] Percy Bysshe Shelley remarked in his essay, *A Defence of Poetry*, 1821, "Poets are the unacknowledged legislators of the world".

[44] Note that Plato regarded lawmaking, rooted in a search for divinely inspired

Thus, we are using the term "poetry" in this essay in the Platonic sense—equivalent to that used by the Catholic philosopher, Jacques Maritain:

> Poetry...is the free creativity of the spirit, and the intuitive knowledge through emotion, which transcend and permeate all arts, inasmuch as they tend toward beauty as an end beyond the end. Then poetry, like Plato's *mousike*, is taken in a primary, most universal sense.[45]

This primary and universal sense of poetry as that which tends "toward beauty as an end beyond the end" (that is, beyond the mere surface appeal of aesthetics), must be understood in the Platonic sense of the coherence of Truth, Beauty and Goodness as Creative Presence.

Section Three: *"Poiesis"* and *"Logos"*

In the quotation just cited, Maritain points to the activity of poetry as "the free creativity of the spirit, and the intuitive knowledge through emotion," and we will now examine the particular sense in which *"poiesis"* or creative "making" is connected with *"logos"* or intuitive "knowing"—that is, the connection between the creative process and the poetic intelligence that is expressed in the poem itself.

In an oft-cited passage, Maritain has remarked on the relationship between poetry and metaphysics as follows:

> The divination of the spiritual in the things of sense, and which expresses itself in the things of sense, is precisely what we call Poetry. Metaphysics, too, pursues a spiritual prey, but in a

standards, as a type of poetry: *Laws*.811c-e.

[45] Maritain, Jacques, *Creative Intuition in Art and Poetry*, Bollingen/Pantheon, 1955, p.393.

very different manner, and with a very different formal object. Whereas metaphysics stands in the line of knowledge and of the contemplation of truth, poetry stands in the line of making, and of the delight procured by beauty. The difference is an all-important one, and one that it would be harmful to disregard. Metaphysics snatches at the spiritual in an idea by the most abstract intellection; poetry reaches it in the flesh, by the very point of the sense sharpened through intelligence. Metaphysics enjoys its possession only in the retreats of the eternal regions, while poetry finds its own at every crossroad in the wanderings of the contingent and the singular. The more than reality which both seek, metaphysics must obtain in the nature of things, while it suffices to poetry to touch it in any sign whatever. Metaphysics gives chase to essences and definition, poetry to any flash of existence glittering by the way, and any reflection of an invisible order. Metaphysics isolates mystery in order to know it; poetry, thanks to the balance it constructs, handles and utilizes mystery as an unknown force.[46]

Maritain emphasizes that there is a cognitive dimension within both poetry and metaphysics, but while metaphysics is directed to disembodied principles and essences, poetry is not conceptual but connatural, rising to the surface of things. As we shall see, the argument of this paper is that there is a more integral relationship between poetry and metaphysics than this passage from Maritain allows: "*poeisis*" or "making" relates to "*logos*" or "meaning" in an ontological sense, through which the poetic interest in phenomena (the "flesh" or "crystallized essence" of Reality) is derived from their shared ontological participation, which the poetic sensibility discerns as the noumenal radiance (the "spirit" or "Presence" of Reality) within things. It is in the intersection of Truth and Presence that metaphysics and poetry meet. The poem is a conveyance of Truth *as* Presence. It "re-Presents" Reality by making its Presence felt. It is in this sense that "*poeisis*" should be understood—in Steiner's words, as "meaning made form."[47]

---

[46] Maritain, Jacques, *Frontiers of Poetry*, trans. J.W. Evans, Notre Dame, 1974, p.128.

[47] Steiner, George, *Real Presences*, University of Chicago Press, 1989, p.187.

Turning to its etymology, the term "poetry" is derived from the Greek "*poiesis,*" which signifies "making" or "creating"—activities that, as we shall argue, are connected archetypally to Creation in the metaphysical sense. Creative expression, as we shall see, implies intelligence, both hermeneutically and teleologically, insofar as it translates meaning into form. To better understand "*poiesis*", we must seek to better understand the nature of this intelligence, or "*logos.*"

"*Poiesis*" denotes a creativity that has its archetype in the Logos. Both are concerned with Presences. Thus, George Steiner notes: "A *Logos*-order entails... a central supposition of 'real presence'."[48] In a similar way, one could define "*poiesis*" as the expression of Truth as Presence. As we have noted earlier, in Traditional metaphysics, the term "*Logos*" is the creative threshold between God and man. It is, in its transcendent aspect, the Divine Logos—that is, the uncreated Being which is the Supreme Creator and the archetypal font of all creation; and, in its immanent aspect, it is the supra-rational Intellect—that is, the seat of the Adamic soul, of the kardial intelligence of the Heart, and associated with the gift of human speech, or the Adamic privilege of "naming." The act of "naming" is the evocation of Truth as Presence, and is central to the interplay between the creative process of the artist and its archetypal source. It lies at the heart of both Revelation and Intellection. As we shall see, Revelation is a "naming" by God that occurs at the archetypal level, by which the Word is made flesh, while Intellection is the "naming" by man, by which that which is named is retraced to its archetypal roots.

From the perspective of the Divine Logos, creation is an ongoing and supra-temporal creative process[49], through which the

---

[48] Steiner, George, *Real Presences*, University of Chicago Press, 1989, p.96.

[49] With regard to the continual nature of creation, Meister Eckhart comments: "Do not fondly imagine that God, when he created the heavens and the earth and all creatures, made one thing one day and another the next. Moses describes it thus it is true, nevertheless he knew better: he did so merely on account of those who are incapable of understanding or conceiving otherwise. All God did was: he willed

created world is continually destroyed and simultaneously remade afresh by the Creator in each moment. Creation, therefore, is an ongoing "re-Presentation." What is of particular significance for our purpose here is that the creative expression of poetry is a reflection of the ongoing creative act of the Divine Logos, or, what was referred to earlier as the "perpetuation of the process of Creation." The true poem is the Word made flesh. It reveals the soul of reality—as it is now, in this present moment of creation—through a creative act that renders reality as metaphysically transparent to transcendence.

The prototype of the Poet is, in this sense, God Himself. Inasmuch as God is "the perfect poet", so mankind, the "*imago Dei*," is endowed with a poetic intelligence that is adequate to the Truth. So, Browning proclaims:

> ...God is the perfect poet,
> Who in his person acts his own creations.[50]

The notion of God "acting his own creations" contains the truth implied by the metaphysical doctrine that there is a transcendent spiritual reality that infuses and sustains all things. This is expressed in the dictum "All is One" or, for example, in the Muslim creed, "*La ilaha illa 'Llah*" ("There is no reality but God Himself"). This substantive truth of the Sole Existent, is also implied in the cosmological doctrine, "as above, so below," and has as its corollary the metaphysical doctrine of verticality that is evident in Eckhart's dictum, "Form is a revelation of Essence."[51] According to these doctrines, phenomenal reality is an aspect of the noumenal reality that illumines the higher consciousness of the Intellect. And so, we derive from this worldview a deeper significance of poetry: just as God is the "perfect poet" who is "acting in his own creations," so

and they were." Citation from *Meister Eckhart*, by Franz Pfeiffer, Leipzig, 1857, and translated by C. de B. Evans, London, Watkins, Volume 1, 1924, p.7.

[50] Browning, Robert, *Paracelsus*, 1835.

[51] Eckhart, Johannes (Meister) , *Ibid*, p. 380.

too man—illumined by his Intellect—must aspire to be the perfect poet by envisioning and expressing the sacredness of reality.

The scriptures relate that Primordial Man was "taught the names of things"[52]—that is, endowed with the Adamic gift of speech. There are two significant aspects related to this privilege which we wish to emphasize: the first relates to its epistemology, the second to its metaphysical content.

Dealing with the epistemological significance of "naming", the Adamic gift signifies an important link between the gift of expression and the gift of vision on which it is premised. Man can only say what he sees. And what he sees can only be recognized in the light of its Source, which is the ontological touchstone in man of recognition. Man as microcosm is a reflection of the macrocosm. What he perceives can only be recognized by him insofar as it is an aspect of his innermost Self. Language signifies aspects of mystery and alterity that are intimate and ontological. Thus Steiner notes: "There is language, there is art, because there is 'the other'."[53] There is thus a connection between the sacredness of language and the sacredness of the things named. The poet evokes the mystery and intimacy of things through the sublimity of language. As Emerson observes, "Every word was once a poem."—and "Language is fossil poetry."[54] Mankind recognizes the Presence of God within creation by knowing "the names of things"—which is through Intellection. "Naming" signifies "knowing" (that is, knowledge discerned through the "Intellect"—*Intellectus*), which in turn signifies cognition of "being" (that is, the essential core or "Spirit" of things—*Spiritus*). "To name a thing" is to enter into its ontological center, so that the object "named" reverberates intimately with-

---

[52] *Genesis*, 2:19: "And out of the ground the Lord God formed every beast of the field, and every fowl of the air; and brought them unto Adam to see what he would call them: and whatsoever Adam called every living creature, that was the name thereof." See also, the Koran, *Surat al-Baqarah*, 2:31: "And He taught Adam the names of all things."

[53] Steiner, George, *Real Presences*, University of Chicago Press, 1989, p.137.

[54] Emerson, Ralph Waldo, *Essays and Lectures*, The Library of America, NY, 1983, from *The Poet*, in *Essays, Second Series*, p.457.

in the center of the "naming" Self. It signifies humanity's innate knowledge of the essential nature of things, and of their archetypal roots in the Divine Logos or Primordial Word. What we wish to emphasize here is that the Intellect is the *objective* consciousness of man, rooted as it is in the Divine Logos, and not the *subjective* consciousness of the egoic and psychic soul. Further, that the Poetic Genius lies in "naming" the phenomenal world by *objectively* transcending it, yet preserving the phenomenon by perceiving the noumenal through it. The poet is therefore "he who knows, that is to say, who transcends, and names what he knows."[55]

As for the metaphysical significance of "naming," Adamic speech has its prototype in the Divine Speech, reflecting the fact that the created Logos—or Intellect—is the objective reflection of the uncreated Logos—or Creator. Thus, *"poeisis"* is a reflection of *"logos"*—that is, of the Primordial Word[56], which is its template. It is in this sense that George Steiner has noted" "there is poeisis 'because' there is creation."[57] Meister Eckhart's lapidary observation is central to our argument here: "Words derive their power from the original Word."[58]

Poetry is firstly, an audition of the Primordial Word—its discernment through the intuitive recollection of the poetic intelligence; and secondly, the invocation of the Primordial Word—its expression as a coherent whole, a remaking or "re-membrance" of Oneness out of multiplicity, which coheres within the Heart of the

---

[55] Jouve, Pierre-Jean, *En miroir*, Mercure de France, p.170.

[56] The "original Word" is the archetypal source of all created beings, signified by the Verbum Deum (referred to in the Johannine Gospel) or the Primordial Word from which all things are made. [*Gospel of John*, 1:1-3: "In the beginning was the Word, and the Word was with God, and the Word was God. The same was in the beginning with God. All things were made by Him, and without Him was not any thing made that was made."] In Christianity, the Primordial Word or Logos is associated with the theological teaching of the Incarnation, but the broader metaphysical doctrine of creation as the Primordial Word—the Word made flesh—is found in all faith traditions.

[57] Steiner, George, *Real Presences*, University of Chicago Press, 1989, p. 203.

[58] Eckhart, Johannes (Meister) , *Ibid*, p. 99.

poet. Audition and invocation are both aspects of "remembrance" in the Koranic sense of "*dhikr*", which connotes both the cognitive and invocatory aspects of remembrance. To "remember", in this sense, is to render the 'other' as fully present in its relationship to oneself, and reciprocally to be fully open to 'alterity'. The audition of the Primordial Word is what is generally referred to as "inspiration". It is an affirmation of the spiritual Origin of things, that things have a soul or spirit, to which the inner spirit of cognition can be receptive. This cognitive receptivity is the foundation of poetic vision—"seeing" and "feeling" the soul of things. The nature of the connection between Truth and artistic creativity lies in its orientation or receptivity to metaphysical transparency. The poet, through being open to transcendence, becomes the vessel for the creative activity of the Divine Creator. The poet's receptivity to transcendence is itself a mode of intuitive knowledge—the intellectual source of the poet's creative inspiration, the channel of his auditory intuitions and invocatory expression.

If the prototype of the Poet is God Himself, from the human perspective one might say that the quintessential poem is the Divine Invocation or prayer. The primary impulse of poetry and of prayer is the resonance of the sacred in the inner temple of the Heart—which corresponds to the audition of the Primordial Word. Just as God, after creating the world, saw that it was Good[59], so the poem must resonate as Good within the heart of the poet. The secondary impulse is the creative expression of "naming" or clothing of that resonance with the form of speech—which corresponds to the invocation of the Primordial Word. In its highest form, poetry is prayer, a correspondence between the Invoker, the Invoked, and the Invocation, and the poet's tongue is, as it were, the divine rosary. Poetry and prayer are both forms of remembrance. To invoke God through the sacred Word is to "re-member" God out of the dis-membered fragments of the world—like Isis gathering up the scattered remnants of her husband Osiris's body. Remembrance

---

[59] *Genesis*, 1:31, "And God saw every thing that he had made, and, behold, it was very good."

is an act of being whole. It is an aesthetic sensibility—one that extends into the minute particulars of phenomena. It is to be understood in the Koranic sense referred to earlier, whereby the true poet, mirroring the unceasing creativity of the cosmic Creator, "remembers God unceasingly," seeing everything as "charged with the grandeur of God" (Hopkins).

Poetry is thus a logotic invocation of the spiritual Presence that resides in the heart of created things.[60] Such invocation has an ontological significance. There is a fundamental connection between between the poetic sensibility—that is, the receptivity of the poet's soul to intuit the verities according to the objective measure of his Intellect—and the poet's ability to intelligibly express their essential nature—to remake them through form and to render their essential reality as Present within the substance of the particular form. At its highest level—that of Adamic speech, or "the language of the birds"—human expression is an invocatory participation within the Divine Presence through "naming." By naming things, Adam calls forth the soul of each creature. The poet too—in an act of creation that mirrors the Adamic gift, which is the human métier—summons the soul of things, expressing their mystery and intimacy as aspects of the underlying Spirit. It is in this sense that Bachelard can conceive of poetry as "the phenomenology of the soul."[61]

Adam can only name what God has first uttered. God creates through "naming"—which is the act of Revelation, in its sense of "the Word made flesh." The Word is a metonym of the act of cre-

---

[60] Emerson, Ralph Waldo, from *The Poet*, in *Essays, Second Series, Ibid*, p.466. "What a little of all we know is said! What drops of all the sea of our science are baled up! and by what accident it is that these are exposed, when so many secrets sleep in nature! Hence the necessity of speech and song; hence these throbs and heart-beatings in the orator, at the door of the assembly, to the end, namely, that thought may be ejaculated as Logos, or Word."

[61] Bachelard, Gaston, *La poétique de l'espace*, 1958—*The Poetics of Space*, trans. from the French by Maria Jolas, Beacon Press, Boston, 1994, p.xxi.

ation. God creates through His Speech[62], which is the source and archetype of His Divine Qualities and Attributes found in creation, and thus the Primordial Word is the essential substance of its composition. Creation is therefore the Self-disclosure of God through the theophany that is composed of aggregations of His archetypal Qualities and Attributes. In Muslim theology, these are known as the "Most Beautiful Names"—*al-asma'al-husna*, emphasizing the integral connection between creation and Beauty. Creation is the expression of Beauty[63] or the theophanic luminosity of transcendence. In the words of Emerson, "The Universe is the externization of the soul"[64]—the "soul" being understood here as the Logos. All created things are the words of God.[65] Revelation can thus be understood as creation out of the uncreated Logos, in the trajectory of *descent*, the poetic unfolding of Oneness into multiplicity.

---

[62] All faith traditions associate creation and speech. The will of the Creator is expressed through speech—through the Divine Command and utterance of the Primordial World, which is the origin of each created being. The following passages from various scriptural texts will suffice as illustrations of the associations between creation and speech:

> Utterance (*Vak*) brought forth all the Universe. He (*Prajapati*) pronounced "*Bhu*" (Earth) and the Earth was born. [*Satapatha-Brahmana*, vi, *passim.*]

> He spoke and they were made. [Psalms, cxlviii:5.]

> Verily His command and Being is such that when He wills a thing to be, He but says unto it: "Be!" and it is. [Koran, *Ya Sin*, 36:82.]

[63] According to a *hadith*, "God is Beautiful, and loves Beauty." In an integral sense, Divine Self-disclosure (Arabic, "*tajalli*") is the streaming forth of the radiance of Beauty, while Self-realization is the unveiling (Arabic, "*kashf*") of Spiritual luminosity.

[64] Emerson, Ralph Waldo, from *The Poet*, in *Essays, Second Series, Ibid*, p.453.

[65] According to one of the great Muslim metaphysicians, Ibn al-'Arabi, existence is synonymous with the Divine Names. He writes: "The whole cosmos is the locus of manifestation for the Divine Names" and "In reality, there is nothing in existence but His Names"—Ibn al-'Arabi, Muhyi al-Din, *Al-Futuhat al-makkiiyya*, Volume II, 34:1 and 303:13, translated by William C. Chittick, in *The Sufi Path of Knowledge: Ibn al-'Arabi's Metaphysics of Imagination* (Albany, NY: Suny Press, 1989), at pp. 44, 48-49.

"Poiesis"—which is an act of Intellection—is creation out of the created Logos, in the trajectory of *ascent*, the poetic enfolding of multiplicity into Oneness so that all things can be seen in the light of the One.[66] The poet excavates reality by acts of metaphysical "remembrance" and the poem invokes reality by "representing" it in terms of its archetypal qualities that are recognized as aspects of the innermost Self[67]. Thus, in the words of Eckhart, "In making a thing, the very innermost Self of a man comes into outwardness."

In a key passage, Brian Keeble has expressed the relationship between the prototype of divine creation and the human act of creation as follows:

> ...in the act of creating God externalizes Himself whereas the artist or workman in the act of making internalizes himself. By making outwardly, in an act of pure worship, man fashions his own internal essence. That is to say, he returns to the perfection of his own nature. Here we have the perennial idea of human vocation as part of the conformity of all things to their true nature as an expression of the Divine will.[68]

The poet, as an artist, is thus engaged in returning "to the perfection of his own nature". It is for this reason that great poetry, like beautiful art, is both penetrating and luminous. It penetrates

---

[66] Schuon remarks: "there are two poles for the manifestation of Divine Wisdom and they are: first, the Revelation 'above us' and, secondly, the Intellect 'within us'; the Revelation provides the symbols while the Intellect deciphers them and 'recollects their content, thereby again becoming conscious of its own substance. Revelation is a deployment and intellect a concentration; the descent is in accord with the ascent." (*Understanding Islam*, Frithjof Schuon, Unwin, London, 1976, p.57).

[67] In an essay on Edward Johnston's view of calligraphy, titled "Archetype as Letterform: The "Dream" of Edward Johnston", Brian Keeble has written, "As each man bears the signature of God in his deiformity, so each work from the hand of the scribe bears the signature of its creator": "*God and Work: Aspects of Art and Tradition*", by Brian Keeble (World Wisdom, Bloomington, Indiana, 2009), p.37. Poetry is both the expression and the inner resonance of this "signature".

[68] Keeble, Brian, "*God and Work: Aspects of Art and Tradition*", (World Wisdom, Bloomington, Indiana, 2009), p.45.

the merely phenomenal aspects of reality, delving beneath surfaces, stripping away all veneers until it exposes to its audience the unvarnished Truth that is preserved in the phenomena—the naked and vulnerable Heart of its creator, the spiritual Center that illumines all. The true poet is one "who is more alive than other people"[69] because he sees the world, its gracious and effulgent radiance that is pregnant with meaning, as a quality of his own soul. It is there, in the sacred chamber of his soul that the meaning of the poem finds its resonance—for the meaning of the poem is none other than a quality of the innermost Self.

Before we move further with our argument, let us pause for a brief summary. In this brief outline of *"poeisis"* and *"logos,"* we have seen how creativity and meaning are connected ontologically, and how the creative impetus of the poet/artist derives from the archetype of Divine Creation. As Revelation is Divine Utterance, so poetry is its reflection. It is the Intellectual re-making of the world through "naming." The poet remakes his innermost Self outwardly through the poem. Poetry is both an audition and an invocation of the Primordial Word, the Presence that underlies all phenomena, which resonates in the poem and mirrors the Heart of all things. It is "remembrance", both as cognitive receptivity that enables us to "see" and to "feel" the soul of things, and as the invocatory expression that "re-members" or makes whole the fragments of ordinary perception. In the next sections, we will look more closely into these two aspects of poetic cognition and expression.

Section Four: Poetic Vision—Seeing with the Eye of the Heart

Aquinas has written, "Art is an intellectual virtue."[70] Poetic Vision engages both an aesthetic and an ethical sensibility. An aesthetic

---

[69] Leavis, F.R., *New Bearings in English Poetry*, 1932, Peregrine reprint, 1963, p.19: "Poetry matters because of the kind of poet who is more alive than other people, more alive in his own age."

[70] Aquinas, Thomas, *Summa Theologica* I-II, q.57.a.3c.

sensibility is rooted in a sense of wholeness, of the underlying harmony of things. This in turn corresponds to an ethical sensibility rooted the integral and sympathetic spiritual insight that the boundaries between the 'self' and the 'other' are porous. Harmony and connection: these perceptions are embedded in the spirit, but to perceive harmony and connection, the vision must be open to transcendence. It requires a particular quality of vision to "see the invisible". It requires "eyes of faith", that is to say, an engagement of the active intelligence in the receptive mode[71]. The poet's ability to penetrate beyond the surface of things is an exercise in self-excavation. The poet sees the world according to his mode of reception, and what he sees in turn influences his looking[72]. This dialectical vision requires an ongoing engagement, in which things are seen afresh in each moment—and, perceived as ever-renewing theophanies, are reflections of ourselves, pregnant with meaning. Through this dialectical engagement is the ontological growth that comes through the decisive defeat of the egoic self "by constantly greater beings."[73]

We have referred in the preceding portions of this paper to the cognitive nature of poetry, as an orientation to Truth, and the necessity that poetic discernment be tethered to the Intellect. The quality of attention that is called for in poetic discernment requires the objectivity of detachment. The poet must observe the world with "cold detachment" from a "distanced gaze."[74] The locus of

---

[71] For a fuller discussion of the term "faith", see "The Secularization of Faith in the Modern World", p.154.

[72] "Context is at all times dialectical. Our reading modifies, is in turn modified by, the communicative presence of its object."— Steiner, George, *Real Presences*, University of Chicago Press, 1989, p.163.

[73] The reference is to a poem by Rilke (*Selected Poems of Rainer Maria Rilke*, trans. Robert Bly, NY, Harper & Row, 1981, p.107):
Winning does not tempt that man.
This is how he grows: by being defeated, decisively, by constantly greater beings.

[74] "Poetic feeling does not derive simply from the expression of the emotions; nevertheless, unbridled egotism, a form of infantilism, is difficult to avoid in the early stages of writing. Also, there are numerous levels of emotional expression

this gaze is the Center of one's innermost self—the Eye of the Heart. To abandon this objectivity is to reduce the sympathetic connectedness that is implicit in aesthetics to mere sentimentalism and to reduce the "Originality" of art to "a means of expressing individual idiosyncrasies and forms of subjectivism."[75] It is, in other words, to forsake the poetry of accomplishment for the poetry of surfaces.

Poetry, if it is to "cohere" morally and aesthetically, must first cohere with the intelligence. It must accord with Reality and must be intelligible and seen in the veritable light of Truth: that is to say it must resonate within the Heart of the poet and the discerning audience as true. This is in accord with the Platonic and metaphysical dictum, "Truth is seen by the eye of the Heart."[76]

Maritain remarks on the integral nature of poetic intuition and its kardial locus in the following passage:

> The first thing, I think, which we have to mention in this connection is the essential requirement of totality or integrity... Poetic experience brings the poet back to the hidden place, at the single root of the powers of the soul, where the entire subjectivity is, as it were, gathered in a state of expectation and virtual creativity. Into this place he enters, not by any effort of voluntary concentration, but by a recollection, fleeting as it may

---

and to reach higher levels requires cold detachment. Poetry is concealed in the distanced gaze. Furthermore, if this gaze also examines the person of the author and overarches both the characters of the book and the author's third eye, one that is as neutral as possible, the disasters and the refuse of the human world will all be worthy of scrutiny. Then as feelings of pain, hatred and abhorrence are aroused so too are feelings of concern and love for life."—Xingjian, Gao, *The Case for Literature*, Nobel Prize Acceptance Speech, anthologized in *Nobel Lectures From the Literature Laureates, 1986-2006*, The New Press, 2007, p.89.

[75] Brian Keeble has written of the "tyranny that urges innovation in defiance of all meaningful criteria". He states, "To suppose that art is the product of 'creative freedom' alone, subjectivizes the richly complex process whereby a work of art comes into being, is comprehended and valued." "*God and Work: Aspects of Art and Tradition*", by Brian Keeble (World Wisdom, Bloomington, Indiana, 2009), pp.64 and 72.

[76] Plato, *Republic*, 533d.

be, of all the senses, and a kind of unifying repose which is like a natural grace, a primordial gift, but to which he has to consent, and which he can cultivate, first of all by removing obstacles and silencing concepts....In such a spiritual contact of the soul with itself, all the sources are touched together, and the first obligation of the poet is to respect the integrity of this original experience. Any systematic denial of any of the faculties involved would be a sort of self-mutilation. Poetry cannot be reduced to a mere gushing forth of images separated from intelligence, any more than to a discursus of logical reason...[77]

Here we see that the poetic sensibility is "a spiritual contact of the soul with itself." The point of contact is the Heart, "the hidden place, at the single root of the powers of the soul," and entry therein is through "recollection" and "unifying repose"—the opening of the receptivity of the intelligence to the grace of transcendence. The "hidden place" of Maritain recalls for us "the hiding places" of Wordsworth in *The Prelude*:[78]

> ...the hiding-places of my power
> Seem open; I approach, and then they close;
> I see by glimpses now; when age comes on,
> May scarcely see at all, and I would give,
> While yet we may, as far as words can give,
> A substance and a life to what I feel:
> I would enshrine the spirit of the past
> For future restoration.

Writing of this passage, Seamus Heaney has remarked as follows:

> Implicit in those lines is a view of poetry which I think is implicit in the few poems I have written that give me any right to speak: poetry as divination, poetry as revelation of the self to the self, as restoration of the culture to itself; poems as elements of continuity, with the aura and authenticity of archaeological finds, where

[77] Maritain, Jacques, *Creative Intuition in Art and Poetry*, Bollingen/Pantheon, 1955, pp.238-239.

[78] Wordsworth, William, *The Prelude*, XI, 336-343.

the buried shard has an importance that is not diminished by the importance of the buried city; poetry as a dig, a dig for finds that end up being plants.[79]

Echoing this sense of poetry as "a dig," Derek Walcott has remarked that "the process of poetry is one of excavation and self-discovery".[80] This "self-discovery" is a "recollection" or "remembrance" of who we are in our innermost core and our recognition of our intrinsic connectedness to things. It is our discovery of the Transpersonal Self. Thus, poetry is, as Heaney calls it, a "revelation of the self to the self". The poet's "knowing" does not excavate temporal memory but the innate wisdom-self that is buried within the Intellect. It seeks what lies beyond merely phenomenal reality. It is in this sense of "knowing" that Pamuk can say, "A writer talks of things that everyone knows but does not know they know."[81]

Elsewhere (in his Nobel Prize acceptance speech[82]), Heaney has described the activity of the poet as a kind of Pythagorean search for harmony, as though the poet were "straining towards a strain, seeking repose in the stability conferred by a musically satisfying order of sounds. As if the ripple at its widest desired to be verified by a reformation of itself, to be drawn in and drawn out through its point of origin." This "point of origin" is none other than the Heart—the spiritual Center within us. Heaney has noted that the purpose of poetry is "to touch the base of our sympathetic nature while taking in at the same time the unsympathetic nature

---

[79] Heaney, Seamus, *Preoccupations: Selected Prose 1968-1978*, Faber 1980, from the essay, 'Feeling into Words,' p.41.

[80] Walcott, Derek, *The Antilles: Fragments of Epic Memory*, Nobel Prize Acceptance Speech, anthologized in *Nobel Lectures From the Literature Laureates, 1986-2006*, The New Press, 2007, p.196.

[81] Pamuk, Orhan. *My Father's Suitcase*, Nobel Prize Acceptance Speech, anthologized in *Nobel Lectures From the Literature Laureates, 1986-2006*, The New Press, 2007, p.10.

[82] Heaney, Seamus, *Crediting Poetry*, Nobel Prize Acceptance Speech, anthologized in *Nobel Lectures From the Literature Laureates, 1986-2006*, The New Press, 2007, p.167.

of the world to which that nature is constantly exposed."[83] The poetic dialogue is conducted radially, between the circumference and the Center, and between these poles, the poetic tensions strain, resolving only in the innermost sanctum of the sympathetic Heart. Heaney credits poetry with "making possible a fluid and restorative relationship between the mind's center and its circumference"[84] because it is there, at the core of one's being—in what Heaney has referred to as the "temple inside our hearing,"[85] from where the poet can proclaim, "now the ears of my ears awake/ and now the eyes of my eyes are opened,"[86]—that all outward oppositions resolve into an inner harmony.

To enter the sanctum of the Heart, one does so by recollecting its Presence in "unifying repose"—or, in the famous words of Wordsworth, "emotion recollected in tranquility." However, this phrase is best understood as the impersonal emotion of an unselfconscious receptivity—of spiritual love. Eliot explains this as follows:

> It is not in his personal emotions, the emotions provoked by particular events in his life, that the poet is in any way remarkable or interesting. His particular emotions may be simple, or crude, or flat. The emotion in his poetry will be a very complex thing, but not with the complexity of the emotions of people who have very complex or unusual emotions in life. One error, in fact, of eccentricity in poetry is to seek for new human emotions to express; and in this search for novelty in the wrong place it discovers the perverse. The business of the poet is not to find new emotions, but to use the ordinary ones and, in working them up into poetry, to express feelings which are not in actual emotions at all. And emotions which he has never experienced will serve his turn as well as those familiar to him. Consequently, we must believe that "emotion recollected in tranquility" is an inexact formula. For it is neither emotion, nor recollection, nor, without

---

[83] Heaney, Seamus, *Ibid*, p.168.

[84] Heaney, Seamus, *Ibid*, p.153.

[85] Heaney, Seamus, *Ibid*, p.166.

[86] cummings, e.e., "*i thank You God for most this amazing.*"

distortion of meaning, tranquility. It is a concentration, and a new thing resulting from the concentration, of a very great number of experiences which to the practical and active person would not seem to be experiences at all; it is a concentration which does not happen consciously or of deliberation. These experiences are not "recollected," and they finally unite in an atmosphere which is "tranquil" only in that it is a passive attending upon the event. Of course this is not quite the whole story. There is a great deal, in the writing of poetry, which must be conscious and deliberate. In fact, the bad poet is usually unconscious where he ought to be conscious, and conscious where he ought to be unconscious. Both errors tend to make him "personal." Poetry is not a turning loose of emotion, but an escape from emotion; it is not the expression of personality, but an escape from personality. But, of course, only those who have personality and emotions know what it means to want to escape from these things.[87]

The poet's "escape from personality" is simultaneously an opening into the grace of transcendence. But the mystery of transcendence is rooted in the intimacy of immanence. The poetic emotion is not rooted in his personal subjectivity but in the suprapersonal subjectivity of the objective, Atmanic Self and in the heightened sensibility of Presence. This higher "emotion" is linked to the "intuitive knowledge" of the Intellect—what Coleridge terms "the union of deep feeling with profound thought"—"deep feeling" or "emotion" here referring to a sympathy or connectedness with things, and "profound thought" or "intuitive knowledge" here referring to the poetic vision which is an "imaginal" quality, as we shall see. Eliot goes on to explain:

> The emotion of art is impersonal. And the poet cannot reach this impersonality without surrendering himself wholly to the work to be done. And he is not likely to know what is to be done unless he lives in what is not merely the present, but the present moment of the past, unless he is conscious, not of what is dead, but of what is already living.

[87] Eliot, T.S., "Tradition and the Individual Talent". *The Sacred Wood and Major Early Essays.* Mineola, New York: Dover, 1998, p. 33

The poetic sensibility is thus a heightened form of awareness, a divination of the phenomenological basis of reality, of its sacred "logotic" Presence in the phenomenon. It is the means of apprehending reality based on its deeper spiritual dimension that "saves the phenomenon" and that unveils Being in the very processes of becoming. The poetic intelligence is a noetic impulse, not a flight from reality, but an ascension to a higher dimension. This ascent is "imaginal" in the sense used by Corbin in his explanations about the Active Imagination ("*khayal*") of Ibn al-'Arabi, and in the definition of "Imagination," as used by other poets such as Coleridge, Blake and Shelley.

The imaginal faculty is the Intellect's transcendent and translucent vision of participative Presence. Emerson describes it as "a very high sort of seeing, which does not come by study, but by the intellect being where and what it sees, by sharing the path, or circuit of things through forms, and so making them translucid to others."[88] In the Coleridgean sense, Imagination was "the living power and the prime agent of all human perception," and in an explicit reference to its logotic foundation, Coleridge described it as "a repetition in the finite mind of the eternal act of creation in the infinite I AM." He distinguished the creative genius of transcendent Imagination from the mechanical and aping faculty of Fancy.[89] Imagination was associated with an "esemplastic" quality[90]—a term coined by Coleridge to refer to the power of the visionary "to shape into one" the fragmentary things of ordinary perception. By viewing the world imaginally, one is able to transcend the limitations of ordinary consciousness and to enter the hidden world that informs the phenomenal world of surfaces. Imagination is therefore "the primordial poetic sensibility that is necessary to experience

---

[88] Emerson, Ralph Waldo, from *The Poet*, in *Essays, Second Series, Ibid*, p.459.

[89] Coleridge, Samuel Taylor, *Biographia Literaria*, chapter XIII.

[90] Coleridge, Samuel Taylor, *Biographia Literaria*, ed. James Engell and W. Jackson Bate, Vol. 1, 168, Vol. 7 of *The Collected Works of Samuel Taylor Coleridge*, ed. Kathleen Coburn, Princeton, 1983.

the world in all its fullness and all its complexity."[91] In this same sense, Blake regarded Imagination as a creative portal into the transcendence where one might "see a world in a grain of sand" or experience "eternity in an hour."[92] This explains the central place that Imagination occupied in the Blakean worldview, reflected for example in his observations, "The world of Imagination is the world of Eternity"[93] and "The Nature of my Work is Visionary or Imaginative; it is an Endeavor to Restore what the Ancients call'd the Golden Age."[94]

It is significant that Blake also regarded the poet as a kind of prophet, and termed Imagination—which he regarded as "the Poetic Genius" or "True Man"—as "the spirit of prophecy."[95] The idea of prophecy referred to here is related to the idea that the poet, like the prophet, is a "seer"[96]—that is, one who apprehends reality in its divine light. Thomas Merton explains this quality of vision:

[91] Cheetham, Tom, *After Prophecy: Imagination, Incarnation, and the Unity of the Prophetic Tradition, Lectures for the Temenos Academy*, Spring Journal Books, New Orleans, 2007, p.22.

[92] Blake, William, *Auguries of Innocence*.

[93] Blake, William, *The Last Judgment, Milton*, Book I.

[94] Blake, William, Johnson, Mary Lynn, and Grant, John E., eds. *Blake's Poetry and Designs*. New York: Norton, 1979, p.xxiv.

[95] Blake, William, *All Religions are One*: "The Religions of all Nations are derived from each Nation's different reception of the Poetic Genius, which is every where call'd the Spirit of Prophecy."

[96] Inayat Khan comments as follows: "The source of poetry and of the prophetic gift is no doubt one and the same: poetry receives its inspiration from the same source as prophecy only if the poet is a real poet. Nevertheless, a poet is not necessarily a prophet, but a Prophet is certainly a poet... Poetry and prophecy have their roots in every soul. There is a faculty of intuition from which poetry and prophecy both are born... The distinct work of the poet is to prepare the heart to receive that light which comes; and the work of the prophet is to bring that light and pour it into the hearts of men." Khan, Inayat, *The Hand of Poetry: Five Mystic Poets of Persia—Lectures by Inayat Khan*, Omega Publications, 1993, pp.2 and 9.

... the true poet is always akin to the mystic because of the "prophetic" intuition by which he sees the spiritual reality, the inner
meaning of the object he contemplates, which makes that thing
not only a thing worthy of admiration in itself, but also and above
all makes it a *sign of God.*[97]

It is through the imaginal faculty that the poetic vision operates, through the functioning of grace and through the innate
intelligence that "strains towards a strain," towards the very ineffable core of reality. This straining or digging or feeling our way
intuitively to the sacred core of things takes us in the direction of
Mystery, to the outer reaches of reality, yet it also takes us in the
direction of Intimacy, to the very core of our Self, revealing "the
self to the self." It is in this sense that, in the words of Bachelard,
"The poet speaks on the threshold of being."[98] We shall have
more to say later about Mystery and Intimacy and the relationship
between them as aspects of the poetic vision, but first we need to
examine more closely the relation between the "imaginal faculty"
and the "image." The key to understanding this relation lies in the
Traditional understanding of the "symbol."[99]

According to Tradition, "Particular natural facts are symbols
of particular spiritual facts" and "Every natural fact is a symbol of
some spiritual fact."[100] All existing things participate in a metaphysical template of a "discontinuous continuity" and therefore
they can be perceived either in their profane or "veiled" mode as

[97] Merton, Thomas, *Echoing Silence: Thomas Merton on the Vocation of Writing,* ed.
Robert Inchausti, New Seeds, Boston and London, 2007, p.86—anthologized from
The Literary Essays of Thomas Merton, New Directions, 1981, p.345.

[98] Bachelard, Gaston, *La poétique de l'espace,* 1958—*The Poetics of Space,* trans.
from the French by Maria Jolas, Beacon Press, Boston, 1994, p.xvi.

[99] The Traditional use of the term "symbol" is very different from the modernist
use. For example, in the writings of Julia Kristeva, the "symbolic" pertains to the
structures of language and the syntactical laws and regulations of life, while the
"semiotic" pertains to the Greek *chora* and "precedes evidence, verisimilitude,
spatiality, and temporality": Kristeva, Julia, *Revolution in Poetic Language,* trans.
Margaret Waller (New York: Columbia U.P., 1984), pp.25-26.

[100] Emerson, Ralph Waldo, *Essays and Lectures,* The Library of America, NY,
1983, from *Nature,* chapter IV, Language, p. 20.

disconnected entities or in their sacred or "metaphysically transparent" mode of connectedness. It is this latter perception that is symbolic. Thus, Martin Lings proposes one definition of symbol "as that in which the relationship of connection predominates over that of disconnection"[101]—the "connection" herein referring to the radial power to connect to the spiritual Center, represented by the Supreme Archetype or uncreated Logos.

Coleridge famously defined a "symbol" as follows:

> a Symbol . . . is characterized by a translucence of the Special in the Individual, or of the General in the Especial, or of the Universal in the General; above all by the translucence of the Eternal through and in the Temporal. It always partakes of the reality which it renders intelligible; and while it enunciates the Whole, abides itself as a living part in that Unity of which it is the representative.[102]

There are two aspects of this definition we wish to elaborate on: first, the representative nature of the symbol, and second the notion of translucence.

The representative nature of the symbol springs from the fact that "there is no fact in nature which does not carry the whole sense of nature."[103] Thus, "the whole sense of nature"—or, in other words, its essential and archetypal reality—can be perceived in particular things. The symbolic vision is the ability, in the words of Coleridge, to "perceive the absolutely indivisible as infinitely

---

[101] Lings, Martin, *Symbol & Archetype: A Study of the Meaning of Existence*, Quinta Essentia, 1991, p.8.

[102] Coleridge, Samuel Taylor, from "The Statesman's Manual," p. 30, in *Lay Sermons*, ed. R.J. White, Vol. 6 of *The Collected Works of Samuel Taylor Coleridge*, ed. Kathleen Coburn, Princeton, 1972.

[103] Emerson, Ralph Waldo, from *The Poet*, in *Essays, Second Series, Ibid*, p.454." ... the world is a temple, whose walls are covered with emblems, pictures, and commandments of the Deity ... that there is no fact in nature which does not carry the whole sense of nature; and the distinctions which we make in events, and in affairs, of low and high, honest and base, disappear when nature is used as a symbol."

distinguishable"[104] and at the same time to sense "the omnipresence of all in each".[105] In this way one can regard all things as potential symbols[106], and so everything is grist for the poet's mill. More importantly, however, "the whole sense of nature" is necessarily an aspect of our innermost Self, and symbols are therefore vehicles of apprehending this omnipresent reality.[107] Metaphysical symbolism is, in de Bruyne's phrase, "an aesthetic expression of ontological participation"[108]—which is to say that the symbol is not merely a "sign," but is also a means of self-transformation. The alchemical nature of a symbol arises from its ability to reflect ontological possibilities within the soul. In the words of Martin Lings, "every material symbol reflects its counterparts in the soul."[109] The symbol is effective insofar as it awakens the spiritual possibilities latent within the soul. What the poetic genius apprehends in nature is the innate qualities that reside within the soul itself. This is the

[104] Coleridge, Samuel Taylor, *The Notebooks of Samuel Taylor Coleridge*, ed. Kathleen Coburn, Vol. 3, NY, Bollingen, 1957, entry 4058.

[105] Coleridge, Samuel Taylor, *The Notebooks of Samuel Taylor Coleridge*, ed. Kathleen Coburn, Vol. 2, NY, Bollingen, 1957, entry 2372.

[106] Martin Lings notes however, that the word 'symbol' "is normally reserved for that which is particularly impressive in its 'glorification'" of the Divine Reality: Lings, Martin, *Symbol & Archetype: A Study of the Meaning of Existence*, Quinta Essentia, 1991, p.6.

[107] This is the basis of the scriptural invitation to examine the "signs": for example, in the Koran, it is stated, "God cites symbols for men in order that they may remember" (*Ibrahim*, XIV:25); and "We shall show them Our signs upon the horizons and in their selves" (*Surat Fussilat*, XLI:53). There are three sources of Truth in Islam, all rooted in Allah: these are the Revelation as Scripture (the Koran, in Islam, which is the "criterion" of Truth), as the Objective Creation (the "horizons" or macrocosm), and as the Subjective Self (the microcosm). Similarly, St. Augustine remarks, "Wherever you turn, by certain traces which wisdom has impressed on her works, she speaks to you, and recalls you within, gliding back into interior things by the very forms of exterior things." (*De lib. arb.*, II, 41).

[108] de Bruyne, Edgar, *L'Esthétique du moyen âge*, Louvain, 1947, p.93.

[109] Lings, Martin, *Symbol & Archetype: A Study of the Meaning of Existence*, Quinta Essentia, 1991, p.15.

core of the poetic vision and the source of the poem's ability to resonate within the sacred chamber of the Heart.

With regard to the translucence of the symbol, the important point to grasp is that a symbol that is seen in the light of its spiritual significance—through "cleansed doors of perception"[110]—has the effect of liquefying the material world and rendering it metaphysically transparent. The imaginal vision of the poet sees things not "through a glass, darkly" but "face to face."[111] Therefore it has justly been said, "The poet is the priest of the invisible."[112] The poetic vision in this sense is akin to the great unveiling (*"kashf al-mahjub"*) of which the Sufis speak, where only the "Face of God" is seen.[113] Things of the world are no longer seen as opaque, but as metaphysically transparent to transcendence. In the words of Emerson, "the poet turns the world to glass,"[114] In essence, the imaginal vision enables us to perceive the world as pure spirit. Cutsinger has com-

---

[110] Blake, William, *The Marriage of Heaven and Hell*: "If the Doors of Perception were cleansed, everything would appear to man as it is, infinite."

[111] "For now we see through a glass, darkly; but then face to face: now I know in part, but then shall I know even as also I am known" (1 *Corinthians*, XIII.12).

[112] Stevens, Wallace, *Adagia*, 1957.

[113] The poetic vision perceives the theophanic Countenance of the Divine—see the Koranic Verse, *Al-Baqarah*, II:115—"Wherever you turn, there is the Face of God."

[114] Emerson, Ralph Waldo, from *The Poet*, in *Essays, Second Series, Ibid*, p.456. "We are symbols, and inhabit symbols; workmen, work, and tools, words and things, birth and death, all are emblems, but we sympathize with the symbols, and, being infatuated with the economical uses of things, we do not know that they are thoughts. The poet, by an ulterior intellectual perception, gives them power which makes their old use forgotten, and puts eyes, and a tongue, into every dumb and inanimate object. He perceives the thought's independence of the symbol, the stability of the thought, the accidency and fugacity of the symbol. As the eyes of Lyncaeus were said to see through the earth, so the poet turns the world to glass, and shows us all things in their right series and procession. For, through that better perception, he stands one step nearer to things, and sees the flowing or metamorphosis; perceives that thought is multiform—that within the form of every creature is a force impelling it to ascend into a higher form; and, following with his eyes the life, uses the forms which express that life, and so his speech flows with the flowing of nature."

mented as follows about Coleridge's understanding of the function of poetic symbols:

> Symbolic de-solidifications, by conducting the mind through the surface of things and into their prematerial heart, are meant to introduce us to a world of forms and energies and archetypes, from which our own, that is, the physical, is being drawn. But this archetypal level, like the symbols that lead into it, exists solely for the sake of transmission. To enter it is to pass through it and into a still higher level, not of spirit on its way into matter, but of spirit *without* matter... This higher is nothing less than the world of God, and the world that God is.[115]

It is important to note, however, that in its highest form, the poet's vision is not an abstraction of reality: this is because creation is not superfluous. Nor is the poetic vision pantheistic: this is because God is not superfluous. What the poet perceives is the Creative Presence of God—the inner Beauty present within the seer's own inner being[116], radiating into a symbolic apprehension of the divine theophany—of God at work in all things. It is an inner presentiment of the "perfect poet" who, in the words of Browning cited earlier, "acts his own creations." Perceiving things in the light of their symbolic nature, the poet apprehends that "Everything

---

[115] Cutsinger, James S., *The Form of Transformed Vision: Coleridge and the Knowledge of God*, Mercer, 1987, pp.84-85.

[116] In the context of a discussion of "art", Brian Keeble has written of the twin heresies of naturalism (to falsify the nature of reality "by limiting it to its appearances, forgetting that, logically, appearances are of something") and of abstraction (falsifying the nature of intelligence in "supposing that reality is all in the delight the mind feels in its own correspondence to certain values of pattern and symmetry"). He comments, "It is perhaps not too difficult to see that behind these twin heresies are two equally partial and unconscious theories of the beautiful—at their crudest, the one exclusively objective and the other exclusively subjective. In the objective view beauty is thought to reside in the appearance of the things we perceive. In the subjective view the objective reality of the thing perceived is granted but beauty is thought to belong to the act of emotive assimilation... In other words, neither view can accept that beauty is in the order of being." *God and Work: Aspects of Art and Tradition*, by Brian Keeble (World Wisdom, Bloomington, Indiana, 2009), p.61.

that lives is holy" (Blake). The poetic vision penetrates through to the sacred core of reality. It perceives how "God is incarnate in every human life" (Raine)[117], and how God "plays in ten thousand places" (Hopkins), recognizing the trace of His Presence as "the dearest freshness deep down things" (Hopkins).

We have earlier remarked that poetic discernment is a form of "recollection"—it is a remembrance of who we really are and of what truly is. We might now define poetry as the vision of Creative Presence. Octavio Paz, for example, has made this suggestion in his statement, "What do we know of the present? Nothing or almost nothing. Yet the poets do know one thing: the present is the source of presences."[118] A poet who can communicate at this level imparts to us, his audience, a glimpse of paradise. Thus Merton remarks:

> All really valid poetry (poetry that is fully alive and asserts its reality by its power to generate imaginative life) is a kind of recovery of paradise.[119]

Poetry can therefore be understood as expressing a nostalgia for the Spirit in the midst of ordinary things. It is this expression that lies at the heart of the poetic vision, and it is to the poet's attempt to effectively express this vision that we next turn our attention.

Section Five: Poetic Expression—Saying the Unsayable

Poetic vision has inspired many a poet to song, but equally it has inspired many to silence—for, at its core, it reflects a truth so pro-

---

[117] Raine, Kathleen, *Blake and the New Age*, Allen & Unwin, 1979, p.19.

[118] Paz, Octavio, *In Search of the Present*, Nobel Prize Acceptance Speech, anthologized in *Nobel Lectures From the Literature Laureates, 1986-2006*, The New Press, 2007, p.233.

[119] Merton, Thomas, *Echoing Silence: Thomas Merton on the Vocation of Writing*, ed. Robert Inchausti, New Seeds, Boston and London, 2007, p.98—anthologized from *The Literary Essays of Thomas Merton*, New Directions, 1981, p.128.

found that it recedes from vision, and it takes a particular quality of genius to express the ineffable.

It has been justly remarked that "all art of a spiritual nature arises from silence,"[120] and this is certainly true for poetry. The first step in the poetic process, as we have seen, is apprehending the verities, which is first and foremost an act of contemplation. Merton writes, "The poet enters into himself in order to create. The contemplative enters into God in order to be created."[121] This "entering into oneself" is the excavation of self-discovery that all great poetry entails. But the act of contemplation precedes the act of poetic expression, and all poetry of accomplishment must involve not only an "entering into oneself" but also of "entering into God" and giving oneself to the other in order to partake of its essence.[122] Thus, Emerson writes, "The condition of true naming, on the poet's part, is his resigning himself to the divine aura which breathes through forms, and accompanying that."[123] The poet thereby enters into the logotic truth of the "other" and recognizes it sympathetically as an aspect of his own being.

It is significant that this act of "entering into the other" involves a form of not knowing—reflecting the Mystery of transcendence. This non-knowing is critical to the poetic process:

> Knowing must...be accompanied by an equal capacity to forget knowing. Non-knowing is not a form of ignorance but a difficult transcendence of knowledge. This is the price that must be paid

---

[120] Nasr, Seyyed Hossein, *The Influence of Sufism on Traditional Persian Music*, anthologized in *The Sword of Gnosis*, ed. Jacob Needleman, Penguin, Baltimore, 1974, p.330.

[121] Merton, Thomas, *Echoing Silence: Thomas Merton on the Vocation of Writing*, ed. Robert Inchausti, New Seeds, Boston and London, 2007, p.92—anthologized from *The New Seeds of Contemplation*, New Directions, 1972, p.111.

[122] The task of the poet is first to transform his own vision through contemplation—see the Biblical admonition, "Do not be conformed to the world but be transformed by the renewal of your mind." *Romans*, 12:2.

[123] Emerson, Ralph Waldo, from *The Poet*, in *Essays, Second Series, Ibid*, p.459.

for an oeuvre to be, at all times, a sort of pure beginning, which makes its creation an exercise in freedom.[124]

Bachelard observes: In poetry, non-knowing is a primal condition. (...) an image is a transcending of all the premises of sensibility.[125] It is in approaching the perimeters of the soul that one approaches transcendence. It is by surrendering oneself to the other that one discovers its presence in one's innermost Self. It is by stepping out into the bounds of Mystery that one paradoxically discovers Intimacy. And once one has plumbed the depths of one's innermost Self, it is from that wellspring of Self that the form of the poem can emerge. This is the meaning of the remark, "Poetry is a soul inaugurating a form."[126]

Karen Armstrong has remarked on the differences and the resemblances between the poet and the contemplative mystic in the following passage:

> It could be said that it is in their goals that poetry and religion differ from one another most. The poet's aim is expression; he has to embody his vision in words. For the mystic 'the end is silence', because the Reality he encounters is far beyond words. But perhaps the difference is not so extreme as it seems at first. Like the mystic the poet constantly feels the tension between words and the reality he sees; he is often striving to say the unsayable and to say it as well as he can. But the likeness is closer than that. The mystic does not remain on the solitary mountain top in an endless trance... Like the poet the mystic also has to incarnate his vision and integrate it in reality.[127]

This incarnation of the poetic vision into poetic expression is fundamental to the poetic process. For, as Merton states:

---

[124] Lescure, Jean, *Lapicque*, Galanis, Paris, p.78.

[125] Bachelard, Gaston, *La poétique de l'espace*, 1958—*The Poetics of Space*, trans. from the French by Maria Jolas, Beacon Press, Boston, 1994, p.xxxiii.

[126] Jouve, Pierre-Jean, *En mirroir*, Mercure de France, p.11.

[127] Armstrong, Karen, *Tongues of Fire: An Anthology of Religious and Poetic Experience*, Penguin edition, 1987, from the Introduction, pp.34-35.

...the mere fact of having this contemplative vision of God around us does not necessarily make a man a great poet. One must not be a "seer" but also and especially a "creator"—a "maker".[128]

Emerson, too, has observed, "The man is only half himself, the other half is his expression."[129] To witness the depths of Reality is to awaken its Presence within oneself. It is to strain to utter the Word in the transcendent moment of its "naming"—to capture the eternal moment in the fleeting passage of time.

All great poetry strives to say the unsayable, insofar as it seeks to express transcendence, yet it derives its voice from the creative Presence of the Heart. It is in the immensity of the Infinite Heart[130], in the sacred inwardness of its immanence in the midst of transcendence, that the creative Word is born, reflecting both the Mystery of transcendence and the Intimacy of immanence in the creative poetic vision of the Unity of Being that is the Heart's creative Presence everywhere.[131] Seen in this light, "For each object,

---

[128] Merton, Thomas, *Echoing Silence: Thomas Merton on the Vocation of Writing*, ed. Robert Inchausti, New Seeds, Boston and London, 2007, p.87—anthologized from *The Literary Essays of Thomas Merton*, New Directions, 1981, p.345.

[129] Emerson, Ralph Waldo, from *The Poet*, in *Essays, Second Series, Ibid*, p.448.

[130] Bachelard likens this immensity to "the pure being of pure imagination" in the following passage: "If we could analyze impressions and images of immensity, or what immensity contributes to an image, we should soon enter into a region of the purest sort of phenomenology—a phenomenology without phenomena; or, stated less paradoxically, one that, in order to know the productive flow of images, need not wait for the phenomena of the imagination to take form and become stabilized in complete images. In other words, since immense is not an object, a phenomenology of immense would refer us directly to our imagining consciousness. In analyzing images of immensity, we should realize within ourselves the pure being of pure imagination. It then becomes clear that works of art are the by-products of this existentialism of the imagining being."— Bachelard, Gaston, *La poétique de l'espace*, 1958—*The Poetics of Space*, trans. from the French by Maria Jolas, Beacon Press, Boston, 1994, p.184.

[131] Coleridge wrote of this vision of Unity of Being in the following terms: "That hidden mystery in every, the minutest, form of existence...freed from the phe-

distance is the present, the horizon exists as much as the center."[132]
At the heart of this vision is the Intimacy of Mystery, whose auditory complement is the Eloquence of Silence.[133]

It has been remarked by F. R. Leavis that the poet's "capacity for experiencing and his power of communicating are indistinguishable...because his power of making words express what he feels is indistinguishable from his awareness of what he feels."[134] However, the greatest awareness may be of things that cannot be spoken, except in similitudes that leave room for Mystery. This limitation upon the poet's powers of expression was recognized by, for example, Keats in his theory of "Negative Capability", which allowed for the ineffability of Beauty—"the sense of Beauty" that "obliterates all consideration".[135] In describing the sublime aspects of Reality,

nomena of Time and Space, and seen in the depth of *real* Being, reveals itself to the pure Reason as the actual immanence or in-being of ALL IN EACH."—Coleridge, Samuel Taylor, from "The Statesman's Manual," pp. 49-50, in *Lay Sermons*, ed. R.J.White, Vol. 6 of *The Collected Works of Samuel Taylor Coleridge*, ed. Kathleen Coburn, Princeton, 1972.

[132] Bachelard, Gaston, *La poétique de l'espace*, 1958—*The Poetics of Space*, trans. from the French by Maria Jolas, Beacon Press, Boston, 1994, p.203.

[133] "The poetic sensibility always leads to that which cannot be spoken, yet which is most Real. The final, paradoxical, stage in the drama of the Lost Speech is to attain the freedom of the true Person and to speak a language whose end can only be the silence of contemplation."—Cheetham, Tom, *After Prophecy: Imagination, Incarnation, and the Unity of the Prophetic Tradition, Lectures for the Temenos Academy*, Spring Journal Books, New Orleans, 2007, p.22.

[134] Leavis, F.R., *New Bearings in English Poetry*, 1932, Peregrine reprint, 1963, p.19.

[135] Keats, John, wrote in a letter of 21 December 1817 to his brothers, George and Thomas Keats:
"I had not a dispute but a disquisition, with Dilke on various subjects; several things dove-tailed in my mind, and at once it struck me what quality went to form a Man of Achievement, especially in Literature, and which Shakespeare possessed so enormously - I mean Negative Capability, that is, *when a man is capable of being in uncertainties, mysteries, doubts, without any irritable reaching after fact and reason*-Coleridge, for instance, would let go by a fine isolated verisimilitude caught from the Penetralium of mystery, from being incapable of remaining content with half-knowledge. This pursued through volumes would perhaps take us no further than this, that with a great poet the sense of Beauty overcomes every other consideration, *or rather obliterates all consideration*."

the poem's greatest eloquence lies in its ability to transcend itself, to let the silence it invokes speak subtly of the profound Intimacy of Mystery.

Just as the "poet is the priest of the invisible", so we have remarked that the quintessential poem is an act of invocation—in effect, a form of prayer. Extending this analogy to the poet's audience, it has been stated by the Nobel laureate, Gao Xingjian, that "the relationship of the author and the reader is always one of spiritual communication."[136] Some poems will be spiritually transparent and will "speak" to the reader. Others may appear as "closed shells." There is a particular quality of attention required from the reader in order to penetrate the "closed shells" of poetry, which is, as it were, the counterpart of the poet's act of "entering into the other." Kenzaburo Oe, writing of Kawabata Yasanuri's interest in Zen poems, has commented on this aspect as follows:

> According to such poems words are confined within their closed shells. The readers cannot expect that words will ever come out of these poems and get through to us. One can never understand or feel sympathetic towards these Zen poems except by giving oneself up and willingly penetrating into the closed shells of these words.[137]

To penetrate the closed shells of poetry calls for a certain quality of attention, for a receptivity that is open to transcendence. It is by penetrating into the innermost depths of oneself that one can participate in the mystery of the poem[138]; and equally, it is by

---

[136] Xingjian, Gao, *The Case for Literature*, Nobel Prize Acceptance Speech, anthologized in *Nobel Lectures From the Literature Laureates, 1986-2006*, The New Press, 2007, p.90.

[137] Oe, Kenzabure, *Japan, the Ambiguous, and Myself*, Nobel Prize Acceptance Speech, anthologized in *Nobel Lectures From the Literature Laureates, 1986-2006*, The New Press, 2007, p.172.

[138] One must allow for the fact that a poem can become enclosed within an obscure or complexly private code of images, symbols, and conceits that effectively prevent the poem from functioning as a poem. For many readers, the mythologies of William Blake or the arcane language of Geoffrey Hill, for example, can pre-

reaching for the horizons that the poetic images point to that we are led into the intimate recesses of the Self. Here, it is important to recall, "The poetic image places us at the origin of the speaking being."[139] This "origin" is at the *barzakh* or the pre-cognitive threshold of archetypes, and at the source of knowledge as "logos" with its associations of Adamic speech and of "naming." This "origin" is the "*awwal*" or spiritual Origin, which is also the kardial Center within each of us. To understand a poem or a poetic image is to engage with it attentively, receptively, to penetrate it ontologically, at the level where we permit it to speak to us about our innermost Self.

For the reader or audience, it is the quality of openness or receptivity that determines how the poem expresses itself. Where poems are rooted in truth, poetic images are symbols that present openings into oneself. They express ontological truths. Thus, great poems have the potential to invoke the creative Presence latent within our souls. This is the essence of poetic expression. In Bachelard's phrase, for the reader of the poem, "expression creates being":

> The image offered us by reading the poem... becomes really our own. It takes root in us. It has been given us by another, but we begin to have the impression that we could have created it, we should have created it. It becomes a new being in our language, expressing us by making us what it expresses; in other words, it

vent their poetry from functioning as poems that speak to the hearts of the vast majority of readers. It is only the elite few who can effectively give themselves up and willingly penetrate into the closed shells of these poems, and one can debate if such poems, though capable of revealing the Truth are in fact the "poetry of accomplishment". On one view, the more profound truths need to make greater demands upon the audience in order to be adequately experienced. But the greatest poetry is capable of addressing itself, and revealing the Truth to, many levels of discernment—for the most profound truths tend to simplicity. Hence, the poetic appeal of, for example, the Parables.

[139] Bachelard, Gaston, *La poétique de l'espace*, 1958—*The Poetics of Space*, trans. from the French by Maria Jolas, Beacon Press, Boston, 1994, p.xxiii.

is at once a becoming of expression, and a becoming of our being. Here expression creates being.[140]

What "takes root in us" is that which was always present in us, though our vision of that Presence may have been clouded by forgetfulness, by the opacity of our material senses, by the murkiness of the Cosmic Veil. The paradox of the poet's art is that of seeking to utter silence: the very means of expression limit what is sought to be expressed. It is only through an act of transcendence, inspired by the poem—leading the reader beyond the limitations of the poem and the self—that the poem can bloom like a precious flower within the heart of the reader, spreading its fragrance on all that the open heart perceives.

Poetry is the art of transcendence. The poet incarnates his spirit within the words of the poem, and that incarnation is paralleled by a promise of resurrection within the heart of the reader. The poet invites the receptive reader to look beyond the words of the poem, to the transcendent Self, to penetrate its meaning. In this sense, the great poet can never merely "say the unsayable"—but he can invoke its kardial Presence within his reader. He can hint to the reader of those mysterious horizons of the Truth that cannot be expressed but only experienced—there, in the most intimate and profoundly silent depths of oneself.

Section Six: Conclusion

In this paper, we have put forward a view of poetic aesthetics based on Traditional metaphysics. Utilizing a phenomenological approach, we have argued for a view of poetry that goes beyond the sentimental, idiosyncratic and subjective expressions which constitute the "poetry of surfaces"—which was rejected in the Traditional world of, for example, the Greeks and in the Koranic vision.

---

[140] Bachelard, Gaston, *La poétique de l'espace*, 1958—*The Poetics of Space*, trans. from the French by Maria Jolas, Beacon Press, Boston, 1994, p.xxiii.

We have argued for a view of poetry that is true to the metaphysical structure of reality, that coheres both in terms of the things of the natural world we see around us and in terms of our inner being. Its vision is not found in the opacity of naturalism or in the abstractions of subjectivism, but in the transcendent substance of the Self. At its core, such poetry—which, drawing on a reference from T. S. Eliot, we have termed the "poetry of accomplishment"—is based on a spiritual imagination which apprehends reality through symbols that evoke within us a poetic vision of inward connectedness and outward translucence, invoking the Creative Presence of the Logos—the continuously refreshing Transpersonal Self in whom we "live and move and have our being." The aim of poetry, corresponding to the human métier, is transcendence. As Brian Keeble has remarked, "For what other purpose would man want an art other than to take him beyond the limited disclosures of his own subjectivity on the one hand and external appearances on the other?"[141]

In his great poem, "Jerusalem", William Blake wrote of "the Eternal Vision, the Divine Similitude... Which if Man ceases to behold, he ceases to exist". It is this Vision that it is the poet's métier to express. Poetry that is grounded in metaphysical Truth operates as both creative vision and the invocation of real Presence. This Presence is hidden both within the poem itself and ultimately within the heart of both the poet and his audience, to whom it is revealed. Poetry is, in Seamus Heaney's words, a "revelation of the self to the self". It is by drawing us outward toward the horizons of Mystery that the poet draws us inward to the heart of Intimacy—to our transcendent Center, whose Presence is everywhere.

The poem is *dhikr* in both its receptive (auditory) and expressive (invocatory) senses: it is a "remembrance" or "recollection" of the eternal verities of our Adamic knowledge, and it is the "invocation" of Presence. It both incarnates the meaning into the flesh of the poem, and resurrects the spirit from its outer shell.

---

[141] Keeble, Brian, "*God and Work: Aspects of Art and Tradition*", (World Wisdom, Bloomington, Indiana, 2009), p.82.

All poetry that has any merit does so because it finds resonance within its audience. In metaphysical terms, nothing resonates except as an aspect of Truth—either because it expresses the Mystery of transcendence or because it expresses the Intimacy of immanence. But in the greatest poetry, these aspects are integrated, being envisioned and expressed in terms of a Unity of Being, so that the poet is a "seer" apprehending the things of this world in the light of their archetypal realities which, though transcending phenomena, are immanent qualities within us and which the poem invites us to experience as aspects of Presence.

We would like to conclude with a few thoughts about the implications of our view of poetics in the light of the conditions of time. The modern world is increasingly secularized and predominantly materialistic. René Guénon has famously referred to the materialistic ethos of Modernism as the "Reign of Quantity". It is an ethos characterized by its denial of transcendence. Shrinking in verticality, the world is expanding horizontally. As outer space is expanding, inner space is becoming compressed. In the absence of the spiritual vision of Imagination, our vision of the world is becoming either externalized into its surfaces or surrealized into abstraction. The world is becoming reduced to its outer skin or to a virtual reality. Religion itself is not immune from these tendencies, and so we find it becoming reduced to either surface fundamentalism or to the diluted pseudo-spirituality of New Ageism. In this ethos, man is losing his theomorphic selfhood[142]. The 'self'—no longer inspired by "Real Presences"—is at pains to construct a bridge to the 'other' and is retreating more and more into outward material pursuits or into the abyss of its own fantasies and abstractions. The Poetic Genius in these circumstances is severely compromised and atrophied. More than ever, it needs to be revived.

---

[142] "If humanism amounts to the process whereby the idea that man is created in the Divine Image is gradually eroded, then modernism is the process whereby man's theomorphic nature is finally eradicated": "*God and Work: Aspects of Art and Tradition*", by Brian Keeble (World Wisdom, Bloomington, Indiana, 2009), p.78.

George Steiner has argued eloquently for the necessity of the aesthetic sensibility to be rooted in transcendence. In his estimation, the world is now in a stage of diminished spiritual literacy that he has termed the "Epilogue" or the "Afterword". Lacking its spiritual moorings, the underpinning aesthetic and ethical sensibility of Poetic Genius is removed. Steiner writes:

> What I affirm is the intuition that where God's presence is no longer a tenable supposition and where His absence is no longer a felt, indeed overwhelming weight, certain dimensions of thought and creativity are no longer attainable.[143]

In these conditions, the poetic impulse is in danger of being degraded into the idiosyncratic novelties and kitsch that Steiner has termed "the pornography of insignificance"[144] or into mere sentimentalism. The former is the parody of that true creative originality that refers the phenomenon to its Origin, while the latter is the parody of that sympathetic impulse that radially reconnects all things to their Source and thereby integrally to each other. Harmony and connection: these are the impulses of the aesthetic and ethical sensibilities that lie at the heart of all creative expression. It is these impulses, rooted in the Imagination, that enable us to see all things—whether a wheelbarrow or simple chair, a shaft of light or a hue of color, an expression or a feeling—as aspects of a Presence in which we participate through the mystery and intimacy of its inwardness. For each of us, the world is unique, and the Divine Presence is uniquely manifest in each and every particular of the theophany. It is only through the Eye of the Heart that we can discern theophany. It is only through the Imagination that we can fire the senses so as to perceive the noumenal radiance within phenomena, and see the Face of God in the minutiae of life. It is only through the "auditory remembrance" of the Intellect that we can hear the resonance of the creative Speech that the Creator is

---

[143] Steiner, George, *Real Presences*, University of Chicago Press, 1989, p.229.

[144] Steiner, George, *Real Presences*, University of Chicago Press, 1989, p.145.

uttering in each moment; and only through its "expressive remembrance" that we can give expression to the creative Voice that is our Adamic gift—the gift of Poetic Genius.

Without the resonance of the Primordial Word, the poet is in danger of losing his creative Voice. In the words of Tom Cheetham:

> The most important thing is for each of us to find our Voice, the Voice that can articulate the Lost Speech. The quest is a personal one, but the result is communal: compassion and communion.[145]

If we are to find compassion and communion, healing and wholeness, it is vital that we revive the Imagination and its symbolist spirit, and that we recover our auditory and expressive Poetic Genius, the Voice that is our Adamic heritage—the Lost Speech of "naming", of summoning forth the soul of things.

[145] Cheetham, Tom, *After Prophecy: Imagination, Incarnation, and the Unity of the Prophetic Tradition, Lectures for the Temenos Academy,* Spring Journal Books, New Orleans, 2007, p.35.

"Neither of the East nor of the West": Universality in Islam

> God is the Light of the heavens and the earth.
> The parable of His Light is as if there were a niche,
> And within it a Lamp: the Lamp enclosed in Glass,
> The Glass as it were a glittering star,
> Lit from a Blessed Tree,
> An Olive, neither of the East nor of the West,
> Whose oil is nigh luminous, though no fire has touched it:
> Light upon Light! God guides to His Light whom He wills.
> And God strikes similitudes for men, and God has knowledge of everything.[1]

The idea of universality has an intrinsic metaphysical appeal. It corresponds to an aesthetic sensibility that perceives an underlying order and harmony in the midst of chaos, and to an ethical sensibility that is premised on an inner impulse of peace and goodness. As this paper will attempt to show, it is precisely these sensibilities of Beauty and Virtue that lie at the heart of the message of Islam and that impress it with its ambience and ethos of universality.

But if the idea of universality has an intrinsic metaphysical appeal, in practice it belies a tension that is also metaphysically rooted. This is the tension between the divine archetypes of Rigor and Mercy, between the need to impose universality as outward conformity to rigid laws, and the need to achieve it by accommodation. The former can lead to a homogeneity that sacrifices diversity in the name of universality, while the latter can lead to an outlook of "laissez faire" that sacrifices principles for the sake of peace. As this paper will argue, both these approaches are flawed. Instead, as we will attempt to show, Islam advocates a principled pluralism that springs from the very substance of reality, of the "Hidden

---

[1] *Surah an-Nur*, 24:35.

Treasure" of the Divine Heart that is the ontological foundation and the Illuminating Lamp of both Beauty and Virtue.

When we speak of the "message" of Islam, this begs the question: where should we look to discern its message? As with all faith traditions, Islam was brought into the world by a messenger, the Holy Prophet Muhammad (peace and blessings be upon him), who first received the divine Word from God through the Archangel Gabriel, and thereafter through a series of intermittent "revelations" that spanned the rest of his life. At one level, therefore, the message can be equated with the codified "revelations" of the Koran, which is itself a compendium of the "*ayat*" or "signs" of God[2] and which describes itself as a "Manifest Light"[3]. In another sense, the Holy Prophet is himself "an Illuminating Lamp"[4], bearing the message that lights the world, and so is also a sign of God. It is noteworthy that both the Messenger (the "Lamp") and the Message (the "Light") are described using the symbol of luminosity and diffusion, which carries the metaphysical connotations of spirituality and universality. But in a broader sense, the "revelation" can be understood in terms of the ever-renewing theophany[5] that is continually destroyed[6] and re-created by the divine fiat[7] in each moment of its existence. Each and every aspect of creation, including oneself, is a translucent "sign" of God, and so humankind is exhorted to discern these signs with "eyes of faith":

---

[2] *Surah Yunus*, 10:1, "These are the *ayats* of the Book of Wisdom."

[3] *Surah an-Nisa'*, 4:174.

[4] *Surah al-Ahzab*, 33:46. This is one of five Koranic capacities of the Prophethood (see 33:45-46). The Arabic term "*siraj*" is translated by Asad as "a light-giving beacon." It can also mean the "sun", and is an emblem of the universality of the Islamic message.

[5] *Surah al-Baqarah*, 2:115, "Wherever you turn, there is the Face of God."

[6] *Surah al-Qasas*, 28:88, "Everything is perishing but His Face."

[7] *Surah al-Baqarah*, 2:117, "...when He wills a thing to be, He but says to it, 'Be!'—and it is."

And in the earth are signs for those whose faith is profound—and in yourselves: can you not see?[8]

What we are exhorted to discern is the nature of our existential reality and our existential purpose—those divine messages that are imprinted in the "signs" which are found in "the utmost horizons" and within ourselves[9]. The essence of these messages is contained in the two testimonial declarations or *"shahadat"* that constitute the basic creed of Muslims, *"La ilaha illa' Llah"* and *"Muhammadun Rasulu 'Llah"*: "There is no god but God" and "Muhammad is the messenger of God". The first declaration sums up the doctrine of *"tawhid"* (the integral Unity of Reality), while the second pertains to the doctrines of *"nabuwwah"* (Prophecy) and *"ma'ad"* (the Return to God) and speaks to the salvation and perfectability of man, of the possibilities of Union and Realization. Referring to these two declarations, Frithjof Schuon has commented as follows:

> The first of these certainties is that "God alone is" and the second that "all things are attached to God"... All metaphysical truths are comprised in the first of these "testimonies" and all eschatological truths in the second.[10]

"God alone is": this metaphysical truth is the key to a Muslim's discernment of reality. Cognitively, this formula engages the understanding that at its core unity embraces universality, but, more importantly, it signifies a mode of "seeing" in which everything is metaphysically transparent to transcendence. If "God alone is", then "Wherever you turn, there is the Face of God."[11] This central doctrine of universality is much more than theoretical in a merely conceptual sense. In the deeper sense, where *"theoria"* denotes

---

[8] *Surah adh-Dhariyat*, 51:20-21.

[9] *Surah Fussilat*, 41:53, "In time We shall make them fully understand Our messages in the utmost horizons and within themselves, until it becomes clear to them that it is the Truth."

[10] Schuon, Frithjof, *Understanding Islam*, George Allen & Unwin, 1963, pp.16-17.

[11] Schuon, Frithjof, *supra*.

"seeing", the doctrine has hermeneutical and phenomenological implications that are rooted in a particular cosmological understanding of creation, which, as we shall see, is itself founded upon the metaphysical structures of Beauty and Compassion.

According to Islamic cosmology, all creaturely qualities and attributes are derived from their divine archetypes residing within the "treasure-house" of God, and are thence deployed within creation in an aggregated measure. Thus, the Koran states, "There is nothing whose treasuries are not with Us, and We send it down only with a known measure."[12] All existential qualities are therefore attenuations of the divine archetypes of perfection. These archetypes are attributes (*"sifat"*) of the Divine Essence, that is, of that quintessential substance of Reality that constitutes its quiddity (or *"dhat"*). As such, they are aspects of metaphysical Beauty—which is the radiance of the Divine Essence—and so are termed "The Most Beautiful Names."[13] Conventionally known as "The Ninety-Nine Names of Allah", they are to be understood as the limitless archetypal aggregations of existential reality whose source is the divine treasury and, ultimately, the Divine Essence which is the "Hidden Treasure" of the celebrated *hadith qudsi* of Creation, "I was a Hidden Treasure and My loving nature impelled Me to be known, and so I created the world in order to be known."[14] The archetypal qualities and attributes derived from the Divine Essence have both a hierarchy and complementarity. The hierarchy relates to His Essence, Attributes and Acts, while the complementarity pertains to the masculine and feminine polarities inherent in cre-

---

[12] *Surah al-Hijr*, 15:21. The "known measure" (*"qadar"*) refers to both the finitude of God's creation and to the unique combinations of His ever-renewing theophany. See also *Surah al-Qamar*, 54:49, "Indeed, We have created all things in a known measure."

[13] These are termed *"al-asma'al-husna"*. Surah al-Araf, 7.180, "And all the Most Beautiful Names belong to God, so call on Him by them, and quit the company of those who belie or deny His Names..." See also *Surah Ta Ha*, 20:8, and *Surah al-Hashr*, 59:24, "To Him belong the Most Beautiful Names."

[14] See note 27, *infra*.

ation, which are themselves archetypally rooted in the hypostases of masculine Absoluteness and feminine Infinitude that pertain to the transcendence and immanence, respectively, of Reality. Thus, "masculine" qualities such as Rigor, Majesty, and Hiddenness, are complemented by "feminine" qualities such as Mercy, Beauty, and Manifestness. All creatures are compounded of these qualities in a divine "measure", and are therefore aspects of the divine theophany.

Of all the creatures, it is man alone who is graced with knowledge of the Divine Names. In other words, it is man alone who is privileged to know God. The Koran discloses that God "taught Adam the names of all things."[15] The Arabic term *"ism"* ("name") is to be understood here as referring to the Divine Names, that is, to the theophanic attributes of created things. The ability to recognize the attributes and natures of things is a key component of the Adamic heritage of mankind. But, more significantly, the Koran also discloses that Adam, exemplifying humanity, was created in the divine form, "proportioned"[16] out of clay, and enlivened with the *"ruh"* or divine spirit, which was blown into him by God.[17] Spiritualized man is thus a microcosm of reality. The Divine Names are ontologically imprinted within him, as they are within the macrocosm that he reflects. There is nothing in creation that does not bear the imprint of its Maker—though it is man alone who is privileged among the creatures to recognize this imprint and thereby to perceive the divine theophany.

We noted earlier that all creation is the existential manifestation of "The Most Beautiful Names", and so everything is an aspect of metaphysical Beauty. There is nothing in creation that cannot be seen, if rightly perceived, as an aspect of Divine Beauty. The

---

[15] *Surah al-Baqarah*, 2:31.

[16] See note 17, *infra*. "Proportioned" here refers not only to the "fashioning" of the clay, but also to the "measuring out" of creaturely attributes from the divine treasure-house of qualities: see note 12, *supra*.

[17] *Surah as-Sajdah*, 32:9, "Then He fashioned him in due proportion, and breathed into him the divine spirit..."

Koran states, "It is God who made beautiful everything that He created."[18] Creation therefore expresses the divine nature, hence the *hadith*, "God is beautiful, and He loves Beauty." Inasmuch as Beauty is the radiance of the divine, the recognition of God is the discernment of God through His Beauty—in other words, through His theophanic Presence in all things. Muslim doctrine is thereby in accord with the Scholastic precept that "beauty relates to the cognitive faculty"[19], but as its cause, because the ability to recognize Beauty extrinsically relates to the intrinsic source of that recognition, which is the presence of inner Beauty, or Virtue. Thus the Arabic root, "*hsn*", refers to "Goodness", both intrinsically, as Virtue, and outwardly as its divine radiance, or Beauty. Intrinsic Beauty, or Virtue, is the very substance of the Intellect and so the cause of knowledge. It is the beauty within us, operating through the intelligence of our aesthetic sensibility, which enables us to discern the sacred radiance of the divine. It is through "the eyes of faith", located in the Heart[20]—that is, through the faculty of the transcendent Intellect functioning cognitively as the active intelligence in the receptive mode[21]—that man is able to recognize the Beauty of the "Face of God" in all its primordial manifestations, in Nature and the Self, and in all other earthly reflections of supernatural beauty, such as sacred Art.

The aesthetic sensibility corresponds to the sense of the sacred, to the perception of hierarchical order and harmonious symmetry, and engages the synthesis of being and knowing, and of love

---

[18] *Surah al-Sajdah*, 32:7, "*'Alladhi 'ahsana kulla shay'in khalaqahuu...*" The root, "*hsn*", refers to "goodness", both intrinsically, as Virtue, and as the divine radiance, or Beauty.

[19] Aquinas, *Summa Theologica*, I,5,4 ad.1.

[20] *Surah al-Hajj*, 22:46, "It is not the eyes that are blind, but blind are the hearts within the breast." The Heart is the kardial center of man, the locus of spiritual discernment.

[21] For an elaboration on the meaning of the term "faith" from the perspective of Tradition, see "The Secularization of Faith in the Modern World", p.154.

and knowledge. It perceives universality as an aspect of unity, as radiance—that is, as a radial effulgence from the Heart-Center. It is this radial connection that engages our perception of things in the profoundly integrative and ontological sense. The aesthetic sensibility also corresponds to the "symbolist spirit", that is, the recognition of the metaphysical transparency of creation—that sees the "signs" of God as pointing to the reality that "God alone is", that principial unity is reflected in the world of manifestation, that Heaven is reflected on Earth, that Adam is a symbolic reflection of God. But these correspondences are more than conceptual—they are more even than ways of "seeing": they are ontological, that is to say, they involve a mode of knowledge that is profoundly trans-formative. This is the effective purpose of prayer and ritual: to be ontologically transformed by our remembrance of, and our ritual participation with, the Presence of God. It is in this sense that *"dhikr"* (the invocation of God through His Divine Names, and the remembrance that "God alone is"[22]) and the prescribed rituals that are enactments of our intrinsic poverty and our subsistence in God, can be efficacious modes of Self-realization.

We have described how Islamic cosmology relates to Beauty and to universality in the sense of the divine manifestation and resplendence that is the ever-renewing theophany of the "Face of God." But there is a more profound aspect that we need to explore, which relates to another aspect of the divine substance. If Beauty is the effulgent radiance of the Divine Essence through His creation, the intrinsic nature of the Divine Substance is Compassion. As Adam—or Universal Man—is the microcosm and the reflection of God, so the intrinsic substance of God is reflected in the human soul as Virtue. The realization of this is the métier of man: the enactment of the truth of the second *"shahadah"*: that "all things are attached to God." And to enact and achieve this realization, man must engage in the task of "self-beautification" which is the essence of *"ihsan"* or Virtue. This truth provides a metaphysical

---

[22] *Surah Ibrahim*, 14:25, "God cites parables for men, so that they may remember."

foundation for an objective ethics grounded in the ontological reality of man, and is another aspect of the universality of Islam.

We can cite three illustrations of the Muslim doctrine of the Compassionate nature of God. The first is the Koranic passage in which God states, "My Compassion embraces everything."[23] This statement of the primacy of God's Compassion is linked to its Koranic prescription as a Law binding upon God. In a remarkable passage that appears twice in the Koran[24], God is described as having "willed upon Himself the Law of Compassion" (*"kataba 'ala nafsi-hir-Rahmah"*). No other divine attribute or quality is described or treated in the same way. Compassion (*"Rahmah"*) is therefore clearly singled out as intrinsically pertaining to the divine nature.

The second example of God's Compassionate nature is the well-authenticated *Hadith Qudsi*, cited by both Bukhari and Muslim, in which God states, "Verily, My Compassion outstrips My Wrath."[25] As we will see later, this *hadith* indicates that while the created universe manifests a variety of divine attributes, corresponding to the complementary masculine and feminine polarities described earlier, there is a quintessential quality that transcends all existential polarities and constitutes the very nature and intrinsic substance of God. The closest human approximation of this quintessential divine quality is Compassion—but it is a supreme quality of such grace and perfection, that it pertains to the Divine Essence and Spirit alone and is unknowable in any purely human sense.

The third example of God's Compassionate nature pertains to the *hadith* of the Hidden Treasure, cited earlier, according to which God was impelled by "love"[26] to create the world. According to the great Muslim metaphysician, Ibn 'Arabi, Divine "love" is a

---

[23] *Surah al-Araf*, 7:156.

[24] *Surah al-An'am*, 6:12, and 6:54.

[25] *Sahih al-Bukhari*, Hadith 3194.

[26] The Arabic text of this celebrated Hadith Qudsi is *"kuntu kanzan makhfiyan fa ahbabtu an u'rafa fa-khalaqtu al-khalq likay u'rafa"*. The term *"ahbabtu"* is derived from the root *"lubb"*, designating "love".

form of God's Compassion (*"Rahmah"*), pertaining to His innermost nature, the Divine Essence, the innermost consciousness or secret Heart (*"sirr"*) of Reality. Creation springs forth from and returns into the Divine Womb (*"rahm"*) through a projection and reintegration that is likened to the divine act of breathing. This metaphoric process is termed the Breath of Compassion (*"nafas al-Rahman"*): *"Rahman"* is God's ontological "all-embracing" and illuminating Compassion, while *"Rahim"* is His reintegrating Mercy. It is also noteworthy that it is precisely these two qualities of God—*"Rahman"* and *"Rahim"*—that are singled out in the Basmalah[27] that begins all Muslim prayers and commences all Surahs, except one, of the Koran.

Ibn 'Arabi has elaborated on the meaning of the *hadith* of the Hidden Treasure to explain the concept of *"wujud"*. The term is usually translated as "being" or "existence", which refers to the Sole Reality or Being of God. But insofar as God is also present in His theophany, there is also a sense in which existence has *"wujud"*, though—because "God alone is"—this is in reality only the *"wujud"* of God. In this theophanic sense, the term can also mean the *"mazhar"* or Presence of *"nur"* or Light. By virtue of this metaphor, *"wujud"* is also Light "for it is manifest in itself and makes other things manifest."[28] According to William Chittick, "Ibn 'Arabi is saying that the Hidden Treasure is both beautiful and luminous,"[29] because the divine love that impels creation is the Beauty and the Light of His *"wujud"*—that is, the ontological contents of His Self-disclosure within creation. Ibn 'Arabi explains, "the cause of love is Beauty"[30]—again pointing to the intrinsic Beauty or Compassion of God, which radiates like Light into the creation it thereby causes to "be" by the grace of his *"wujud."*

---

[27] "In the Name of God, the Most Compassionate, the Most Merciful."

[28] Chittick, William C., *Ibn 'Arabi: Heir to the Prophets*, Oneworld, Oxford, 2005, p.42.

[29] *Ibid.*, p.43.

[30] Chittick cites *Al-Futuhat al-makkiyya*, Cairo, 1911, volume II, 326.24.

The image of creation as illumination embeds within it the idea of diffusion, and so of universality. God is Light by His very nature, and is thereby a Self-illuminating Lamp. It is in the very nature of Light to radiate: the Good is not there to illuminate itself. Creation is the self-disclosure ("*tajalli*") of God. It is the illumination of the Divine Spirit—of Goodness, Virtue, or transcendent Compassion, that radiates outwardly as Beauty. But it is only the eyes of Beauty that can perceive Beauty. The task of man is therefore "to make oneself beautiful" ("*ihsan*") by prayer and by spiritual disciplines of detachment. By invoking and remembering God constantly, and by practicing detachment from contingency, one is led to the realization of one's intrinsic poverty and nothingness. This realization of emptiness ("*fana*") is also a realization that our innermost self is nothing but the "*wujud*" of God[31]—hence, its plenitude ("*baqa*"). This realization constitutes the self-unveiling of the primordial nature ("*fitra*")—the Heart of man. It is only from the vantage of this beatific Center that order and harmony can be "*seen*." And it is only by opening the Heart to its innate Compassion that one's participative connection with all of creation can be "*felt*." Self-realization thereby engages a kardial, sympathetic vision—the fusion of knowledge and love, of knowing and being—which is the basis of the reality of "attachment to God". This has profound ethical implications: for all relationships, though outwardly diverse and self-referential, are inwardly experienced as relationships with the Sole Subsisting Self—God.

Islam teaches that the diversity within creation springs from a single Source, which is its origin and to which it will return.[32] The Koran states that mankind was created "from One Soul."[33] "God

---

[31] This is one meaning of the phrase, "*La ilaha illa' Llah.*"

[32] The Koran paradoxically states in *Surah al-Hadid*, 57:3: "He is the First and the Last, the Most Present and the Most Hidden, and He has full knowledge of all things." God is therefore metaphysically transcendent and immanent, the Source and the Destination, the Most Present to the "eyes of the spirit" and the Most Obscure to the "eyes of the flesh."

[33] *Surah al-Nisa*, 4:1, "O Mankind! Be conscious of your Sustainer, who has made

gave everything its creation"[34] and "all things go back to God."[35] This essential relationship of divine origination and return, rooted in a common spiritual paternity—among humanity, and between humanity and all creatures—is the foundation of the universal ethos of Islam. The One Soul (*"Nafsin-wahidatun"*) or universal Adamic spirit of humanity is the primordial nature or *"fitra"* of man. Thus, according to a famous *hadith*, "Every child is born according to *fitra*. Thereafter its parents make it into a Christian, a Jew, or a Magian." The soul's *"fitra"* is its innate disposition to Goodness, its intrinsic Virtue that gives it the ability to radiate Beauty, and is also its innate disposition to Beauty that is the cause of its attraction to Beauty, both within itself and in the world. The *"fitra"* is the spiritual presence of God in man, his spiritual predisposition, which derives from the Compassionate Light of God. It is the source of his spiritual orientation, and is the basis of his perception of the divine theophanies. It is *"fitra"* that is the foundation of humanity's sympathy for the rights of others. It is this Heart-centered disposition to Goodness and Beauty that constitutes the core of human intelligence, evident in its ability to recognize the higher Self, and in its aesthetic and ethical sensibilities.

In the Koranic episode of the Primordial Covenant[36], God asks the pre-existential soul of man—the Adamic *"fitra"*—to bear witness to its divine patrimony. In doing so, the soul fulfills the primordial covenant of man to bear witness in existence to the two metaphysical truths of Reality that are encapsulated in the *"shahadat"*: the ontological reality of Beauty (the truth that "God

you from one soul, and from it created its mate, and from two spread abroad a multitude of men and women..."

[34] *Surah Ta Ha*, 20:50.

[35] *Surah al-Hadad*, 57:5.

[36] *Surah al-Araf*, 7:172, "And when your Lord brought forth from the children of Adam, from their loins, their descendants, and made them bear witness concerning themselves, saying: Am I not your Lord? And they responded: Yes. We bear witness! Remember this, lest you say on the Day of Judgment: Truly, we were unaware of this."

alone is"—corresponding to the soul's aesthetic sensibility), and the ontological reality of Virtue ("all things are connected to God"— corresponding to its ethical sensibility)—and that together represent the universal truths of Islam. Each created thing has a "right" (*"haqq"*) according to its hierarchical ranking, which is discernible by the intelligence of the soul. Each "right" is owed a corresponding "courtesy" (*"adab"*). This is the foundation for Muslim ethics. The fiduciary responsibilities (*"amanat"*) of mankind are rooted in the faith (*"iman"*) of man—in his ability to fulfill his primordial covenant by "realizing the Real." It is by becoming mirrors of the Beautiful Light of *"wujud"* and by expressing its quintessential quality of Compassion, that we can be true to ourselves and fulfill our fiduciary obligations. This is the heart of universal message of Islam.

Yet, as we stated at the outset, there lies a metaphysical tension that underlies the quest for universality. This is the tension between the need to impose outer conformity and the need to accommodate diversity. Within Islam, these needs are expressed as conservative religious fundamentalism, and as liberal syncretism, respectively. Both approaches are flawed from the perspective we have delineated above. What we have termed "fundamentalism"[37] expresses itself by an excessive formalism (reducing the "spirit" to the "letter" of the Law) and an exclusivism that is marked by a strong rejection of pluralism. The reasons for these tendencies are evident: they are compensations for the lack of a Center that can embrace both outer forms and inner substance, or multiple expressions of Truth. Lacking the metaphysical foundation for such a Center, universal order is therefore imposed from the outside and judged in terms of outward conformity. By contrast, what we have termed "syncretism" expresses itself in an indiscriminate embracing of diversity that minimizes all formal differences in the name of ecumenical tolerance. Once more, this approach is grounded in the lack of a metaphysical Center, and results in the dilution of stan-

---

[37] For a fuller discussion of this term, see *"Fundamentalism: A Metaphysical Perspective"*, p.32.

dards and the privileging of procedural pluralism over principled pluralism, and of accommodation over substance and form.

The central doctrine of *"tawhid"* which lies at the heart of Islam is founded on the mystery and intimacy of Reality. God is both transcendent and incomparable (*"tanzih"*) and immanent and the source of similarity (*"tashbih"*). It is therefore as misguided to emphasize only His mystery by devaluing His Manifestness (*"zahir"*) in the formal world, as it is to emphasize only His intimacy by devaluing His Hiddenness (*"batin"*) in His Essence[38]. To overvalue formalism in the name of religion (the error of "fundamentalism") is to commit *"shirk"* (blindness toward God) by de-spiritualizing God and His creation. Similarly, to essentialize all forms of religious expression (the error of "syncretism") is also to commit *"shirk"* by denying the formal significance of His theophany and of His Beauty. The Straight Path of Islam requires us to embrace Reality fully, and thereby to perceive Truth *as* Presence.

In several key passages, the Koran states:

> All mankind was once one single community; [then they began to differ], and God sent them Messengers[39] as bearers of good tidings and as warners, and revealed to them the Scriptures with the Truth, to judge between people with regard to their divergent views. And those to whom [the Scripture] was given, after clear proofs had come unto them, did not differ except through mutual jealousy. And God by His Grace guided the true believers unto the Truth, from whence they differed: for God guides unto the Straight Way him that wills to be guided.[40]

> And We never sent a messenger before you, save that We revealed to him, saying, "There is no deity but I, so worship Me."[41]

---

[38] See note 33, *supra.*

[39] There are numerous Koranic references to God sending messengers for each community. See for example, *Surah Yunus*, 10:47; *Surah ar-Ra'd*, 13:38; *Surah Ibrahim*, 14:4; *Surah Anbiya'*, 21:7-9; *Surah Ghafir*, 40:78.

[40] *Surah al-Baqarah*, 2:213.

[41] *Surah al-Anbiya'*, 21:25. See also note 40, *supra.*

> And unto you [O Prophet] have We entrusted this Message, setting forth the Truth, confirming what is true of the prior revelations, as a Guardian of it...For each We have prescribed a Law and a Way. And had God willed, He could have made you one single community. But [He made you as you are] so that He might test you by means of what he has entrusted to you. So vie with each other in Virtue. Unto God you will all return, and He will clarify your understanding about your differences.[42]

The clear implication of these verses is twofold: it demonstrates, on the one hand, the falsity of a fundamentalist's rejection of pluralism (for God has willed diversity, prescribing for each community a separate "Law" and "Way"), and on the other, the falsity of the syncretist's compromise of substantive pluralism (for the "Law" is the Truth: "There is no deity but I, so worship Me"; while the "Way" is Virtue: "So vie with each other in Virtue").

While Islam rejects fundamentalism and respects the various faith traditions—each with their unique articulations of the underlying Truth—it does not extend this pluralistic embrace of other faith traditions to the level of a syncretic accommodation. Each community has its own prescribed "Law" and "Way", but only as aspects and diverse expressions of Truth and Virtue. Forms are the revelation of the Divine Essence and are metaphysically important. Further, as the Koran states[43]: "piety does not consist in your entering houses from the rear, [as it were,] but truly pious is he who is conscious of God. Hence, enter houses through their doors, and remain conscious of God, so that you might attain to a happy state." One interpretation of this passage is that forms, while subservient to purpose, are nevertheless important. Except by the Grace of God, in this world the Law cannot be essentialized to the point where its forms cease to matter.

The metaphysical tension between the "Rigor" of the fundamentalist and the "Mercy" of the syncretist is not resolved except by recourse to one's natural disposition or "*fitra*". Islam is the final

---

[42] *Surah al-Ma'idah*, 5:48. Yusuf Ali records this as 5:51.

[43] *Surah al-Baqarah*, 2:189.

articulation to mankind of God's primordial message. That is why it is also regarded as the "primordial religion" (*"din al-fitra"*). It emphasizes that the disciplines of the Law and Way are to open the Heart's inner capacity for Compassion—that is, the quintessential quality of Compassion that transcends all metaphysical polarities. The Koran repeatedly states[44] that salvation is attained, by the Divine Grace, through "God-consciousness"[45]—which has two aspects: first, faith (*"iman"*) which manifests in self-surrender (*"islam"*) to Truth; and second, the assumption of Beauty and Virtue (*"ihsan"*) through piety and good works:

If any human being, man or woman, is virtuous and has faith, that person will enter paradise and shall not be wronged by as much as the dint of a date-stone. And who could be more faithful than he who surrenders his whole being to God, and does good works, and follows the creed of Abraham...?[46]

The elements of Truth (expressed as faith and self-surrender) and Virtue (expressed in piety and good works) are the Law and the Way of the "primordial religion." Their particular and diverse articulations in each faith tradition are revealed to each community in its own idiom[47] as a manifestation of the Compassion that has impelled the creation of the world and that sustains it in each moment. This Compassion is Beauty—the Hidden Treasure of the Heart. It is the *"wujud"* whose *"mazhar"* is the Lamp of the transcendent Heart. Man can only perceive universality to the extent that he embodies it within himself as its microcosm. He can only embrace it to the extent he transcends himself. He can only perceive its radiance to the extent he illuminates it. Its luminosity

---

[44] This is a constant refrain in the Koran. See, for example, *Surah al-Baqarah*, 2:25, 62, 82, 112, and 277.

[45] We are following Muhammad Asad in rendering *"muttaqi"* as "the awareness of His all-presence and the desire to mould one's existence in the light of this awareness"—Asad's translation and commentary of the Holy Koran, Gibraltar, 1980, p.3.

[46] *Surah an-Nisa'*, 4:124-125.

[47] *Surah Ibrahim*, 14:4, "We never sent a messenger but with the language of his folk."

signifies the true meaning of "Revelation". Only through our self-emptying can we be filled by its radiance, and only through our stillness can its flowing be felt—the flowing of the Sacred Light whose source is "neither of the East nor of the West" and whose Center is everywhere.

Education in the Light of Tradition:
A Metaphysical Perspective

"It is no longer enough to know the rules. We have to understand what lies behind the rules".

Charles Le Gai Eaton[1]

"Let no man deceive himself. If any man among you seemeth to be wise in this world, let him become a fool, that he may be wise".

1 Corinthians, ch. 3, v. 18[2]

We use the term "education" in conventional parlance as though it were synonymous with the school system, so that to be "educated" often means no more than to be a university graduate or possess a college degree, or to be recognized as having been trained in a particular discipline, skill or technique. There is also the broader sense in which the term "education" is equated with experience, carrying the connotation that learning involves more than passing exams or having a merely theoretical understanding of a subject: it also involves the practical dimension of a lived experience. After all, "only small fish swim in schools". Both these aspects—the theoretical and the practical—form a part of the Traditional conception of education, but with some significant differences. The aim of this paper is to provide an overview of these differences from the perspective of Traditional metaphysics. But to do so, we will also need to debunk a few modernist preconceptions about Tradition.

---

[1] Le Gai Eaton, Charles, *Remembering God: Reflections on Islam*, ABC International, 2000, p.233.

[2] St. Symeon's commentary on this passage is as follows: "Anyone who thinks himself intelligent because of his scholarly or scientific learning will never be granted insight into divine mysteries unless he first humbles himself and becomes a fool..." —cited in volume 4 of *The Philokalia*, translated by G.E.H. Palmer, Philip Sherrard, and Kallistos Ware (Faber, London, 1995), pp.46-47.

By way of an overview of our subject, we note that while conventional secular education is primarily aimed at training the individual to earn a living, Traditional education is aimed at training the individual in self-realization or the art of living. From a theoretical perspective, Tradition teaches the discernment of Reality ("*theoria*" signifying "seeing", not merely conceptualization), and from a practical perspective, it teaches the methodologies of Realization and self-transformation. Traditional teachings offer "an education in philosophy, in Plato's and Aristotle's sense of the word, for whom it means ontology and theology and the map of life, and a wisdom to be applied to everyday matters"[3]. While the outlook of a secular education—even in the fields of the humanities and the liberal arts—is almost exclusively materialistic, that of Tradition—even in the utilitarian fields of teaching practical skills and crafts—extends into the vertical realm of Heaven, which is the source and prototype of Earthly purpose and endeavor.

At the outset we need to dispose of certain potential misunderstandings about Tradition. Any discussion regarding education immediately raises the concern of the possibilities of abuse and indoctrination, and provokes questions of the legitimacy of both educational content and pedagogical authority. We live in a world that largely takes for granted the wondrous miracle of existence, but at the same time is greatly impressed by the marvels and novelties of modern technologies. It is a world whose outlook is dominated by faith in science. Given this domination, it is important to clarify at the outset that Traditional metaphysics is itself an intellectually grounded science of reality. In this, it is not at odds with secular science, though Tradition has a broader cosmological perspective—that extends vertically and is not confined to the horizontal dimension that is the concern of modern science—and consequently it also has a broader epistemological foundation. Thus we see that Traditional metaphysics endorses scientific facts and all perceptions of reality premised upon reliable sensory observa-

---

[3] Coomaraswamy, Ananda K., *Why Exhibit Works of Art*, from *Studies in Comparative Religion*, (Summer 1971), pp.173-182.

tions and proper scientific reasoning and experimentation, so long as these facts and methodologies are understood to pertain to the materialistic worldview that is the focus of modern science, and do not encroach beyond these legitimate bounds. When they do, it is not authentic science that is guilty of the encroachment but ideological "scientism". The epistemology of "scientism" confines knowledge to outwardly verifiable physical realities and thereby improperly denies legitimacy to those metaphysical realities which, being of a transcendent order, cannot properly be made subject to its limited epistemology. In recognition of this transcendent dimension, Tradition teaches that man has been given eyes to see the Invisible, and it therefore carefully distinguishes between the irrational follies of the passive intelligence—which, according to Tradition, science is fully justified in criticizing—and the supra-rational or transcendent realities of the active intelligence in its receptive mode—which have been universally attested to by sages and by spiritual philosophers throughout time, and which science is not equipped to examine in the same way as it does material realities. To adapt a line from Shakespeare, there are more things in heaven and earth than are dreamt of in the philosophy of conventional science.

As scientism poses a barrier to understanding Tradition, so does the secularist bias of modernism. The meaning of several terms that we will be using in this paper—terms such as "tradition", along with a host of others, such as "religion", "faith", "revelation", and "orthodoxy"—have been devalued in modernist usage, and are viewed with skepticism, if not actually maligned by the modernist outlook in its assumptions and teachings. The underlying causes of this devaluation of meaning are the denial of transcendence that characterizes secular dogmatism, and the distortions of sacred language by religious fundamentalists. A critical function of Traditional education must therefore be to redeem this language from its modernist abuses and to recover its sacred etymology and the true meaning of sacred words.

Here, it is important to recognize that modernism has led to the deracination of religion. While it is beyond the scope of this paper to discuss how and why this has occurred, we can note that many misrepresentations of authentic religion are carried out in the name of conventional religion. These abuses, which are generally labeled as "fundamentalism", take a variety of forms, are marked by their excessive formalism (emphasizing the letter over the spirit) and their rigid exclusivism (emphasizing homogeneity and outward conformity over diversity and pluralism). These distortions are themselves a component of modernism, and are not a part of Traditional education or its respect for the divine gift of human intelligence, even if Traditional settings or texts are employed to promote such abusive teachings. They have contributed greatly to the devaluation of sacred meaning, and are, notwithstanding outward appearances, a reflection of the denial of transcendence within the sanctum of conventional religion itself.

The implications of the denial of transcendence—both in the secularist and fundamentalist senses of modernism—are catastrophic because of the resulting distortion of reality. When Earth is viewed in isolation from Heaven, man is cut adrift from his divine source, and becomes disoriented, both in terms of identity and purpose. All attempts to construct a sense of order or purpose in life become relativized and lack any objective foundation. Decentered man is perched perilously between the extremes of hypertrophic narcissism and existential nihilism. The only apparent hope for salvation within the secularist ethos of modernism is Reason. Yet, Reason alone cannot construct a foundation for the meaning of life that is not itself capable of rational challenge. It is only by transcending discursive Reason through the higher faculty of the universal Intellect—whose epistemological legitimacy can be experientially verified by Traditional techniques, and which is grounded in an intellectually-rooted understanding of "faith"[4]— that we can hope to recover the basis of objectivity. Though social contracts and rational consensus may yield truths that conform to

---

[4] By "faith", we mean, cognitively, the active participation of the intelligence in the receptive mode of knowing, and, volitively, the conforming of the will to its guiding intelligence. See *"The Secularization of Faith in the Modern World"*, p.154.

the Intellect, consensually-based values are unreliable, particularly in an age of "manufactured consent", and are more likely to be manipulated and rationalized than to be grounded in objective metaphysical Truth. Also unreliable are the pseudo-religious alternatives of occultism and "New Age" experimentation with syncretic religion, which are not grounded in sound metaphysics, and all-too-frequently conflate the psyche and the spirit—and therefore are objectively unreliable.

All of this points to the conclusion that there is a critical role in Traditional education to expose the false premises of modernism—not only in secularism and scientism, but also especially in the abuses of religion—and to offer an alternative worldview based on the timeless and objective premises of Traditional metaphysics, which perceives all faith traditions as supra-formal expressions of that universal Reality which is Truth, Goodness, and Beauty.

Having addressed these preliminary barriers in modernity to viewing education in the light of Tradition, we will now examine what we mean by a Traditional education. The term "education" derives from the Latin roots "*ex*" ("from" or "out of") and "*ducere*" ("to lead" or "to guide") and signifies the meanings "to lead out of" or "to draw from", all of which presupposes a source. From the Traditional perspective, this source is the Absolute Reality or that transcendent font of Being in which we participate existentially, and which is therefore immanently accessible to us, both ontologically as the being we possess in life, and epistemologically as the innate Adamic "knowledge of naming"[5] that we can draw upon to "recognize" things. All education is a drawing-forth from this font of Truth, from our innermost Being, which can be the only legitimate criterion of knowledge. Thus, there is no learning without our recognition (or remembrance, in the Platonic sense of *anamnesis*) of the pre-existing and innate knowledge that is latent within our soul.

Traditional education therefore engages the art of directly accessing knowledge from the divine font of Truth that is the tran-

---

[5] *Koran* 2:31: "And He taught Adam the names of all things"; see also *Genesis* 2:19-20.

scendent and immanent Source of all knowing and being. In Book IV of the *Mathnavi*, the Sufi mystical poet and metaphysician, Jalal ud-Din Rumi (1207-1273), distinguishes two kinds of intelligence: one is the conventionally acquired and fragmented "plumbing-learning"[6] of the lower intelligence, while the other is God-given and emerges from within us like a fountain. This latter is the direct Source-based learning of the superior Heart-centered Universal Intellect—which it is the object of a Traditional education to draw upon. Rumi states:

> The intellect is of two kinds: The first is acquired. You learn it like a boy at school,
> From books, teachers, reflection and rote, from concepts and from excellent and new sciences.
> Your intellect becomes greater than that of others, but you are heavily burdened because of your acquisition...
> The other intellect is a gift of God. Its fountainhead lies in the midst of the spirit.
> When the water of knowledge bubbles up from the breast, it will never become stagnant, old, or discolored.
> If the way to the outside source should become blocked, there is no reason to worry since the water keeps on bubbling up from within the house.
> The acquired intellect is like a stream led into a house from outside.
> If its way should be blocked, it is helpless. Seek the fountain from within yourself![7]

Traditional education, then, is based on the direct apprehension of Truth by an intellectual quest of "seeking the fountain from within"[8]. However, this search presupposes a certain relationship

---

[6] This term is from Coleman Barks' translation of the passage quoted below, from Book IV of Rumi's *Mathnavi*, lines 1960-1968.

[7] Translated by Chittick, William C., in *The Sufi Path of Love: The Spiritual Teachings of Rumi*, SUNY, Albany, 1983, pp.35-36.

[8] The precept inscribed in gold letters over the portico of the great temple at Delphi proclaims: *"gnothi seauton"* ("know thyself"). This basic command is central to Traditional epistemology, with its implication nothing can be truly known until it

regarding authority, which has its roots in Traditional metaphysics. While the font of knowledge resides within, it is nevertheless a fool who would have himself for a master. This is because the unguided and undisciplined mind, prone to beguilement by the illusory and centrifugal aspects of the contingent world, will not necessarily discern or conform to the authority inherent in the hierarchic ordering of Reality. Traditional cosmology is based on a hierarchy that places the One above the many, Heaven over Earth, the vertical over the horizontal, and, on condition of this verticality, the right in ascendance over the left. Man is raised up above all creatures only by virtue of his willingness to bow before God, and those who hold authority do so only by virtue of the principle of *"noblesse oblige"*. Just as there is a legitimate outward hierarchy between the Outer Guide and the disciple, so there is a legitimate inward hierarchy among the faculties, among which the pre-eminent faculty is the Inner Guide or Intellect: this is depicted in the famous Hindu image of the Divine charioteer (representing the Heart-centered Intellect) who wields the reins (of discursive reason, the lower intelligence) that control the unruly steeds (of willfulness and unbridled passion) that propel the chariot (of the body) through life. Thus it is stated in the Upanishads:

> Know that the Self is like the Lord of the chariot, and the body is his chariot. Know that the intellect is the charioteer and the mind the reins. The senses, they say, are the horses, the objects of the senses their roads. When the Self is in union with the body, the senses and the mind, the wise call Him the enjoyer.[9]

The relationship between the Inner Guide and the Outer Guide defines the contours of authority in a master-disciple relationship. Because no one can be educated who is unwilling to learn, Traditional methodologies require the initiation of the disciple. The spiritual teacher will not normally initiate one who is unprepared

---

has been authenticated within the Self.

[9] *Katha Upanishad* III.Up.3-4.

to learn. Preparedness requires not only a sufficient indication of the disciple's willingness to submit to the teacher's authority as Outer Guide, but also of the disciple's readiness to orient to the innate powers of the Inner Guide. The role of the teacher is to teach according to the evolving levels of competence of the disciple and to guide his efforts, while the role of the student is to make the efforts demanded of him, to obey the teacher and to be receptive to his teachings and to the graces of the spiritual states bestowed on him as divine gifts[10], but always in conformity to his faith and his critical Intellect. Within the parameters of sympathetic receptivity and spiritual courtesy—which require the disciple to love and honor the teacher—and of the Law—which is both "right thinking" (or "orthodoxy", in its strict etymological sense) and "right conduct" (or "orthopraxy")—Traditional education is premised upon the pre-eminence of the inner over the outer, and therefore of the Inner Guide over the Outer Guide. Hence the adage, "If you meet the Buddha on the path, slay him!"[11] Far from being a prescription for individualism or a licensing of exemption from the Law, this adage speaks to the liberating goal of spiritual education. Just as a parent directs and guides a child through the stages of its education until it reaches its maturity—whereafter the child, as an adult, becomes responsible for its own decisions, thereby in a sense outgrowing its dependence on the parent—so too the disciple is guided by the teacher to the threshold of spiritual maturity, whereafter the disciple crosses the threshold accompanied only by the Inner Guide whom the Outer Guide has fully awakened. Prior to such awakening, there remains the constant danger that the dis-

---

[10] In Traditional education, the efforts of the disciple enable him to attain certain "stations" ("*maqamat*" in Arabic), but these are distinct from the spiritual "states" ("*ahwal*" in Arabic) that are conferred by Grace.

[11] This paradoxical adage must not be misunderstood: it is only when the Inner Guide is functional—as active intelligence, rather than as passive conformity—that it will intelligently appreciate and properly accede to the legitimate authority of the Outer Guide. Obedience to the Law and submission of the egoic self to the greater Self (represented by the Outer Guide or Master) are vital components of any Traditional education.

ciple will succumb to intellectual pride or the temptations of the will—both beguilements of the egoic self. It is to protect against these dangers, among others, that Tradition counsels the guidance of a spiritual teacher and requires the disciplines of initiation.

We referred earlier to the fact that, in general, Traditional learning encompasses a doctrine of Reality and a methodology for Realization. Beyond the various conventional forms of literacy, Tradition instructs us in the various dimensions of spiritual literacy. While conventional education offers us the understanding, training and techniques to develop those skills that are necessary to operate the self and the world in a mechanistic and utilitarian sense, Traditional education aims to initiate us into the mysteries of life through the divine imagination, symbolic knowledge and spiritual disciplines that will, by the divine Grace, awaken us to the depth and height of our transcendent senses. Thereby, we can expand our awareness of things, discerning them with the "eyes of our eyes" and with the "ears of our ears". By perceiving the universe through these inner senses—which are aspects of the Intellect—we become aware of its underlying harmony of the divine theophany, the beauty of the "Face of God". This awareness and vision in turn reconnects us to the universe through a participative sympathy that is the root of all spiritual ethics. By living our lives integrally, in conformity with this theophanic vision and the awareness of our intrinsic harmony with all creatures, we are alchemically transformed into spiritually alive and engaged souls. This transformative vision is an antidote to the dehumanizing and soul-destroying influences of the materialistic world of modernism that René Guénon has famously referred to as "The Reign of Quantity".

By the gift of this transformative vision—which Traditional training teaches through a combination of contemplative and hermeneutic techniques that fall under the broad heading of "prayer"—we can come to see the world as a unified whole, rather than as the fragmentary world of mind and matter. Matter is just one dimension within a vertical and hierarchic continuum of reality that descends from the One Absolute Source through multiple contingent levels of reality that are transcendentally and supra-formally unified. The ever-renewing theophany can then be seen as a creative aspect of the Presence that mercifully reintegrates and replenishes creation within its divine womb. This discernment enables us to appreciate the fragility and bounty of the gift of life and of a world that is destroyed and remade in each moment as an act of divine compassion and love. Through the blessing of this vision, we can awaken to our individual purpose in life, to express those special qualities and attributes with which our souls are compassionately and uniquely endowed. We can situate our relationships within an ethical dimension that connects us with the rest of creation. We can understand our existential purpose within the context of the larger dynamic of life as a descent from our Place of Origin, and as an ascent to our Place of Return—both these abodes being the One ground of being which is Ever-Present and is our innermost Center. By appreciating our intrinsic poverty in relation to that transcendent Center, we are able to detach ourselves from the contingent aspects of reality, and at the same time to discover within that Center the source of our abiding joy, transcending the sufferings and illusions of this world. Thus we can awaken to our own existential purpose, and to our own creative gifts and powers, conscious of the blessings we have to offer other creatures, and that they have to offer us. We can embrace the world sympathetically, aware of its complementarity and inter-dependence, united in our diversity, seeing our reflection in it and its reflection in us.

To see the world in this special way, one must be trained to look with the Inner Eye of the Heart—the Eye of the Intellect. This requires a proper orientation—the search for the Center everywhere. To combat the centrifugal tendencies of the world, the Traditional teacher initiates the student in the hermeneutics and techniques of "prayer". In general, these involve the remembrance or witnessing of one's existential context, that God alone is, that creation is a theophany emerging continually from the infinite bounty and compassion of the divine, that all creatures are united in the hierarchical order of the divine matrix, which defines both their individual rights and their ethical responsibilities, and that man must therefore worship his Creator and must respect His

Divine Face in all His creatures. Prayer, then, is more than a liturgy or the recitation of a prescribed formula. It is a perpetual hermeneutic, of which beauty and virtue, and all their complements such as love and wonder and gratitude, are the resonance. Prayer is an opening into mystery and intimacy, and, above all, an engagement with Presence. It is the central component of Traditional praxis, the practice of a quality of attention by which one can be fully engaged and present in life, in sympathetic participation with the Other as a part of our Self.

The development of an ethical sensibility is a vital component of a Traditional education. According to Traditional metaphysics, the cosmos is substantively "good" and its ongoing creation and integration within the divine womb are sustained acts of divine compassion. Mankind, who is formed in the divine image, is created to reflect these divine qualities of goodness and compassion. Virtue is the inner substance of reality, and so of beauty, which is its outward expression. By contrast with this Traditional view, modernist theories of ethical behavior reduce ethics to mechanistic prescriptions justified by utilitarian needs or consensual preferences that are not rooted in any principled notion of objective Truth. By contrast, the ethos of Tradition is predicated on a metaphysical structure of reality in which the Other is *seen* and, more importantly, *felt* as an aspect of the Self. It is through this participative connection of sympathy that metaphysical truth is embodied as virtue.

The counterpart of virtue is beauty. The development of an aesthetic sensibility is therefore another vital component of a Traditional education. In Traditional metaphysics, "beauty" is the radiant effulgence of the divine. It is the presence of the Center in the periphery. The aesthetic sense therefore corresponds to the sense of the sacred and to the wholeness and harmony that is implicit in the divine order. It is only by finding the Center within us that the underlying order and the criterion of relationships can be known. It is only by discerning the Center in all things that one can achieve harmony and the abiding peace that is its corollary. In any Traditional education, the sense of the sacred is honed through the discipline of *ascesis*, the detachment from contingency. By this discipline, one creates the conditions of detachment that will remove the veils of egoic illusion that cloud our perception and that tempt our baser senses. It is through clarifying and cleansing our perceptions that we can perceive the Real. As man is a microcosm of the universe, it is by "polishing the mirror of the Self" that one can perceive the reflection within it of the divine theophany of the macrocosm. It is only through the inward gaze that opens into "the deepest freshness deep down things" that one can discover how "Nature is never spent"[12] but is an ever-renewing theophany. It is this continually replenishing fountain of life that is the core of beauty. It is ungraspable and fluid, yet abidingly present and still. It is therefore simultaneously mysterious and intimate. The Traditional doctrine of beauty therefore engages us in the Traditional praxis of ascetic discipline, by which we are enabled to detach ourselves from contingent reality and to open into the substantive presence of beauty, harmony and peace, which is the substance of our innermost Self. According to the Vedantic formula, "*sat-chit-ananda*", the abiding and blissful peace of "*ananda*" is an attribute of "*chit*", the ontologically participative consciousness of "*sat*", the transcendent Absolute who is the Sole Existent and our innermost Center or Self.

To sum up, these are the elements of a Traditional education: an initiation into the mysteries of Truth as Presence; the doctrine of Reality and Unity, and the method of Realization and Union; the "saving barque"[13] of prayer; the cultivation of the ethical sensibility of "virtue", and the aesthetic sensibility of "beauty". This is the wisdom that Tradition seeks to impart. The knowledge it seeks to convey is not merely of outer things, but is ontological—a part of our being, out of which it is drawn. The lessons that it offers are an antidote to the limited vision of reality that hubristically claims the part to be the whole, and that would deny us our noble

---

[12] These quotations are from Gerard Manley Hopkins' poem, "God's Grandeur".

[13] Schuon, Frithjof, *The Play of Masks*, World Wisdom Books, 1992.

birthright—the "kingdom of heaven", the divine treasure that lies buried within.

Part Three:

Book Reviews

Book Review:
Science of the Cosmos, Science of the Soul:
The Pertinence of Islamic Cosmology in the Modern World
By William C. Chittick
(Oxford, 2007, Oneworld)

During the course of the last three decades, William C. Chittick
has, through a remarkable series of scholarly publications and translations, introduced his many students and readers to the texts and
insights of a variety of traditional Muslim sages, two in particular—
Rumi[1] and Ibn 'Arabi[2]. These sages and their insights are a part of
what Chittick identifies as the "intellectual tradition", which is by
no means restricted to the Muslim world but is a universal heritage
found at the root of all faith traditions. In his previous publications, Chittick has let these sages speak to us in their own words,
and has largely refrained from commenting about the significance
of their spiritual insights to issues confronting the contemporary
world. This book is a departure for Chittick in that he offers it as
a commentary on the contemporary relevance of the intellectual
tradition.

The focus of Chittick's thesis is the epistemological distinction between two ways of knowing: the unmediated "intellectual"
('aqli) knowledge of self-realized wisdom which is associated with
the intellectual tradition, and the mediated "transmitted" (naqli)
knowledge of accepted authorities which is associated with modernism. Intellectual knowledge is intrinsically rooted in the soul's
depth, in the unitary vision of the "heart", and in the self-realizing
intellect's potential to actualize its innate and divinely endowed
predisposition (fitra) to wisdom. By contrast, transmitted knowledge is deracinated, cut off from its intellectual roots, and is built
instead upon a foundation of hearsay and the acceptance of con-

[1] The Sufi Path of Love, SUNY, NY, 1983

[2] The Sufi Path of Knowledge, SUNY, NY, 1989; Imaginal Worlds, SUNY, NY,
1994; The Self-Disclosure of God, SUNY, NY, 1998

ventional authorities, the "scientific priesthood" of modern-day experts and specialists who command a blind allegiance to their rigid ideology of scientific rationalism. Cut off from that unitary vision that pertains to the spiritual predisposition of humanity, transmitted knowledge is both fickle and malleable, rooted in dogmatism rather than in direct cognition, and susceptible to exploitation by those who invoke external authorities to shape the consensus of contemporary "wisdom."

Chittick sees modern science as "fundamentally a transmitted science, not an intellectual science" because the modern scientist, while trained to privilege knowledge verified by experimentation within a "sensualist and empirical epistemology," is primarily trained to accept transmitted knowledge based on the consensus of the scientific community and its experts, rather than to independently seek knowledge through direct unmediated experience and realization. Chittick quotes Brian Appleyard: "Scientists who insist that they are telling us how the world incontrovertibly is are asking for our faith in their subjective certainty of their own objectivity." This epistemological distinction between intellectual and transmitted knowledge points to a cosmological rupture found at the heart of the modern scientific worldview, and rooted in the Cartesian bifurcation of mind and matter—of the psychologized knowing subject and the materialized known object. According to this perspective, the world is reduced to mechanism and knowing to instrumental reasoning. The modernist epistemology thus lacks what Tu Weiming calls the "anthropocosmic vision," the integral correspondence between the microcosm that is man and the macrocosm that is the larger universe—a correspondence that is central to the unitary vision of all traditional cosmologies. In the materialized universe, man is removed from the world because the world is cut off from "the unseen realm that is the home of the human spirit." As a result, modern science aims at controlling the world that it is in effect separated from, while intellectual science aims at self-mastery and thereby harmonization with the world within which it participates.

Early Muslim scientists were certainly interested in exploring the mechanisms of the created world, but, unlike the contemporary scientists whose knowledge is fragmented, non-participative and dissociated from any unifying cosmological vision, traditional Muslim scientists premised their intellectual quest for knowledge on the principle of *tawhid*, the unitary cosmological vision which related all things to God. The outer universe of the world reflected the inner universe of the self, and therefore, for Muslim scientists, who operated within the intellectual tradition, "the purpose of studying the macrocosm (was) to come to understand the powers and capacities of the microcosm." This unitary vision defined man's privileged role as steward and vicegerent within the world, and his purpose as taking on the qualities of the divine through the realization of the divine names and attributes present within creation and in his soul. Accordingly the traditional Muslim scientist saw the material universe as an aspect of a spiritually rooted and unfolded universe that integrally included oneself, and pursued knowledge for the greater purpose of being a fully realized human being (*muhaqqiq*)—one with the Real and with the created world. Pre-modern Muslim scientific knowledge was thus a facet of faith (based on the presupposition of "the transcendence, infinity, and absoluteness of the One Reality", which transcends definition, standing in "the standpoint of no standpoint"), though, as Chittick explains, no less intellectual for that because it was premised on *tahqiq* or verifying and realizing the truth for oneself, rather than on *taqlid* or imitating or following authority.

The goal of knowledge in the intellectual tradition is what Chittick terms "the *tahqiq* of *tawhid*," which is not merely to discern the truth through "awakened intelligence" but to conform to it by a spiritual transformation that demands both intellectual and moral perfection. In other words, to "know" reality is to "be" it. Intellectual discernment entails "unitary vision" (*tawhid*—requiring one "to see all things in relation to God"), while spiritual conformity entails the alchemical transformation of "virtue," the union of knowledge and being (*tahqiq*—requiring "both right thought and right activity"). The ethical significance of this epistemology is evident—to see things in relation to God means that each thing can be accorded its *haqq*, its rights in accord with the responsibilities entailed by the *haqq*. Chittick reminds the reader that, "In the premodern discourse, rights and responsibilities were two sides of the same coin, both founded on the Absolute *haqq* that is God."

Chittick's outline of the foundations of the intellectual tradition, which we have briefly described, forms the basis of his critique of modernism. Central to this critique is the difference between traditional and modernistic conceptions of the multiplicity of creation. While the former views multiplicity in relation to the Oneness that originates, sustains and integrates it, the latter fragments reality through processes of relativism or reductionism. The intellectual tradition focuses on the unitary vision of Absolute Reality ("*tawhid*"), whose Oneness embraces a multiplicity of derivative and subordinate realities ("*takthir*"), so that "*takthir* is kept subordinate to *tawhid*, which is to say that the many is seen as forever governed by the One". By contrast, modernism has abandoned the unitary vision of *tawhid*, and focuses only on the multiple gods of *takthir*, misguidedly absolutizing them in their own right, without subordinating their relative reality to the One Absolute Reality.

Underlying this misperception is the loss of the symbolic spirit and the impoverishment of the mythic discourse because of the reduction of "scientific" reality to quantifiable and measurable, material "facts", with the consequent disregard of any unseen and transcendent realities that might be discernible by the higher intellect that is referred to in traditional discourse as the "Eye of the Heart". By reducing reality to scientific quanta, modernity has perforce marginalized the qualitative aspects of reality that are not readily accessible to those limited methods of scientific epistemology that are privileged by the modernist ideology.

The result is a worldview that is increasingly superficial, the Reign of Quantity about which René Guénon has compellingly written. By disassociating qualities from quanta, and by reducing the world to mere mechanisms that are unrelated to the Absolute Reality and the divine attributes and qualities they reflect, knowledge becomes merely arbitrary and disengaged from any meaningful cosmic participation. Chittick remarks: "What appears arbitrary to Islamic thinking is any system of naming that ignores the transcendent dimensions to things and wrenches them from their qualitative contexts. It is these contexts that allow us to see how they are connected with greater wholes, with the world of the Unseen, and with the ultimately Real."

The corollary of modernism's loss of the unitary vision of Reality is the cause of a further criticism of modernism that Chittick levels: its loss of purpose and meaning. The lack of correspondence between the microcosmic subject and the macrocosmic object inevitably results in a disengaged reality, ultimately devoid of any objective meaning. By denying the unitary nature of meta-cosmic Reality, as both immanent and transcendent, modern man has effectively shut himself off from the cosmos and from those qualitative attributes that his knowing can take on in the depths of his being in order to be fully human. In Muslim terminology, without *tawhid,* or relating all derivative realities (including the self) to God, there can be no *tahqiq,* or actualized wisdom and cosmic harmonization through taking on the attributes of the divine.

Chittick offers many profound insights in this book that are of immense value to those who are concerned about the state of the contemporary world. Speaking of the state of modern Muslim thought, Chittick comments, "there can be no rehabilitation of Islamic thought unless Muslim thinkers put the *tahqiq* of *tawhid* back at the center of their concerns." This perception is grounded in the view that Islam is not merely an ideology, as it is for the so-called "fundamentalists", but an awakening into self-transformation that radiates as divine compassion. In another passage, Chittick laments the current state of the world of clashing fundamentalisms and points to the spiritual degeneration that underlies it: "When people fail to see the divine face wherever they look, they fall either into the one-sided transcendentalism that is characteristic of religious fundamentalism or the atheism and agnosticism that are characteristic of secular and scientific fundamentalism." In other words, the malaise of modernity is rooted in its loss of the spiritual vision that characterizes the intellectual tradition.

A careful examination of the author's arguments will reveal that Chittick is not unduly critical of science. He justly observes that, "science can provide no direct insight into the nature of the unseen realm that is the home of the human spirit." And again that, "The quest for wisdom is qualitative, because it aims at the actualization of the qualities present in the divine image and named by the names of God. The scientific quest for knowledge and theoretical prowess is quantitative, because it aims to understand and control an ever-proliferating multiplicity of things." Chittick's criticisms in this area relate principally to the ideological claims of an over-reaching ideology of science (that he terms "scientism") and its epistemology—grounded in the material and physical world accessible to the senses and to instrumental reasoning, that deny or devalue the spiritual and metaphysical realms that are invisible to them. In several sections of the book, Chittick criticizes the scientific epistemology that has usurped the legitimacy of the higher intellect and its intuitive ways of knowing; for instance, he states:

> "Science gains its power from rejection of any sort of teleology, brute separation of subject and object, refusal to admit that consciousness and awareness are more real than material facts, exclusive concern with the domain of the senses, and disregard for the ultimate and the transcendent."

> "Scientism gives absolute importance to scientific theories and relativizes all other approaches to knowledge."

> "Scientism is a rationalizing ideology that has all the persuasive powers of technology, education, and the media to back it up. It provides the de facto theology for the civil religion of modernity."

The effects of a blind faith in this civil religion, are profound and, as Chittick reminds us, potentially devastating: "Scientific 'objectivity' and 'disinterest' become at best ignorance, at worst moral failing and spiritual disaster." In an early chapter of the book,

Chittick engages with the reader in a thought experiment, imagining what it might be like for a traditional visitor from the past to travel to our modern world. Chittick contrasts the traditional, integrated, hierarchical, devolved, and teleological worldview of this imaginary traveler, Ibn Yaqzan ("Son of Awake", or a *muhaqqiq*—awakened soul), with the modern, fragmented, flattened, polytheistic, schizophrenic, worldview of *takthir*. In a key passage that appears later in the book, Chittick remarks, "An impoverished and flattened universe is the mirror image of an impoverished and flattened soul. The death of God is nothing but the stultification of the human intellect. Social and ecological catastrophe is the inevitable consequence of psychic and spiritual dissolution. Cosmos and soul are not two separate realities, but two sides of the same coin, a coin that was minted in the image of God."

Authors who write books critical of the centrifugal trajectory of the modern world are often justly criticized for offering a one-sided, pessimistic, and fatalistic view of life. However, Chittick's approach, while undeniably critical of modernism, avoids this outcome by also reminding the reader of the centripetal trajectory of "the ascending arc" of Return, and of the saving grace of Divine Mercy, and the book thereby uplifts and operates to effectively empower those who yearn for meaning and transcendence. By reminding us of our true intellectual heritage, Chittick's critique of modernism belies the futility and pessimism of the outer conditions of the modern world by awakening us to our inner purpose and meaning—to the possibility of our "remembrance" of Reality as Compassion and its embodiment within us as "virtue".

Book Review:
Conversations with Wendell Berry
University Press of Mississippi, August 2007
(Literary Conversations Series)
Edited by Morris Allen Grubbs

Wendell Berry is not easily labeled. Known as a poet, author, and man of letters, he is also a farmer, agrarian reformer and environmentalist, a cultural and economic critic, and a defender of communitarian and family values and lifestyles, whose ideas are rooted practically in a sense of fidelity to place and community and in a commitment to community-based living. He was born into a farming heritage in Kentucky in 1934. After studying creative writing under Wallace Stegner at Stanford in 1958, he traveled abroad in Europe under a Guggenheim Fellowship in 1961, before returning to the USA to teach English briefly in the Bronx in New York, and then, in 1965, purchasing a farm and homestead, Lane's Landing, in his native Kentucky, and settling there with his family. For several years Berry pursued an academic career, teaching creative writing at the University of Kentucky till 1977, but he has since devoted himself to cultivating his farm, and tending to the needs and concerns of his family and community, while maintaining a prolific career as a writer. The recipient of several writing awards, Berry's ideas—in particular, his views on stewardship and sustainable communities—have gained the attention and garnered the support of traditionalists and critics of modernism over the years. Berry is a Fellow of the Temenos Academy in England.

Conversations with Wendell Berry is an anthology, edited by one of Berry's former students, which gathers in one place for the first time his various interviews spanning the period 1973 to 2006. Reading these interviews, one can discern a remarkable thematic coherence and consistency of thought, while observing, in his responses to the changing currents of time and topic, the perennial value of his ideas. This review of the anthology will attempt to provide an overview of the themes that emerge from his conversations, as far as possible in Berry's own words.

At the heart of Berry's worldview is the community. Berry speaks of a "community" as a "commonwealth," which is "a holding in common of many different things of value," an inclusive "pattern of practical relationships" and "a pattern of loyalties". "A good community is one in which people understand that in order to have certain good things, they have to have them in common." This idea of community is necessarily economic, and is based on the notion of a fidelity to place, to sharing space, and to improving the quality of life for all who live in that shared space, based on their common concerns and values. "When enough people in a place know themselves as members, then I believe the place will change for the better. That's a statement of faith necessarily, because most of us now don't live in such a place... most of us live in places and in neighborhoods dominated by the influence of individualism, by the endless justified selfishness of the consumer economy, and by the principle of competition."

The idea of community could easily be qualified to limit the definition to suit dominant elements in the group, as it is in some modernist discourse—for example, in secularist polemics of exclusion (think of the *hijab* controversy in France) or limits to reasonable accommodation (think of the Heurouxville controversy in Quebec); but Berry is clear that the vision of a community requires a greater magnanimity and pluralistic foundation than some modernistic communitarian views might allow. Berry is critical of the idea of an "intentional community": "I think the idea that you can have an intentional community is about as misleading as saying you can have an intentional life. If you're going to have a decent and stable community, you've got to produce the cultural and social forms by which to deal with the unexpected and the undesirable. The intentional community idea assumes that when you say love your neighbor as yourself, you have some kind of right to go out and pick your neighbor. I think that the ideal of loving your neighbor has to take on the possibility that he may be somebody you're going to have great difficulty loving or liking or even tolerating."

But where does one draw the line in defining the community and the outcast? Berry's broader approach to community is not defined by outer emblems of affiliation but by the commitment to the principle of neighborly love. This involves: "loving one another, taking care of one another, being thankful for the gifts of heaven and earth and our human forbears, taking good care of those gifts." For Berry, the community is the servant of its individual members, and this service, which is the seedbed of its culture, extends from the economic sphere—the cultivation of the land and its boun-ties—to the spheres of upbringing and education—the cultivation of values. As a corollary, Berry's notion of pluralism is founded on his particular view of community and its fidelity to people and place, which he distinguishes from broader or narrower notions of pluralism that are relativistic or superficial: "The pluralism that extends hospitability to just anything is not valid. There are stan-dards. Real pluralism extends respect—not tolerance—toward all rooted, locally adapted cultures that know what works and what doesn't work in a given place. That kind of pluralism doesn't exist now. In fact, as soon as a culture becomes rooted, our so-called pluralism *withdraws* its respect, labeling it provincialism or anach-ronism."

Berry's generous view of 'community' is related to his environ-mentalism and is based on the intimate relationship between man and the environment. "There is no line that you can draw between people and the elements they depend on. That's why this term 'environment' is so bothersome to me. 'Environment' is based on that dualism, the idea that you can separate human interests from the interests of everything else. You *cannot* do it. We eat the envi-ronment. It passes through our bodies every day, it passes in and out of our bodies. There is no distinction between ourselves and the so-called 'environment.' What we live in and from and with doesn't *surround* us—it's part of us. We're *of* it, and it's *of* us, and the rela-tionship is unspeakably intimate." But while there is no ultimate boundary between man and the environment, Berry nevertheless acknowledges a hierarchical basis to life and the responsibilities this entails: "Humans...have responsibilities that go above and below.

We're supposed to be humble and reverent toward the things that are above us and magnanimous to those things that are below us."

Underlying Berry's notions of community and environment is the sense of interconnectedness and interdependence, and reverence and responsibility, that are central to the meaning of faith for him. In one interview, Berry confides: "My approach to religion has pretty much been from the bottom up. I never was much good at the top-down version, and my understanding of religion has grown from my understanding of the things of time, from family and community life." He is critical of the conventional teachings of the Church: "The 'church'—in its organized forms—has always loved itself for excluding, and sometimes for killing, unbelievers and heretics. Christianity (in its Western forms, at least) has also tended to exclude nature—the body's life and all it depends on. Which is to say that it has not been interested enough in our economic life. It has been too easy to be 'a good Christian' while destroying the world that (we are told) God loves." Berry cautions against the effects of a materialistic and outwardly pietistic religion: "religion itself is increasingly industrialized: concerned with quantity, 'growth', fashionable thought and an inane sort of expert piety." Instead, Berry advocates a return to the heart of Christ's teachings, in particular their emphasis on love: "I think that if Christians quit worrying about being 'Christians' or church members and just undertook to do what Christ told them to do—love one another, love their enemies, take care of the helpless and the friendless and the unworthy and the no-account—then the 'church' might sooner or later dissolve into something much better." Berry views religion as an ecological idea, involving a shift in viewpoint from the idea of the Church to the whole of Creation—a shift that requires humankind to exercise the faculty of the spiritual imagination: "When St. Paul said that 'we are members of one another', he was using a far more inclusive 'we' than Christian institutions have generally thought. For me, this is the meaning of ecology. Whether we know it or not, whether we want to be or not, we are members of one another: humans (ourselves and our enemies), earthworms, whales, snakes, squirrels, trees, topsoil, flowers, weeds, germs, hills, rivers, swifts, and stones—all of 'us'. The work of the imagination, I feel, is to understand this."

Inevitably, these notions of interconnectedness and interdependence that lie at the heart of Berry's worldview are central to his views of economic life. Berry defines the economy in a way that pays due attention to "externalities," unlike many modernist economic theories: "Economy is our way of making a living. It connects the human household with the good things that sustain life. This involves the money economy and many other things that our present idea of 'economics' excludes: good work, good care of the materials and other gifts of nature, faithfulness to one another in all relationships." For Berry, good economics is tied to good community: "I think this starts with an attempt at criticism of one's economy... What are the things that one buys? How necessary or useful are they? What is their quality? Are they well grown or well made? What is their real cost to their producers and to the ecosystems in which they were produced? Almost inevitably when one asks these questions, one discovers that they are extremely difficult and sometimes impossible to answer. That frequently is because the things we buy have been produced so far away as to make impossible any stewardly interest on the part of the consumer. And this recognition leads to an even better question: how can these mysterious products brought here from so far away be replaced by products that have been produced near home? And that question, of course, leads to all manner of thoughts and questions about the possibility of a better, more self-sufficient local economy. What can we neighbors do for one another and for our place? What can our place do for us without damage to us or to it?" These kinds of questions and the approach they imply compel Berry to be critical of the exploitative globalized economy, which he views as a false kind of pluralism, one that is potentially destructive of the environment: "Today, local economies are being destroyed by the 'pluralistic', displaced, global economy, which has no respect for what works in a locality. The global economy is built on the principle that one place can be exploited, even destroyed, for the sake of another place. That is a bad kind of pluralism. There are standards relating to culture that go beyond the self-interest of any group. We must, first and foremost, ask what objective measures we can use in our efforts to live in the world without destroying it." For Berry, the problems of poor economics and of the lifestyle diseases that result from them are derived from the alienation of people from land and community. Things have grown too big, too complex, and we are losing our connection with reality, forfeiting control to systemic changes in a way that is threatening all we should truly value: "... we've lost the sense of connection between ourselves and the natural world... and this connection is economic necessarily." This is the principal reason that Berry is a proponent of locally self-sufficient communities. He cautions: "Creatures who grow beyond the carrying capacity of their habitats will die. So the right question is: will we restrain ourselves, or will we die?" The economics he advocates are based on prudence and responsibility: "Shorten the supply lines. Bring your economic geography back into your own view."

Berry advocates the need for real engagement with complexity in dealing with life. This requires an inner harmony and integrity. It requires a reconnection with the world, a reordering of elements so that a just response to complexity can then emerge: "Simplicity means that you have brought things to a kind of unity in yourself; you have made certain connections. That is, you have to make a just response to the real complexity of life in this world. People have tried to simplify themselves by severing the connections. That doesn't work. Severing connections makes complication. These bogus attempts at simplification ignore or despise the real complexity of the world. And ignoring complexity makes complication—in other words, a mess." In order to truly reconnect with the world, we must pay loving attention to the things that matter: "I want to live in a good place, and I know that people can't live in good places unless they know where they are and pay the closest, kindest attention to what they do there." This kind of attention requires us to be concerned about our relationship to our neighbors and our collective relationship with the land we share: "The primary concern has to be the cultural relation between people and land." This means that we need to learn not to want to live just anywhere, but in a particular place; to be a loyal steward of our habitats and the creatures we share it with; to cultivate our shared lands responsibly, conserving them and sustaining them; to be loyal to one's particular community while being open to all its members; to commit to a dignified life for all and to work responsibly in this cause as an engaged member of the community. Central to reconnection is the notion of "love" as a discipline: "Love is not just a feeling; it's a practice, something you practice whether you feel like it or not." Berry gives the example of a farmer having to milk a cow: this must be done when the cow needs milking, not when the farmer feels like it. This takes a fidelity rooted in the discipline of love—of both community and land. "I think we're developing a society now whose dominant effort is to get out of work. It's probably a measure of our decadence that we can talk about a 'work ethic'. Work isn't an ethic, work's a necessity."

Berry's ideas compel a rethinking of modernist premises in a variety of areas, and he has indeed much to say about the false premises of modernism, particularly as these might impact the community-based quality of life that he advocates. In one interview, Berry speaks of "the modern divorce between economy and religion—which is really just a version of the devastating old dualism of body and soul." In another interview, he is critical of the myth of progress, which, at its worst, becomes in his view a kind of determinism: "It substitutes this infinite advance toward better and better life in the material sense for the old pilgrimage, which you make by effort and grace, to become a better person." He also bemoans the loss of loving affection in the modernist emphasis on sexuality, rightly castigating promiscuity as a form of self-depreciation and exploitation: "To me, love is the source from which all else springs, and that is why the modern 'sophisticated' exploitation of sexual love is so regrettable, depressing and, I think, dangerous." He is critical of the sexual revolution: "The sexual revolution, based on the superstition of safe sex, is as big a failure as the 'peaceful atom (bomb)'. In the last 400 years, our attention has moved from the countenance to the specific sexual anatomy. When we read Shakespeare or Chaucer, we find that the great source of power is in the eyes... This change in focus of sexual love from the countenance to the genitals means that certain responsibilities are being refused. The countenance involves the spirit, the soul. If you deal with people in terms that require you to meet their eyes, you are dealing with them as living souls, not just as bodies. Further, if you deal with them as living souls you recognize instantly that certain things are demanded; for one, you must acknowledge them as people with lives, needs, problems. Of course, if we can keep the countenance out of it, we don't have to take responsibility for the complexity of the encounter. We can remain in our 'animal nature.' However, once we exclude responsibility from the encounter, we have also obliterated its power."

For those who are familiar with his writings, and also for those who are approaching Berry's thinking for the first time, this book of conversations and interviews is a fine introduction, overview, and synthesis of the themes and ideas that lie at the heart of his worldview—a perspective that invites a reorientation to the Center and that has much wisdom to offer us in these disorienting times.

Book Review:

The World Turned Inside Out: Henry Corbin and Islamic
Mysticism
By Tom Cheetham
Spring Journal Books, Conn., 2003

Green Man, Earth Angel: The Prophetic Tradition and the Battle
for the Soul of the World
By Tom Cheetham
SUNY, New York, 2005

After Prophecy: Imagination, Incarnation, and the Unity of the
Prophetic Tradition (Lectures for the Temenos Academy)
By Tom Cheetham
Spring Journal Books, Louisiana, 2007

This trilogy of works centers on the metaphysical thought of the
French Islamic scholar, Henry Corbin (1903-1978). A student of
Scholasticism under Etienne Gilson, and a close associate of Louis
Massignon (whose position he succeeded, as Director of Islamic
Studies at the Sorbonne), Corbin was not only a pre-eminent theologian but also a mystical philosopher. Influenced by the German
theological tradition of Boehme, Luther, Hamann, Heidegger, and
Barth, among others, Corbin developed a philosophy of mystical
hermeneutics, which drew greatly from Christian and Muslim
mystics and philosophers who viewed reality phenomenologically,
as an unveiling of the inner Light of transcendent Reality. A major
figure (along with Jung, Eliade, and Scholem) at the Eranos confer-
ences, Corbin spent many years living in the Muslim world and was
regarded in the West as an authority on medieval Muslim philosophy (particularly the teachings of Avicenna, Suhrawardi, and Ibn
'Arabi). Also, as head of the Franco-Iranian Institute in Tehran, he
was a specialist in Irano-Islamic studies (particularly Suhrawardi's
revival of Zoroastrian angelology), Persian Sufism (in particular,

Mulla Sadra), and Shi'a theosophy (including Isma'ili gnosis and hermeneutics). Corbin's legacy has been immense, ranging from his influence upon traditionalist metaphysicians or those with traditionalist leanings (notably, Seyyed Hossein Nasr, Toshohiko Izutsu, William C. Chittick, Sachiko Murata, Hermann Landolt, Kathleen Raine and Philip Sherrard), and extending beyond into the fields of literature and psychology (his ideas have influenced, for example, the literary critic, Harold Bloom and the Jungian scholar, James Hillman).

Dr. Cheetham is a scholar of Corbin, and a fellow of the Temenos Academy, which—through its journal and lectures devoted to the Arts of the Imagination, and to Perennial Philosophy, both arguably key aspects of Corbin's thought—has promoted Corbin's work for several decades. Cheetham also maintains an online blog on Corbin at "http://henrycorbinproject.blogspot.com".

In *The World Turned Inside Out*, Cheetham has provided perhaps the best available introduction to Corbin's thought for the general reader. The second and particularly the third volumes of this trilogy, *Green Man, Earth Angel*, and *After Prophecy*, respectively, are more interpretive works, exploring the relevance and significance of Corbin's ideas for our lives and the issues that confront us in the modern world. Those volumes will be of especial interest to readers of *Sacred Web*, given their interpretive focus. In the comments that follow, we have chosen to review the works collectively, as a trilogy, rather than individually. For readers unfamiliar with Corbin's writings, they might do well to read the books in the order they were written. For others who may be more familiar with Corbin's ideas—and this review will attempt to provide the reader with an outline of the key ideas—and who wish to sample but one book in this trilogy, we would recommend the final volume which anthologizes Cheetham's lectures for the Temenos Academy.

In considering Corbin's ideas, Cheetham remarks on the "astonishing variety of influences" that shaped them—"Christian theology, Heideggerian phenomenology, and Islamic mysticism fused with Zoroastrian angelology; all united by a deep reverence for what in Islam is called the Primordial Revelation: the book of nature." Cheetham traces the early philosophical influences of Heidegger in Corbin's hermeneutics and phenomenology, clarifying that unlike for Heidegger, whose quest for the "history of Being" remained situated entirely within the Western philosophical tradition, Corbin's research extended beyond and came to be largely influenced by Irano-Islamic metaphysics, which led him in the direction of a transcendentally rooted understanding of "Being" as "Presence"—an understanding based on the reality of the "*mundus imaginilis*", the realm of the Creative Imagination. The reality of the imaginal world (Cheetham states: "Corbin called it the *mundus imaginilis*, the imaginal world, to underscore the fact that it is not *imaginary* or unreal") was central to Corbin's worldview. This domain of reality was "a median and mediating power" between the sensible and the intellectual, the metaphysical threshold ("*barzakh*") of transcendence and of immanence. By contrast, Heidegger (in George Steiner's appraisal of him) based his metaphysics on an effort to view reality as immanence without transcendence. In Cheetham's words, "Heidegger tried to erect a philosophy denying the need for the category of the Person and the transcendence implicit in that Being." Corbin, however, regarded "Being" not as an escape from the particulars of mundane reality into the realm of abstraction, but as an opening into the "spiritual corporeity" of Divine Presence rooted in Personhood.

Corbin's true influences in this regard were the Sufi and Shi'ite metaphysicians about whom he later wrote, including in particular, Avicenna (981-1037), Suhrawardi (1155-1191), Ibn 'Arabi (1165-1240), and Mulla Sadra (c.1571-1640). Corbin was introduced to Suhrawardi's works by Massignon, and the influence on him of this twelfth-century Persian mystic was seminal. Corbin later wrote: "[T]hrough my meeting with Suhrawardi, my spiritual destiny for the passage through this world was sealed. Platonism, expressed in terms of the Zoroastrian angelology of ancient Persia, illuminated the path I was seeking." From Suhrawardi, the founder of the Illuminationist School of Persian mysticism, Corbin learned of the importance of the intermediary imaginal realm as the means of the visionary perception of the "sacral light" that was central to Zoroastrian faith and to the Abrahamic traditions. Thus in the Zoroastrian tradition, the Celestial Light of Ohrmazd and His six Archangels in Avestan cosmology, is opposed to the Darkness of Ahriman. The Light is embodied for all created beings in their Fravarti or personal angel and soul's guide, and illuminates the path of the soul's personal embodiment of the Light through spiritual transformation. Similarly, the Light of God appears as the "Burning Bush" in Judaism, the apparitions of Gabriel to Mary and Muhammad, and as the symbolic "Light upon Light" of the Surah of Light in Islam. These are images of the divine theophany and of the soul's destiny to actualize on earth the "Energy of sacral Light" through spiritual transformation.

From the Muslim texts that he studied, Corbin learned how life could be viewed as a "dramaturgy", an awakening of the soul through its encounter with its archetypal image in the "*imago mundi*"—with the personified presence of the soul's Heavenly Twin, its Guiding Angel or Fravarti. The soul's encounter with its "Angel" is to be understood here as its submission to the active Intelligence. The Angel is identified with such figures as the Paraclete in the Gospel of St. John, or Khidr in the Koran, with the Archangel Gabriel, and with the *Logos* or Angel Holy Spirit. Corbin was greatly influenced here not only by Suhrawardi's revival of Mazdean angelology, but also by the Kubrawite phenomenology of lights and colors developed by the central Asian school of Sufism of Najm al-Din Kubra (1146-1220), and his followers Najmeddin Razi (d. 1256) and Alaoddawleh Semnani (1261-1336), as well as the illuminationist metaphysics (of illumination as the "intensifica-tion of being" and inner light) associated with the Persian, Mulla Sadra. This "imaginal" encounter with the Angel, with "the light of that Presence which is the ultimate source of all personification" formed the basis of the soul's individuation, its ethical valorization and its harmonization with the world. Cheetham notes: "It is not too much to say that Corbin's entire work revolves around the ontological priority of the individual. It is the Presence of the Angel that provides the conditions for the possibility of the experience of the Person."

It is only through our interiority and heliotropic orientation to the Angel Face that we can hope to unveil the theophanies of the soul and the world. The Angel is the inner Guide, the exegete, the Intellect, the "Khidr of your being." It is also the hermeneutical principle or *ta'wil*, the opening to the Origin, unveiling the Divine Face that is uniquely and "imaginally" discernable by each visionary. Here, knowledge and being interpenetrate. How we see the world is dependent on the quality of our vision. What we perceive is dependent on how we choose to see. According to the doctrine that "like can only be known by like", what is known corresponds to the mode of being of the knower: Light can only be perceived by light. We can come to know the hierarchies of being through a growth of consciousness—through *dhikr* or prayerful and contemplative remembrance, which is central to Corbin's praxis of spiritual awareness and transformation. Cheetham remarks that for Corbin, "Prayer is the supreme form of the creative imagination, and as such is the ultimate exercise of human freedom." It is through the discipline of *dhikr* or the intensification of spiritual awareness that we are enabled to ascend to the divine. Our growth in spiritual consciousness effects our alchemical transformation into an ontologically higher "mode of presence," so that our growth in knowing corresponds to the intensification of our being as light.

The mediate realm of "imaginal" archetypes and the symbolic significance of the "image" that corresponds to the visionary's degree of receptivity are central to Corbin's ideas. They are the basis of his theophanic worldview of creation as the "Face of God", and of his doctrine of the Guiding Angel that is the soul's heavenly counterpart and the means of its spiritual transformation into the "Body of Light." It is in this context that one can understand Corbin's critique of the official Church doctrine of the Incarnation by which Jesus is the hypostatic union of God and man, a divine person with two natures—fully human and fully God. Historically, the doctrine of the *Logos* reconciled Christian theology with Greek philosophy in respect of the possibility of the Supreme Being's ability to relate personally to His creatures. But if the *Logos* was identified with Christ, it became necessary to consider the theological difference between the Father and the "human" personality of Christ as the Word of God. The Council of Nicea in 325 had rejected the Arian view that Christ, though the first among creatures, was not co-eternal with God, decreeing instead that Father and Son were of one substance—*homoousis*. In a further elaboration of this position, the Council of Chalcedon in 451 had decreed the official doctrine of Incarnation—that the Son was consubstantial with the Father, being "of two natures in one person" so that the divine and human were united substantially, yet by nature distinct. Corbin found the official doctrine of the Incarnation to be deeply flawed because it had reduced the theophanic significance of the Incarnation to a mere doctrine, a dogma rather than a "*dokema*" or theophany. By allowing God to be seen as entering history and so into social and material reality, the Incarnation had effectively secularized the sacred and dissolved the transcendent God into the natural world. By adopting the viewpoint that Jesus *was* God, the Church had effectively compromised the metamorphic function of the Logos as a theophanic vision. Corbin preferred to regard the Incarnation in terms of a fusion of docetism (the view that Christ was an apparition of God) and early Ebionitism (the view that Christ was a Prophet, a human messenger of God). He emphasized that a thread of docetic angelology—that of the True Prophet and Guiding Angel—runs through each of the Abrahamic faiths and this was a key to his ecumenic regard for the monotheistic faiths as an Abrahamic Harmony that he termed "*Harmonia Abrahamica*." Corbin's docetic interpretation of the Incarnation eliminates any schism between matter and spirit, so that Christ's reality is not based on a bifurcation of Christ's dual nature but on the theophanic reality of his unique personhood, representing each human being's potential for spiritual transformation and the realization of his or her own personhood. The Incarnation was the reality of the Word made flesh—not matter. The significance is that "flesh" is not impersonal or abstract (like matter) but is the concretely unique personified fragment of the Real Presence of God. Rightly understood, Corbin claimed that Christ was the Angel Holy Spirit, a theophanic vision and archetypal embodiment of Personhood, of the Real Presence of the Person—both "ensouled flesh and personal substance," the imaginal reality and potential of each soul.

Cheetham discusses how Corbin's views share some similarity with those of the Catholic theologian, Hans Urs von Balthasar, and how it also differs from Balthasar's Trinitarian emphasis which it rejects. Balthasar interprets the Incarnation in terms of God's self-giving (*kenotic*) love through Christ, who is the immanent and intimate aspect of God's transcendent mystery. But while for Balthasar Christ is the absolute guarantor of objectivity (the only Son of the Father), for Corbin Christ is the Heavenly Twin who appears in various other guises as the Soul of the World and is the source of all Presence. Christ is the *Christos Angelos*, the theophanic vision of God coming into contact with humanity only by transforming the latter. Cheetham summarizes: "Theophanic psychocosmology is based upon this transfiguration. In it ontology and epistemology are united in a cosmogenesis of the individual." The key to understanding this alchemical "transfiguration" is the role of the transfiguring presence of the Christic Image and its ability to ignite the soul of the seer. In the imaginal realm, thought is united with being and the mode of presence is dependent on the orientation of the soul because "whatever is received is received according to the mode of the receiver."

This "unveiling" of the soul of the self and the world is the hermeneutical counterpart to our orientation to the Divine Face. It is only by our receptivity to the Word that we can decode the true meaning of the cosmic Book—which includes ourself. By orienting ourselves to transcendence, by interpreting the world and our selves imaginally as manifestations of a greater reality, we are able to unveil the innermost Self that pervades all creation. For Corbin, the aim of hermeneutics, which he regarded as the proper function of phenomenology, was the recovery of the interiority of the text of the soul and the world. The aim is to unveil the Face of the Self, to recover the "Lost Speech", the integral Word or *Logos*. But Corbin was clear that *ta'wil*, the hermeneutical orientation to the Origin or *awwal*, "is not theory; it is an initiation to vision." And this vision is transformative. Knowledge is realizational: to *know* is also to *be*.

Reality, in its corporeal intimacy cannot be properly reduced to an abstract idea, nor can its essential mystery be reduced to its outer surface or literal form. Rather, the world must transcend both abstraction and literalism and be perceived imaginally, symbolically, and participatively, as a continually renewing theophany of the unveiling of Presence so that each unveiling is in respect of a unique and individualized manifestation of the divine theophany that is the Face of God. Corbin explained that "the Divine Being is not fragmented, but wholly present in *each* instance, individualized in *each* theophany" because, as Ibn 'Arabi taught, "Each being has as his God only his particular Lord, he cannot possibly have the Whole." This "wholeness" ("holiness") or "Presence" means that each being can, by choosing to see the Other in this participative mode, view the world conjunctively rather than disjunctively, through "a kind of reciprocal imaginative interaction, a sympathy between self and world." This kind of engaged interpretive envisioning entails an imaginative sympathy between subject and object so that what we see in our clarified perception is the unveiling of the Presence of the Supreme Reality of the Divine Subject who manifests that continually renewing theophany within which we immanently participate and which transcends the disjunctive vision of our egoic subjectivity.

Corbin's epistemology is founded on the doctrine of participation and it is sympathy that is the foundation of his ethics. His hermeneutics engage our capacity for angelic vision, for the iconoclastic rendering of the idol as transparent to the light invested in it. This involves a way of seeing that Corbin speaks of in terms of the hermeneutics of "transmuting the idol into an icon." To endow things with ontological presence, to see them in all their spiritual corporeity, one has to perceive them imaginally, with a participative sympathy. This involves breaking "through the mutual isolation of consciousness and its object, of thought and being," writes Corbin, adding: "here phenomenology becomes ontology." As Cheetham explains, "It is sympathy that is the prerequisite of *ta'wil*...It is the ability to open oneself to the presence of things and of persons." This is what Corbin refers to as the "cognitive function of sympathy" or, adopting the terminology of Etienne Souriau, calls "the angelic function of a being." What is at stake here is the recovery of the meaning of spirit as substance, not as dichotomies of mind and matter, but as the embodied Presence of body, mind, and being, poised here and now in what the poet Gary Snyder calls the "mythological present"—as a concrete reality that is a theophany opening into mystery. To open ourselves to such a Presence requires us to have "a sensate, imaginative sympathy" where images carry an ontological force, and where the natures of the world and the soul interpenetrate and so each can meet the "Other" in mutual Presence. As Cheetham notes, "This kind of attention is intensely relational because it is felt, it is sensuous, and it is embodied."

It is easy to understand why, for Corbin, prayer, love, and beauty would play a central role in spiritual transformation. He regarded prayer as the supreme act of the Creative Imagination, as one's orientation to the Pole Star of transcendent Being. Thus it was "the expression of a mode of being" and the means by which Creator and Creature were irrevocably entwined in mutual sympathy. Prayer, thus understood, is the response of each soul to the prophetic summons to experience divine love and beauty through seeing the world as a theophany, through seeking the Angel Holy Spirit in our encounters with the Other, and through incarnating love with other *persons* whom we encounter not merely abstractly, through their *personas*, but as the iconic face of the Beloved, in the esoteric unity of Love, Lover and Beloved.

For Corbin, beauty is the essential divine attribute and the source and reality of our love. To perceive this divine beauty, however, requires a quality of attention and perception that has an ethical foundation, one that is premised on the profound connections between *ascesis* and *aesthetics*, between renunciation and beauty. Cheetham uses this idea to provide a critique of modernity in respect of the loss of this dimension of perception, suggesting that what is required to regain an appreciation of beauty in the world is a quality of detachment. To "refuse to become unconsciously ensnared by the allurements of a commercialized world ... (t)o begin to be sensitive to the manifold effects of this impersonal world on our actions, thoughts, and emotions and so gain some distance from it is already an act of renunciation and of aesthetic discrimination." [Though Cheetham uses the word "renunciation" in this quote, the better term might have been "detachment."] But the detachment that pulls us away from things must be balanced by the sympathy that draws us to them. Aesthetics, Cheetham observes, is rooted in a cosmological *synaesthesia*: "All the beings of the world are connected within and among themselves by the vibrations of harmonic *sympathy*. Our place among them is not one of dominion, but of interconnection." The imagination is synaesthetic, filled with harmonic sympathy: "When harmonic sympathy is fully in operation, then *to speak* is *to be*. Understanding something, we say we can *make sense* of it, and now it is clear that this making sense is not theoretical, but is primarily aesthetic, concrete, and sensuous." It is the function of beauty to awaken us to the spiritually embodied realization of Presence: "When imagination and renunciation are wed, then all the world becomes sensuous and my individual world, my life, can make sense to me. The spiritual world is no longer abstract and distant, but alive and intensely real." Cheetham laments, "The true meaning of the word *substance* has faded from our consciousness. The spirit *is* substantial. Understanding this can help reclaim a sense of the concrete significance of the individual."

In the second and third volumes of the Corbin trilogy, in particular, Cheetham considers Corbin's ideas and their significance in providing a critique of modernism. The defining characteristic of modernism is its loss of a cosmological sense of wholeness, of a hierarchical continuum that includes the verticality of transcendence. Just eight months before his death, Corbin had written: "To confuse Being with being is the metaphysical catastrophe." This "metaphysical catastrophe" has led, in Cheetham's recounting of the implications to modernity of Corbin's ideas, to "three great crises: a rupture between the individual and the Divine, a severing of the felt connection between human beings and the living earth, and a profound breakdown of long-held assumptions about the nature and function of language In traditional terminology, we are witnessing a collapse of the structures that make sense of the relations among God, Creation, Logos, and the human person." These are respectively, the crises of the spirit, the environment, of the loss of meaning.

Cheetham notes that a shift from a conjunctive to a disjunctive mode of perception occurred in Western Europe around the 12th century, resulting in a "withdrawal of participation", a disharmony between man and nature, and the birth of a mechanistic cosmology based on abstract materialism. "It was Corbin's contention that European civilization experienced a 'metaphysical catastrophe' as a result of what we might call the Great Disjunction. This was signaled by the final triumph of the Aristoteleanism of Averroes over Platonic and neo-Platonic cosmology championed by Avicenna. To the defeat of that cosmology is coupled the disappearance of the *anima mundi*, the Soul of the World. The catastrophic event that gave rise to modernity is the loss of the soul of the world."

The loss of the imaginal realm has both materialized and abstracted reality, leading to the loss of the theophanic sense of Presence, the sense of the sacred. Cheetham considers at some length the attempts by modern psychology, particularly through the theories of Jung and his research into traditional alchemy, to recover this lost realm. He cites Corbin's criticism of Jung that his theories were overly empirical and not grounded in sound metaphysics. Readers of this journal will know that traditionalist authors, notably Titus Burckhardt, have criticized Jung's conflation of the spirit and the psyche. This conflation is at the heart of Corbin's critique. Cheetham focuses on Corbin's criticism that Jung failed to transcend the realm of the psychic world, and so to properly distinguish between two kinds of metaphysical darkness: the demonic darkness of nihilism and the hypertrophic (Faustian or Nietzschean) self, and the mystical darkness of poverty that opens into the plenitude of theophanic light. In Corbin's traditional metaphysics, there exists a higher consciousness than our ordinary consciousness, one that is intensely personal, in contrast to Jung's undifferentiated consciousness that is "collective" and unable to transcend the impersonal laws of the natural world. This higher consciousness is signaled by the Black Light of *fana'* (or egoic death), and associated in the spiritual journey with the flight into the Darkness of the *Deus absconditus*, the Hidden Treasure of the celebrated *Hadith* ("I was a Hidden Treasure and yearned to be known, so I created the world in order to be known"). It precedes the Green Light of *baqa'*, of the ultimate theophany, which is associated with pleroma of the *Deus revelatus*. Jung failed to distinguish between these two types of darkness. For Jung, good and evil were psychic projections that needed, as opposites, to be integrated within the self. In Jungian therapy, therefore, the dark side, represented by the psychic *shadow* of our struggle with material darkness, was an element to be integrated within the individuated self, not to be overcome or repressed. But as Corbin explained, only complementary elements could be integrated, not contradictory ones. God was Good, not evil, and therefore the demonic darkness of the Black Light of the psychic *shadow* was to be vanquished by the spiritual transformation of the self into the Body of Light (as the Illuminationists claimed), and not integrated (as Jung claimed). The task of putting on the Body of Light occurs by the simultaneous growth in spiritual consciousness and illumination of being, and represents for Corbin the path of spiritual ascent. Of this ascent, Cheetham observes that even though it involves purgation of darkness, the necessary self-emptying (though not integrative in the Jungian sense) is a path to wholeness: "This ascension does involve increasing wholeness, since one does become more complete, more real, closer to God. To attain the full possibilities of human perfection human beings have to experience to some degree all the attributes of God. But the journey toward the Divine consists in overcoming that which is lower, not in integrating it to become whole. The lower is the less real; one includes it only by surpassing it. The wholeness to be attained is a wholeness of perfection, not a wholeness of inclusion." In the end, the path to Light lies through Darkness: we can know only through our own unknowingness, and we can be born into Being only through our own mystical poverty.

The stance that is involved in spiritual growth, then, is one of self-discipline (*ascesis*), not indulgence, of sympathy (*aesthetics*), not an-aesthetization, of love (*caritas*), not power. Cheetham is rightly critical of the lustful, desensitizing and power-driven forces that pit man against nature and that dominate the modern world. He writes: "... in so far as we live in a world dominated by the products of the human economy, oriented towards producing and gratifying human desires, we will suffer from a dangerous restriction of experience, thought, and expression, and of our capacities for love and relationship, lacking even the memory of the desire for transcendence... A degree of poverty is a prerequisite for the experience of the fullness of this world. This poverty is the result of letting go of a desperate grip upon the world. Creation unfolds only when power is renounced. For the things of this world grow opaque when we try to control and possess them. They withdraw into themselves and block our access to the riches at the roots of things." Paradoxically, we must open into the darkness of the unknown in order to discover the Presence that we, and the world, are. Corbin presents an alternative vision of life grounded in the renunciation of power, in mystical poverty, freed from passions for control, "because everything is gratuitous—it is all a Gift." This higher consciousness is the basis of a spiritual ecology that is implicit in Corbin's ideas. Cheetham is critical of the materialistic scientism that overreaches, that enacts the creed that there is nothing in the universe that cannot, and should not, be unveiled, or that is inviolate. It secularizes and demystifies the world to the point that the soul becomes unmoored, and enters what Corbin terms its "vagabondage and perdition." From Corbin's traditional perspective, the soul and the world should not be pitted against each other, but should be seen as mirrors of each other, as microcosm and macrocosm within the same cosmos. In contrast to the technologies of modernistic science, which are grounded in the lustful desire for power and its ideological assumptions ("that knowledge is synonymous with power, and power is always good, and that knowledge must invariably be exercised by changing the world"), Cheetham advocates the development of counter-technologies in modernity to "help us reveal that everything we need is already at hand." And it is to poetry and the project of recovering the Lost Speech that he turns to search for a solution.

At the heart of Cheetham's critique of modernism is his contention that man has experienced a loss of meaning through his loss of the imaginal realm. Corbin correctly identifies the need for the application of a hermeneutical corrective to address this loss of meaning. In Islamic metaphysics, creation is divine speech, and all creatures are revealed "words of God." The world is an ever-renewing theophany, made and unmade in each moment. For us to perceive the theophany afresh in each moment requires us to be engaged in a "perpetual hermeneutics" of continual openness to its ever-new Presence. This dialogue of inner and outer, the Adamic language of "naming," is the Lost Speech that we need to recover. Meaning is to be sought through transmuting idols into icons, so that we can perceive Truth, in the constantly changing yet ever-present *here* and *now*, as Presence. But the modern world is in danger of becoming, in George Steiner's celebrated description of the post-literate world, an "After-Word", lacking the imagination to perceive "Real Presences." The recovery of meaning in this world requires us to discover the primordial techniques of sympathetic awareness, a kind of therapeutic literacy that Ivan Illich describes as "an ontologically remedial technique." We need to rediscover the power of language as symbolic, of its potential to imaginally awaken within us an awareness of our participation in, and harmony with, that synaesthetic substrate of reality in which spirit and substance are unified. Cheetham writes: "When harmonic sympathy is fully in operation, then *to speak* is *to be*. Understanding something, we say we can *make sense* of it, and now it is clear that this making sense is not theoretical, but is primarily aesthetic, concrete, and sensuous... When imagination and renunciation are wed, then all the world becomes sensuous and my individual world, my life, can make sense to me. The spiritual world is no longer abstract and distant, but alive and intensely real. The true meaning of the word *substance* has faded from our consciousness. The spirit *is* substantial. Understanding this can help reclaim a sense of the concrete significance of the individual."

The loss of the imaginal dimension in modernity is evident in the loss of its primordial poetic sympathy, which Cheetham calls "that forgotten language and the energies that would return us home to a world we dimly recall." We can therefore define the urgent task of modernity as the need to recover the Lost Speech of the angels, or the recovery of the poetic sensibility. The function of *poeisis* is, in this regard, to unveil for us the reality of that personified and qualitative and sensate Presence through language that is both concrete and resonant of transcendence. Cheetham views poets, therefore, as "the guardians of the person and of the soul of the world," both inextricably linked so that "a violation of either is a violation of both." He contrasts poets with scientists. While the latter would leave no room for mystery and wonder in their quest for abstract and literal Truth, Cheetham says this about poets: "They speak to us out of intimacy. They are the guardians of the inviolate individual, of the mystery of the Person." But the responsibility to perform as poets rests with each of us, and it is a heavy responsibility for to lose our poetic sensibility would be to deface the soul and the world: "To the degree that the language of the imagination is lost, to that degree are people and all the elements of Creation de-personalized, turned into objects, into abstractions. The final result is Hell. The final result is a world without a Face."

Cheetham is wary at times of Corbin's mysticism, of his "nostalgia for the Elsewhere and his desire for the Body of Light." He prefers a more grounded counterpoint to his views. For this "coagulating" counterpoint to Corbin's "sublimating" tendencies, Cheetham turns to the polymath thinker, Ivan Illich (1926-2002). He finds in Illich's ideas a complementary but more developed sense of meaning and Presence that opens up a way into the Beyond through the deepest reality of the present. He discusses Illich's dislike for the depersonalizing influences of institutions—including the Church—and of secularism in society, and his critique of Western culture's attempts to (in Cheetham's language) "institutionalize grace and the call that is implicit in the divine face of the other person." For Illich, the Incarnation is central to Christian revelation. It represents the possibility of a profound continuity between "the eyes of the flesh" and the "eyes of fire" that forms the condition of the "ethical gaze." Illich explores the medieval connections between optics and ethics, the view that how we discipline our seeing through *ascesis* can condition how we see. We need to look with eyes of inner light (or *lumen*), rather than be passive recipients of the light of external vision (*lux*). The secularization of images occurs through the loss of inner light or "in-sight", and this has profound implications for moral conduct, leading to the "secularization of the Samaritan" and an outlook that conditions our definition of the "neighbor" instead of allowing us to respond through a willingness to remain open and surprised by our faith, and an interiority that demolishes the constraints of our conditioning. The moral decline of modernism is marked by our loss of the openness and interiority of the ethical gaze, the vision of love, of our potential to perceive the iconic face of all creatures, and by the corresponding loss of our ability to "prolong the Incarnation" by incarnating our spirituality in personal relationships.

The Corbin trilogy deserves a wide readership. Cheetham presents Corbin's ideas accessibly, in a manner that will not deter the general reader who is interested in them. These ideas are important not only because Corbin is a seminal thinker whose influence has extended beyond the fields of his specialization, but also because of the profound implications of his ideas to the issues that confront us in the modern world. Cheetham interprets these ideas for his readers in a personally engaged and critical manner, drawing on related ideas from a wide variety of other thinkers, and demonstrating the connections between Corbin's ideas and theirs in a way that will no doubt inspire the reader to explore their ideas and to seek a deeper meaning in their personal quests for Truth as Presence in their own lives.

Biographical Notes

M. ALI LAKHANI was born in England in 1955. He was educated at the King's School, Canterbury, before reading law at Cambridge, and being called to the Bar in British Columbia, where he has practiced primarily as a barrister since 1979.

In 1998, Ali founded the traditionalist journal, *Sacred Web*, with the focus of identifying the "first principles" of tradition and exploring their relevance to the issues of modernity. *Sacred Web* (appearing in print bi-annually, and with a web site at www. sacredweb.com) is now regarded as one of the pre-eminent traditionalist journals in the English language, and has included essays by the foremost contemporary traditionalist writers, as well as by several prominent religious scholars and writers sympathetic to tradition.

In 2001, Ali was invited to address the International Congress on Imam 'Ali in Iran, where he presented his essay on the "Metaphysics of Human Governance". That essay, which dealt with the teachings of 'Ali ibn Abi Talib on Truth and Justice, garnered the First Prize in English at the conference, and was awarded at a special ceremony held in Tehran in March 2002. A revised version of the essay was included in the anthology, *The Sacred Foundations of Justice in Islam: The Teachings of 'Ali ibn Abi Talib*, co-published by World Wisdom Books and Sacred Web Publishing, 2006.

REZA SHAH-KAZEMI is a Research Associate at the Institute of Ismaili Studies in London and the founding editor of the *Islamic World Report*. He has authored several books, including: *Paths to Transcendence: According to Shankara, Ibn Arabi, and Meister Eckhart, The Other in the Light of the One: The Universality of the Qur'an and Interfaith Dialogue*, and *Justice and Remembrance: Introducing the Spirituality of Imam 'Ali*. His newest book, *Common Ground Between Islam and Buddhism* features introductions by H.H. the Fourteenth Dalai Lama and H.R.H. Prince Ghazi bin Muhammad. His contributions to the traditionalist journals *Sophia* and *Sacred Web* deal with themes relating to the perennial philosophy, tradition, beauty, and prayer.

WILLIAM STODDART was born in Carstairs, Scotland, lived most of his life in London, England, and now lives in Windsor, Ontario. He studied modern languages, and later medicine, at the universities of Glasgow, Edinburgh, and Dublin. He was a close associate of both Frithjof Schuon and Titus Burckhardt during the lives of these leading perennialists and translated several of their works into English. For many years Stoddart was assistant editor of the British journal *Studies in Comparative Religion.* Pursuing his interests in comparative religion, he has traveled widely in Europe, North Africa, India, Ceylon, and Japan. Stoddart's works include *Sufism: The Mystical Doctrines and Methods of Islam, Outline of Hinduism, Outline of Buddhism, Invincible Wisdom: Quotations from the Scriptures, Saints, and Sages of All Times and Places,* and *What Do the Religions Say About Each Other?* His essential writings were recently published by World Wisdom as *Remembering in a World of Forgetting: Thoughts on Tradition and Postmodernism* (2008).

Index

Abraham, 144-145, 245
Absolute, 9, 11-16, 20, 29, 35-36,
   52, 69, 77-82, 85-86, 106, 110-
   111, 120-121, 126-130, 136, 149,
   160, 169-170, 179, 181, 251, 255,
   258, 266
adab, 23-24, 242
al-'Alawi, Shaykh Ahmad, 16
al-Hallaj, Mansur, 148, 169
'Ali ibn Abi Talib, 41, 45, 111, 121,
   167
anamnesis, 57, 189, 251
anthropocentric, 10, 23
Aquinas, Thomas, 55, 69, 180, 185,
   205, 236
Aristotle, xiii, xviii, xix, 65, 68, 92,
   179, 188, 248
Armstrong, Karen, 43, 48, 221
Arnold, Matthew, 194
ascesis, 121, 257, 286, 290, 293
aesthetics, 115, 176, 195, 207, 226,
   286-287, 290
Augustine, 122, 184, 191, 216
Avicenna, 278, 280, 288
ayat, 9, 232

Bachelard, Gaston, 202, 214, 221,
   225
Balthasar, Hans Urs Von, 284
barzakh, 190, 225, 280
Batin, 16
Beauty, xxi, 16-18, 30, 55, 63, 69,
   74, 77, 85, 134, 137-142, 152,
   163, 183, 188, 193, 195, 203,
   218, 223, 231-239, 240-241, 243,
   245, 251
Being, 79, 81, 86, 117, 135, 136,
   137, 142, 155, 179, 181, 183,

197, 203, 212, 222-223, 228, 239,
   251, 280, 282, 285, 286, 287, 289
Berry, Wendell, xvii, xix, 179, 183,
   270
Bhagavad Gita, 31, 86, 88, 117
Bible, the, ix, 192
Blake, William, xviii, 62, 80, 108,
   117, 176, 178-180, 182, 212-213,
   217, 219, 225, 227
Bloom, Harold, xvii, 179, 279
Browning, Robert, 174, 176, 198,
   218
Buddha, xxi, 17, 32, 91, 254
Buddhism, xiii, 35, 118
Burckhardt, Titus, xiv, xv, xix, 45,
   108, 116, 125, 168, 178, 288,

Cartesian, 81, 126, 264
Center, xviii, 3, 5-6, 9-10, 14,
   23-24, 38, 39, 44, 49-51, 61, 69,
   70, 77, 79, 81, 83-91, 93, 96-98,
   103-106, 109-110, 113, 115,-117,
   126, 147, 149-150, 153, 160-162,
   178-181, 188, 205, 207, 209-210,
   215, 225, 227, 237, 240, 242,
   246, 256-258, 277
Cheetham, Tom, xix, 213, 223, 230,
   278-282, 284-292, 293
Chittick, William C., vi, xix, 175,
   203, 239, 252, 263-269, 279
Christianity, xiii, xiv, xv, 22, 35,
   200, 273
Coleridge, Samuel Taylor, 179, 211,
   212, 215, 218
Coomaraswamy, Ananda K., xiv,
   xviii, 52, 61, 123, 176, 178, 248
Corbin, Henry, vi, xvii, xix, xx, 110,
   176-178, 182, 187, 212, 278-293

297

For a glossary of all key foreign words used in books published by World Wisdom, including metaphysical terms in English, consult: www.DictionaryofSpiritualTerms.org.
This on-line Dictionary of Spiritual Terms provides extensive definitions, examples and related terms in other languages.

Praise for
SACRED WEB: A JOURNAL OF TRADITION AND MODERNITY

"I am always delighted to receive the latest issue of *Sacred Web* because, so often, I come across such deeply revealing and enlightening articles, rich in content and diverse in subject matter."
—HIS ROYAL HIGHNESS THE PRINCE OF WALES

"*Sacred Web* provides scholarly and inspiring access to a form of spiritual understanding that is very little understood in our modern society but which is of the greatest importance for our time. Its varied and excellent articles give the reader an insight into the deeper dimensions of our contemporary problems, bringing to life and giving contemporary relevance to the issues of our day."
—KAREN ARMSTRONG, Professor at Leo Baeck College, and acclaimed author of *A History of God*

"Along with *Sophia*, *Sacred Web* is the most important journal in the English language devoted to the study of tradition. Furthermore, it is unique in its interest in the consequences of confrontation between tradition and modernity, an issue which lies at the heart of so many aspects of the life of humanity today."
—SEYYED HOSSEIN NASR, University Professor of Islamic Studies, The George Washington University

"However deluged I am with incoming, time-consuming mail, I always find myself smiling and turning mental cartwheels when I find an issue of *Sacred Web* arriving. Its modest circulation belies the quality of every issue's content."
—HUSTON SMITH, Pre-eminent religious scholar and author of *The World's Religions*

For more information visit www.sacredweb.com